# Examine. Explore. Experiment.

RMIT's School of Media & Communication is home to a vibrant pioneering community of theorists, thinkers and practitioners.

We offer world-renowned programs that are global in focus and practical in application, as well as online and short courses that offer you the flexibility to reach your career goals without putting your life on hold.

From navigating new technologies for audio visual expression, to exploring the societal changes brought about by online and digital culture, RMIT stands at the forefront of innovation. Our world-leading media precinct is fitted with cutting-edge technology, and fosters industry-engaged research collaboration between disciplines.

**Explore the future at rmit.edu.au**

Image by Riley Reynolds

# create.

## • CREATIVE COURSES FOR CREATIVE MINDS •

At SAE, you'll learn the skills you need to create your future in Creative Media. With Fee-Help* available on all Bachelor, Associate Degree and Diploma courses, you can learn now and pay later. Start your creative career sooner; join the SAE crew today. *Visit sae.edu.au for information on FEE-HELP.*

CRICOS: 00312F | RTO: 0273

ANIMATION — AUDIO — DESIGN — FILM — GAMES — WEB & MOBILE

**ENROL TODAY**
**SAE.EDU.AU | 1800 723 338**

SAE QANTM
CREATIVE MEDIA INSTITUTE

**BRISBANE | BYRON BAY | SYDNEY | MELBOURNE | ADELAIDE | PERTH | ONLINE**

 44
 72
 86
 128

# Contents

## SPECIAL FEATURE: *METRO* HITS 200

**8** A Fetching Achievement ADOLFO ARANJUEZ

### Behind the Scenes

**10** The Past Is a Foreign Country PETER TAPP

**12** In the Beginning, There Was Film Appreciation KEVIN ADAMS

  + *Metro* in the 1970s PETER HAMILTON

**14** A Brief History of *Metro* WAYNE LEVY

  + The Bridge LISA FRENCH

**16** Letter from the Editors GRETA PARRY

### Big Screen

**18** Indigenous Representations on Screen and in Print GREG DOLGOPOLOV

**21** Classic Takes: The NFSA Essays BRIAN MCFARLANE

**24** The Changing Face of Genre OLIVER PFEIFFER

**26** Old Journal, New Media DAN GOLDING

**28** Sydney and the Small Screen LIZ GIUFFRE

**30** Penning with Pride GLENN DUNKS

### Beyond the Curtain

**32** Advocacy Meets Analysis: *Metro* and Documentary HANNA SCHENKEL

**34** Three Paths to Asian Cinema MIKE WALSH

**36** Melbourne Plays Itself ANTHONY CAREW

**39** The Reel South: Adelaide and *Metro* NICHOLAS GODFREY

**42** Enabling a Screen Ecology ANDREW PIKE

## AUSTRALIAN AND NEW ZEALAND CINEMA

**44** Terror, Tragedy, Truth: Anthony Maras' *Hotel Mumbai* FELICITY FORD

**50** Breaching Bounds: The Confronting Body in Miranda Nation's *Undertow* ELIZABETH FLUX

**56** Bird's-eye View: Childhood, Grief and Community in *Emu Runner* AIMEE KNIGHT

**62** Tearing Out a New Leaf: *Book Week* and the Unlikeable Protagonist MEL CAMPBELL

**66** In the Crease: Self-referential Storytelling in Ted Wilson's *Under the Cover of Cloud* LEAH JING

## AUSTRALIA ON THE SMALL SCREEN

**72** The Parochial Fantastic: Australian Television Fantasy in *Bloom* and *Tidelands* TRAVIS JOHNSON

**80** Crooked Histories: *Underbelly* and Australian Self-mythologisation DAVE CREWE

## FOCUS ON ASIA AND THE MIDDLE EAST

**86** Quiet Rage: The Fire and Finesse of Lee Chang-dong's Cinema ANTHONY CAREW

**94** Darkness in the Spotlight: Binaries and Brutality in Zhang Yimou's *Shadow* DEBBIE ZHOU

**98** Film à la Mode: Juxtaposing East and West in *Yellow Is Forbidden* REBEKAH BRAMMER

## DOCUMENTARY

**104** The Cost of Country: Capital and Ownership in *Undermined: Tales from the Kimberley* ROCHELLE SIEMIENOWICZ

**110** Home on the Rocks: Blue Lucine on Displacement and *The Eviction* JASMINE CRITTENDEN

**114** Age of Acceptance: Community and Inclusion in Sue Thomson's *The Coming Back Out Ball Movie* STEPHEN A RUSSELL

**118** Rhetoric and Reminiscence: Graham Freudenberg, Political Memory and *The Scribe* ANDERS FURZE

**122** Greener Pastures: Tradition and Modernity in Grace McKenzie's *In the Land of Wolves* GABRIELLE O'BRIEN

## CRITICAL VIEWS

**128** Cinema for Claustrophiles: Virtual Reality at the Adelaide Film Festival and Beyond KIT MACFARLANE

**136** Other Voices: *Grace, Who Waits Alone* and New Australian Underground Cinema DAVID HESLIN

## THE NFSA RESTORES COLLECTION

**142** *Proof* ROSE LUCAS

## METRO MAGAZINE

**MANAGING EDITOR**
PETER TAPP
editor@atom.org.au

**EDITOR**
ADOLFO ARANJUEZ
metro@atom.org.au

**SUBEDITOR**
DAVID HESLIN

**CONTRIBUTING EDITORS**
LIZ GIUFFRE
DAN GOLDING
ROCHELLE SIEMIENOWICZ

**ART DIRECTOR**
PASCALE VAN BREUGEL

**SUBSCRIPTIONS & ONLINE SERVICES**
ZAK HAMER
online@atom.org.au

**COLLECTIONS**
ANNE VAN DER SANDEN
TRACY CHEN

**SUBSCRIPTIONS & ONLINE SERVICES ASSISTANTS**
ANGIE CHAN
ANNELIZ ERESE

**PRINTING**
SHENZHEN TIAN HONG PRINTING

**ADVERTISING**
PETER TAPP
+61 (412) 473 116
editor@atom.org.au

**POSTAL ADDRESS**
PO BOX 2040
ST KILDA WEST VIC 3182
AUSTRALIA

**TELEPHONE**
+61 (3) 9525 5302

**WEBSITE**
www.metromagazine.com.au

**SOCIAL MEDIA**
facebook.com/metroaustralia
twitter.com/metrofilm

Cover: *Undermined: Tales from the Kimberley*
ISSUE 200 | MAY 2019 | ISBN 978-1-76061-100-2
PRINT ISSN 0312-2654 | DIGITAL ISSN 2207-8428

## ATOM BOARD

**CHAIR**
Roger Dunscombe

**DEPUTY CHAIR**
Jenna Grace

**EDUCATION EXECUTIVE OFFICER**
Robert Young

**PUBLICATIONS & AWARDS MANAGER**
Peter Tapp

**COMMITTEE MEMBERS**
Victoria Giummarra
Emma McCulloch
Laura Newman
Kevin Tibaldi
Lisa Worthy

**EDUCATION OFFICER**
Scarlet Barnett

## ASSOCIATE EDITORS FOR REFEREED ARTICLES

- **KEITH BEATTIE**
  Associate Professor, Faculty of Arts and Education, Deakin University

- **FELICITY COLLINS**
  Associate Professor, Department of Cinema Studies, La Trobe University

- **GREG DOLGOPOLOV**
  Lecturer, School of the Arts and Media, UNSW

- **ANNA DZENIS**
  Lecturer, Department of Cinema Studies, La Trobe University

- **BERYL EXLEY**
  Professor, School of Education & Professional Studies, Griffith University

- **TRISH FITZSIMONS**
  Associate Professor, Griffith Film School, Griffith University

- **LISA FRENCH**
  Professor and Dean, School of Media and Communication, RMIT University

- **BEN GOLDSMITH**
  Senior Lecturer, Screen and Media, University of the Sunshine Coast

- **ALEXANDRA HELLER-NICHOLAS**
  Adjunct Research Fellow, Institute for Social Research, Swinburne University of Technology

- **BRIAN MCFARLANE**
  Adjunct Professor, Institute for Social Research, Swinburne University of Technology

- **JANE MILLS**
  Associate Professor, Senior Research Fellow, Journalism and Media Research Centre, UNSW

- **MEAGHAN MORRIS**
  Chair, Inter-Asia Cultural Studies Society, Department of Gender and Cultural Studies, University of Sydney

- **DANA POLAN**
  Professor, Critical Studies, School of Cinema-TV, University of Southern California

- **DAVID ROWE**
  Director, Centre for Cultural Research, University of Western Sydney

- **SUE TURNBULL**
  Professsor, School of Social Sciences, Media & Communication, University of Wollongong

- **CONSTANTINE VEREVIS**
  Associate Professor, Film and Screen Studies, Monash University

- **MIKE WALSH**
  Associate Professor, Department of Screen and Media, Flinders University

- **DEANE WILLIAMS**
  Associate Professor, Film and Screen Studies, Monash University

- **BRIAN YECIES**
  Senior Lecturer in Communication and Media Studies, Faculty of Law, Humanities and the Arts, University of Wollongong

*Metro* is produced by the Australian Teachers of Media Inc. (ATOM) with assistance from Film Victoria.

*Metro* is a partly refereed journal, for authors who request that their pieces be refereed. Manuscripts, of a maximum of 3000 words, should be submitted for blind review with identification of author(s) on a separate page.

**Accompanying photographs** or graphics are preferred. **Electronic images:** 300dpi EPS, TIFF, JPEG or Photoshop – not too small, and please do not embed in Word document.

A *Metro* style guide is available from <http://www.metromagazine.com.au>.

The views expressed in signed articles and reviews do not necessarily represent the views of the editors or ATOM.
© 2019 Australian Teachers of Media (ATOM). *Metro* magazine is indexed by the following organisations: FIAF in the International Index to Film/TV Periodicals • BFI in its online resource Film Index International • Film & TV Documentation Centre's Film Literature Index • Australian Council for Educational Research (ACER) in Australian Education Index • Informit

# 2019 SAE ATOM AWARDS

## ENTRIES NOW OPEN

**ENTER AUSTRALIA'S LEADING FILM AND MEDIA AWARDS FOR THE EDUCATION AND INDUSTRY SECTORS**

If you are a student, a professional, or an independent screen content producer from Australia or New Zealand, there is a category for you. This year's diverse categories will cover film, television, animation, educational resources, and new media including web series, apps, ebooks and games.

**FOR A FULL LIST OF CATEGORIES, OR TO ENTER YOUR PRODUCTION, PLEASE VISIT US ONLINE AT**

## atomawards.org

**FOR FURTHER ENQUIRIES, EMAIL US AT**
awards@atom.org.au

**INVESTIGATIVE AND INQUIRY-BASED CLASSROOM RESOURCES FOR**

# The Australian Curriculum:
# HISTORY

**AU $30 TO $35 PER BOOKLET**

## YEAR 8

**AVAILABLE NOW**

### Depth Study 1: The Western and Islamic World
- Medieval Europe
- Renaissance Italy
- The Ottoman Empire
- The Vikings

### Depth Study 2: The Asia-Pacific World
- Japan Under the Shoguns
- Angkor/Khmer Empire
- The Polynesian Expansion Across the Pacific

### Depth Study 3: Expanding Contacts
- Mongol Expansion
- The Black Death in Asia, Europe and Africa
- The Spanish Conquest of the Americas

### Depth Study 6D (NSW: Expanding Contacts)
- Aboriginal and Indigenous Peoples, Colonisation and Contact History

(Covers Australian Aborigines, North American Indians, New Zealand Maori)

**AVAILABLE NOW 2019 (INCLUDES TITLES FOR DEPTH STUDY 1 AND 3.**

### Depth Study 1: Making a Better World?
- The Industrial Revolution

### Depth Study 2: Australia and Asia
- Making a Nation (Forthcoming in 2019)

### Depth Study 3: World War I
- World War I

**TO SEE SAMPLE PAGES GO TO:
HTTP://ATOM.ASN.AU/SAMPLE_PAGES/**

**FOR MORE INFORMATION AND TO ORDER, VISIT**
theeducationshop.com.au

## YEAR 10

**FORTHCOMING IN 2019**

### Depth Study 1: World War II
- World War II

### Depth Study 2: Rights and Freedoms
- Rights and Freedoms

### Depth Study 3: The Globalising World
- The Environment Movement

## YEAR 12 (VCE) AUSTRALIAN HISTORY

**AVAILABLE NOW**

### Unit 3 (Transformations: Colonial Society to Nation)
- Making a People and a Nation 1890–1920

Part 1 Creating a New Nation
Part 2 The New Nation
Part 3 The Impact of World War I

### Unit 4 (Transformations: Old Certainties and New Visions)
- Crises that Tested the Nation 1929–1945: The Great Depression

Part 1 The causes of Australia's involvement in the world economic crisis of the Depression
The response of Australian governments to the crisis

Part 2 The responses of Australian people to the Great Depression
Cohesion and divisions, Change and continuity

- Crises that Tested the Nation 1929–1945: World War Two

Part 1 What sort of nation was Australia in 1939?
The outbreak of war 1939
'Phony war' September 1939 – March 1940
'All in' April 1940 – November 1941

Part 2 'Total War' December 1941 – August 1943
A balanced war effort August 1943 – August 1945

**TO SEE SAMPLE PAGES GO TO:
HTTP://ATOM.ASN.AU/SAMPLE_PAGES/**

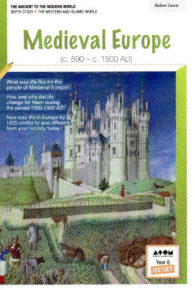

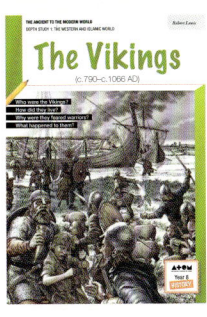
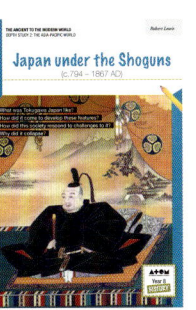
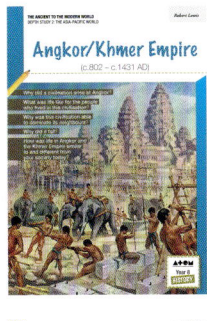

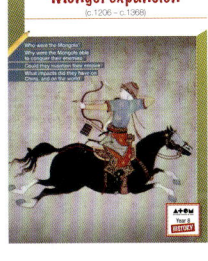
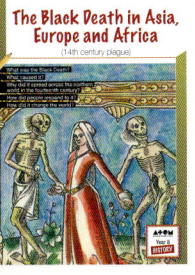
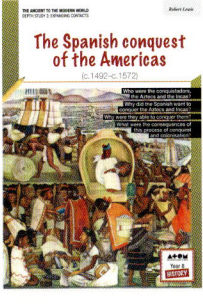
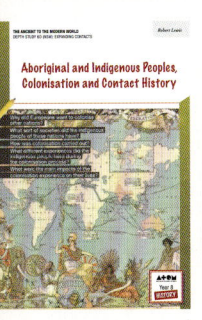

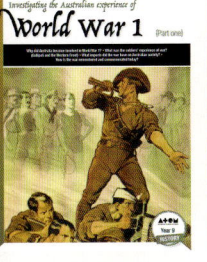
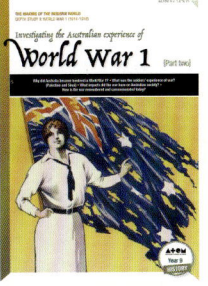

## EACH BOOKLET:

» is written specifically for the Victorian History Curriculum at years 8 or 9

» is a self-contained practical classroom resource that fulfils all curriculum requirements and can be the basis of the entire classroom unit

» engages students by starting with a concept-developing activity that taps into students' current knowledge and understanding of the topic, and uses that as a base for further development

» is Inquiry based – that is, students find out by working out through evidence and other information

» includes a rich variety of information and evidence – stories, documents, pictures, maps, artefacts, graphs, tables

» incorporates different levels of questions and activities to make it appropriate for the greatest variety of learning styles and abilities

» is rich in images, with full-size reproduction of images available online at The Education Shop

» includes a variety of classroom and research activities

» uses scaffolded questions to ensure students are able to progress at appropriate rates of understanding

» provides a variety of possible assessment activities includes 'fun' tasks – such as crosswords, art activities, and word codes

» includes a number of specific 'detective' challenges for students to solve through evidence

» incorporates the most up-to-date information in a way that suits the appropriate year level

» suggests follow-up activities to enable students to use the unit as a springboard for further development of knowledge and understanding

» is fully photocopiable for classroom use by individuals or groups

» includes a teacher guide for using the resource effectively in the classroom

» reflects the reality of classroom needs for a manageable approach in terms of time, resources and effective pedagogy.

### SAMPLE PAGES SHOWING THE VARIETY OF ACTIVITIES INCLUDED:
HTTP://ATOM.ASN.AU/SAMPLE_PAGES/

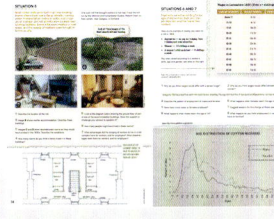

WW1 Part 2     WW1 Part 1     The Industrial Revolution

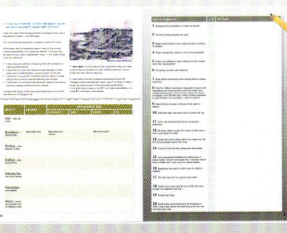
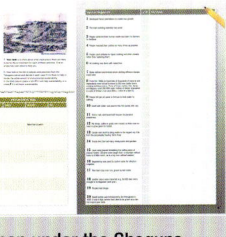

Japan under the Shoguns     Renaissance Italy     The Ottoman Empire

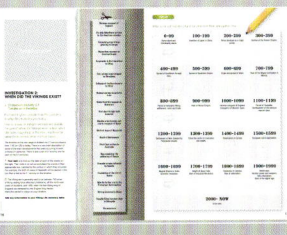
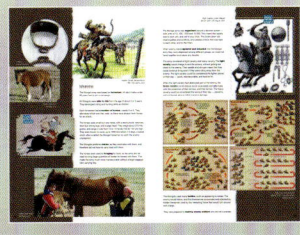
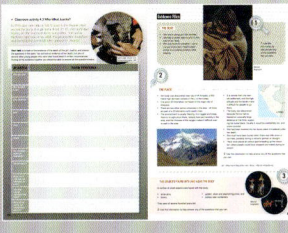

The Vikings     Mongol expansion     Spanish conquest of the Americas

Aboriginal & Indigenous Peoples     The Black Death in Asia, Europe, Africa     Medieval Europe

## METRO HITS 200

 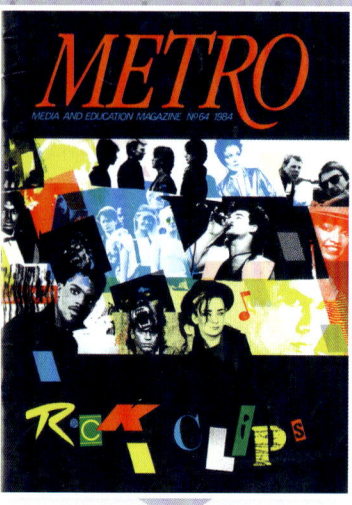 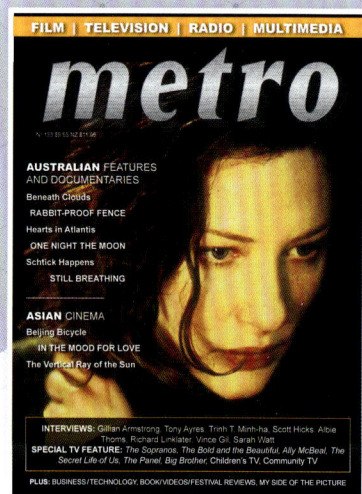

Above, L–R: *M*55; *M*64; *M*133

# A fetching achievement

» ADOLFO ARANJUEZ

Editor, *Metro* (2013–present)

I *could* talk about *Metro*. Except I've commissioned seventeen stellar contributors to do just that, so, instead, let me tell you about the person currently responsible for putting it together.

One of the first things I did when I landed the *Metro* editorship was attempt, with my nervous newbie energy and infinite nerdiness, to make sense of the magnitude of *Metro*'s history. On the publishing side, its style guide – a key document for those of us in the business of editing – was expansive and laden with precedent, but also littered with inconsistency. I set about not just memorising this document but revamping it, and, within my first month, and with input from then–*Screen Education* editor Greta Parry (who was also my subeditor – and I, hers – because we tight @ ATOM HQ), I had a totally clear, totally comprehensive version that I, of course, proceeded to disseminate via all official channels as well as among the other staff. Speaking of, that was another aspect of this 'history' story: I like knowing everyone's business, like Regina George (Rachel McAdams) in *Mean Girls* (Mark Waters, 2004) except not mean, so I proceeded to venerate my Filipino roots and gossip with everyone about the ins and outs of both publication and parent organisation. All in little doses, mind you; can't be too obvious or else I'd have ruined my cool exterior or tarnished any respect my new co-workers had for this precocious youth(ish).

I'm not going to shy away from that last bit, but that's the third 'history' thing: *Metro* is old. Like, only-seven-years-younger-than-my-Boomer-mother old. Getting a gig like this at twenty-four meant colliding head-on with the robustness of that legacy. This magazine had published critics whose words I'd read at uni, in libraries, on the internet while trying to figure out what the hell that ambiguous off-centre long shot meant at the end of that arthouse film. My high school media teacher (and eventual teaching-placement mentor; yes, surprise! I'm a qualified teacher as well), Liza Bermingham, was previously on its board. A favourite uni lecturer, Alexandra Heller-Nicholas, is one of its regular contributors; eventually, more lecturers' names would pop up in our author database (that's right – an internal, technologically facilitated gossip network!). From its humble origins as a newsletter to what is now an internationally sold, industry-respected journal – 'Australia's oldest film and media periodical', as I like to parrot to anyone who'd listen, after getting smug confirmation that, yes, it *does* beat *Cinema Papers* by a couple of years – *Metro* has come a long way.

And so had I. Prior to helming *Metro*, I'd been working in book publishing and hating it – not because I hate books, but because I have zero patience for the delayed gratification of a published manuscript. At the same time, I was also editing for the literary magazine *Voiceworks*, heading its nonfiction department and working as deputy to one of the best people I'd ever met (and whom I and the world are unfortunate to have lost so early; a story for another time). It was always clear to me that I enjoyed *Voiceworks* more than the book-editing gig. The turnaround was short: a few weeks of involved editing and you had finished pieces; within the next month, you had beautiful layouts pretty much mirroring the tangible product. Quarterlies work to a twelve-week cycle, and that synced with my natural predisposition for regularity and rhythm.

So when I got the *Metro* gig, it felt like a reward for that entire slog. And I wanted to do it damn well. By all accounts, over my six years in the editor's chair thus far, I've been doing just that.

I dare say my twenty-three issues of the mag to date are some of my proudest achievements. This is coming from someone whose childhood-bedroom walls were literally papered over with framed awards and medals (fodder for my regular psych visits); who blitzed through school; who got selected as one of Melbourne's literary 30 Under 30; who fills his non-day-job time with professional speaking, teaching and dancing gigs. Aristotelian ethics emphasises the importance of *aretē*: the 'doing' aspect of the 'good life' that also doubly means 'excellence' and 'virtue'. *Aretē* is directed outwards – while you can obviously get something out of it, personally, it's ultimately about contributing what you're naturally good at for a larger whole: a knife is only a knife if it cuts things sharply. I've always had an aptitude for language, for argument, for organisation, for getting people to do what I want and on time but without feeling bossed around (like Regina George), and this job, at heart, is about all of those things. There are days when the dread about a tricky edit or the anger at an author gone AWOL is unbearable. But each time I hold another issue in my hands, seeing how text and images have come together so purtily, I'm met with the same giddy feeling I get every time I've done something good. Not just a 'good job' good, but *aretē* good. Bigger-than-me good. Because, my superb editing and management aside, each *Metro* reminds us that art *does* things: it teaches us, transforms us, tells us about lives we don't live and lines of thought we've yet to entertain. It links us to others' views, lets us understand, smoothens paths to seeing the world differently.

If I felt this way about issues I'd made, imagine how my predecessors must have felt! So I decided to do something to mark this milestone. Putting together this historic 200th issue has been both incredible and hellish. Hellish because, in the lead-up to print, I'd spent several twelve- to fifteen-hour days just getting shit ready (including trawling the ATOM archives and scanning shelves-worth of material), which means I'm an exhausted pile of mush barely retaining upright form as I write this. Incredible because I'd always known about *Metro*'s trajectory, but nothing prepared me for the satisfaction of flipping firsthand through, say, those lo-fi issues from the 1980s and reading the same stuff we talk about now: style's relationship to substance; the importance of representation, especially for marginalised groups; the semiotics of shot sizes; male filmmakers (lol); how the industry needs to better support the arts; how screen storytelling is wondrous for all of us, young and old.

I only have a few specific thank-yous, primarily to managing editor Peter Tapp, who took a chance on me all those years ago, and the ATOM staff, who, I'm sure, are sick of my infamous morning grump because small talk is the devil. Massive thanks also go out to Greta and her successor, David Heslin, who have proven, time and time again, that even an editor with the most immense of talents requires a subeditorial hand (besides patience, trust is another thing I struggle with and, alas, everyone makes mistakes even if we try to prevent them with seven fail-safes – thanks are clearly in order for therapist extraordinaire Dr J as well). A huge thank you, too, to my talented designer Pascale van Breugel, who unceasingly turns in elegant work (especially after the great redesign of 2014) and somehow disarms the stresses of deadline time into non-stresses. And, of course, heaps of thanks to my amazing writers, who keep my magazine ticking, inspire me to be a better writer myself and, really, make this job worth doing.

David pointed out that, second to Peter (who doesn't count because he's superhuman), I'm now officially the longest-running *Metro* editor in the magazine's entire history – please refer to the table below, which I've meticulously put together – and it's a strange, spectacular feeling, as though I've emerged victorious in a battle royale whose contestants didn't know they were playing. It's not a competition, but, like, also I've won. I'm grateful, I'm honoured, and I'm excited to continue furthering the legacy of all who've come before me and made *Metro* and ATOM the stalwarts they are today.

What you're holding in your hands, dear readers, is a capsule of time. In a hundred years, or another hundred issues, some nerd will flip through its pages and say to themselves, 'Dayummn, the world was so different back then – and yet, somehow, it's also still the same.' They'll sigh, then continue: 'But, omg, what were they *thinking* with that layout?'

Clockwise from top right: *M*40; *M*199; *M*95

### METRO EDITORS OVER THE YEARS

| | | | |
|---|---|---|---|
| 1963–1974 | (by committee) | 1998–2001 | Kate Raynor |
| 1974–1975 | Dawn Brown | 1999–2001 | Naji Dellal |
| 1975–1976 | Warren Thomas | 2001–2003 | Liz Conor |
| 1976 | Michael Small | 2003–2006 | Sophie Gebhardt |
| 1977–1981 | Peter Hamilton | 2006–2007 | Zoe Tovey |
| 1981–1983 | Helen Kon | 2007–2010 | Natalie Book |
| 1984–1989 | Sheila Allison | 2010 | Rjurik Davidson |
| 1988 | Paul Kalina | 2010–2011 | John Marnell |
| 1989 | Philippa Hawker | 2011–2013 | Nick Tapper |
| 1989–1998 | Peter Tapp | 2013 | Tim Coronel |
| 1995–1998 | Raffaele Caputo | 2013–present | Adolfo Aranjuez |

# METRO HITS 200: BEHIND THE SCENES

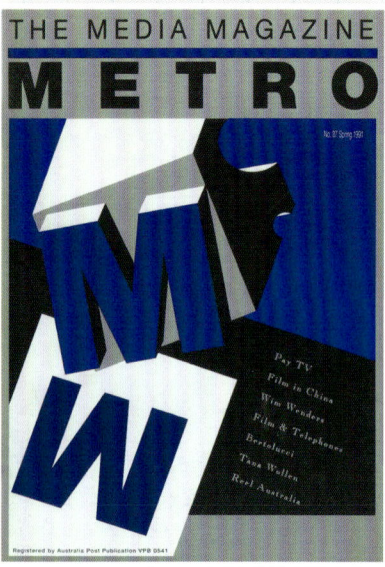

# The past is a foreign country

» PETER TAPP
Editor, *Metro* (1988–1998)
Managing Editor, ATOM (1998–present)

I was offered the job of editing and running *Metro* in late 1988, originally for just two to three days a week. At the time, I was working at *Cinema Papers* as joint editor with Philippa Hawker. Prior to that, I had edited and published *Filmviews* magazine, and worked in distribution at the Australian Film Institute (AFI) and at the State Film Centre of Victoria.

The *Metro* offer was interesting. I had always been passionate about film and media education. *Metro* was an established, well-produced and respected publication with an engaged readership of Victorian media teachers. I saw the potential to build a wider readership and increase the use of Australian films in education, so I took the job. I then approached a number of friends and colleagues whom I had worked with at *Filmviews* and *Cinema Papers* to form an editorial board to help with planning content and commissioning writers. I certainly didn't expect to still be at *Metro*/ATOM thirty years later!

During the 1980s and 1990s, a large proportion of the films that were being used in education were foreign titles. Many teachers and others, including myself, felt that Australian students should be watching programs produced by Australians about Australia. To encourage this, we decided to cover only Australasian film and television in *Metro*. The idea was to be geographically specific, so as to build a reputation for *Metro*'s analysis of Australian titles and to contribute to the recognition and growth of the Australian industry.

By 1995, the editorial team felt we couldn't cover films with strong educational content alongside Australian and New Zealand features in enough depth in *Metro* alone. We needed another magazine dedicated to education and ways film could be used effectively in the classroom, so we launched *Metro Education*, which soon morphed into *Screen Education*. Additionally, ATOM broadened the scope of the magazines and entered into creative partnerships with organisations such as the National Film and Sound Archive of Australia, the AFI, the Australian Film Television and Radio School, the Australian Children's Television Foundation, the Australian Centre for the Moving Image, the ABC, SBS, Fairfax, the Melbourne and Sydney film festivals, and other subject associations.

Also around this time, I decided to introduce some younger editors and assistant editors to take over the production of the magazines. I became the managing editor and worked on creating other revenue streams. This decision injected vitality into the ATOM office. In the years following, I had the pleasure of working with a number of very talented, passionate and hardworking people who contributed enormously to the success and growth of both publications – people like Raffaele Caputo, Kate Raynor, Liz Conor, Zoe Tovey, Natalie Book, John Marnell, Nick Tapper and Greta Parry, most of whom have carved out impressive careers in the publishing industry after working at ATOM.

During the late 1990s and early 2000s, we were lucky enough to receive funding from Screen Australia (then the Australian Film Commission) and Film Victoria. However, I could see the writing on the wall regarding long-term funding from these government bodies, and I knew ATOM had to diversify if the magazines were to survive.

One of the ways we have done this is through EBSCO, a leading international provider of subscriptions for magazines. While EBSCO already handled about 45 per cent of our subscriptions, in the early 1990s it also began selling digital copies of individual articles. When I received our first EBSCO yearly report, I was amazed to see there were a couple of thousand downloads in North America – and from then on, each year, the downloads just kept increasing. This was the first confirmation that Australian educational material was of interest beyond Australian shores. It meant we were not only spreading the word about Australian screen productions, but also encouraging their purchase overseas, in turn enabling more money to go back to Australian filmmakers. But this created a new dilemma: how could we receive a better payment for *Metro* and *Screen Education* articles?

Despite some financial bumps from time to time, we proudly pay all of our contributors. In 2018, ATOM paid over A$200,000 to Australian freelance writers and A$100,000 back to producers and other third parties whose products we market through The Education Shop.

ATOM is a lean and transparent organisation. Working from a small office with a staff of seven, and with a stable of talented freelance writers, we have grown from our ATFA/ATFAV beginnings and take pride in what we produce and the programs we run. Besides the publishing of *Metro* and *Screen Education*, ATOM:

- has built The Education Shop
- produces seventy-plus study guides a year
- has created opt-in email lists (with over 140,000 subscribers) promoting both ATOM's work and Australian screen content
- continues to run the ATOM Awards
- has launched the 1-Minute Film Competition, the ATOM Photo Comp and the Front Page newspaper competition.

How has ATOM been able to achieve this? First and foremost, through the hard work of all its staff and board members over its fifty-six-year history. There are so many people to thank, it's impossible to name them all: the friends and colleagues who agreed to be on editorial boards for both *Metro* and *Screen Education* in the late 1980s and early 1990s; the funding agencies that helped support ATOM for more than fifteen years; the magazine and study guide writers, who are the main contributors to the success of ATOM; and the individuals and companies who have supported the magazines with advertising over its many years. Of course, I would like to thank the current editor of *Metro*, Adolfo Aranjuez, as well as the editor of *Screen Education*, David Heslin, for their outstanding work. I must give particular mention to *Metro*'s art director, Pascale van Breugel, whose flair for design has been integral to the magazine's evolving look and character over the past nineteen years (and counting). And two others who must be mentioned are Zak Hamer and David Eedle, for their work on The Education Shop, awards and competitions.

*Metro* and *Screen Education* are rare; not many screen or media magazines across the world publish such extensive articles and are so beautifully designed and printed. It has been a privilege to work with so many talented, generous and dedicated writers and educators as well as passionate and inspired filmmakers to bring media education and Australian screen content to a wider audience.

**This spread, L–R:** Tapp's first issue, *M79*; issue 3 of *Metro Education*; the cover of *M87* and spreads from *M84* and *M105*, all of which Tapp designed

# In the beginning, there was film appreciation

» KEVIN ADAMS
President, ATFA/ATFAV (1972–1975)
Committee member, ATFA/ATFAV (1965–1978)

Our beloved teaching association didn't really take off until the Association of Teachers of Film Appreciation (ATFA), founded in 1963, became the Association of Teachers of Film and Video (ATFAV) in 1974 and *Metro* in its current form was born. ATOM – first as Association for the Teachers of Media from 1978, then Australian Teachers of Media from 1981 – came about not long after. During my time (including my turn as committee president from 1972 to 1975, after which I was awarded a life membership), I saw it change from a largely film-appreciation-oriented group to a platform that included a wide range of media formats and a diverse range of teachers.

In 1974, we had an extraordinary general meeting at the Trak Cinema in Toorak to discuss the rapidly changing face of the association, the widening of the needs of our new membership base, our film advisory service, and our inclusion of photography and video – that is, we were morphing into a wider vehicle for teachers of media. Following then-treasurer Wayne Levy's huge task of renumbering the issues of ATFA/ATFAV's publications, the first magazine to carry the new *Metro* logo was released, circa March 1974. Then-editor Dawn Brown had been busy getting a government grant, had lobbied many committees, including the Karmel Commission, and was seeking support for premises in Carlton.

By then, I was well and truly on the ATFAV committee. But how did I get into media? It was a combination of survival and a need to engage a small group of difficult students. It was 1966 and I was thirty. I had been a primary teacher for eight years. To enable me to start a degree at Monash Uni, 'The Dept' seconded me part-time to a high school. On day one of Term 1, I was 'parachuted' into Dandenong High (which didn't have me on its staffing list, so I had no teaching allocation). The senior master then introduced me to a group of fifteen boys who'd been banished to the oval until they cut off their Beatle haircuts (some things never change), and suddenly I was their form teacher. They became 4R.

In between driving up and down the highway to Monash and trying to come to grips with subjects and content I'd never taught, I tried to figure out how I'd survive a year with 4R. While they were strong-willed and recalcitrant, there was also something endearing about them.

During my first lesson with them, they said poetry was for girls, Shakespeare was old-fashioned, the novel was boring, and so on. The next day, I arrived armed with handouts of lyrics by The Beatles,

# *Metro* in the 1970s

» PETER HAMILTON
Editor, *Metro* (1977–1981)

'Whitlam!'

That's the one word that best captures *Metro*'s journey in the 1970s. When I first met *Metro* in 1973 – before it was even officially known as *Metro* – it was a roneoed newsletter created by a handful of passionate teachers who shared overlapping, twin goals: promoting cinema studies and super 8 filmmaking in the classroom. A demographic tidal wave was about to lift their efforts into a widely supported educational movement. Baby boomers were just beginning to graduate into employment as teachers; we had come of age opposing the Vietnam War, and many of us were pressing hard for social change, starting in the schools. Gough Whitlam's newly elected government had pulled Australia's forces out of Vietnam, and radical reform of our schooling system enjoyed backing from the top.

I began teaching at Sunshine Tech, where we discovered a crisis in literacy. Many students lacked skills either in their parents' language – in Sunshine, it was mainly Maltese – or in English. These students were disengaged at best, and often hostile to their schooling. So were many students whose only language at home was English. Classes were often riotous. A student arsonist destroyed the typing teacher's beloved portable classroom. That was the vibe!

We discovered, though, that our restless students responded well to curricula inspired by popular culture. In a pivotal exercise, the automotive studies teacher, Ray Newlands, worked with Year 9 boys to reconstruct Ned Kelly's armor. Humanities teachers created a suite of reading and writing exercises inspired by the bushranger's tale. We shot a super 8 reel dramatising Kelly's last stand, and the class trooped off to Footscray for a screening of the Mick Jagger *Ned Kelly* movie (Tony Richardson, 1970).

I had worked as a journalist, including for *Dispatch News* in Indochina during the war, and was comfortable writing about our work in *Metro* and other curriculum publications. One day, Canberra called. A Whitlam-appointed public servant was reading about our Ned Kelly project, and she offered to help me apply for an Innovations grant, a new program intended to bypass school hierarchies and directly fund the initiatives of low-ranked teachers. Our proposal was successful. A grant funded us to develop and test curricula that linked popular culture to literacy and language arts.

Our mission was eased by a technical breakthrough: Sony had introduced the revolutionary Portapak, a low-cost, portable video system that gave students what they crave most: instant feedback!

Bob Dylan and Simon & Garfunkel. It was a no-brainer: if you can't beat them, join them. I announced that these songwriters were modern poets. This didn't go down so well, so I read out the lyrics and drew attention to their obvious poetic qualities; 4R reluctantly agreed. (Fifty years on, I was a bit amused when Bob Dylan was awarded the Nobel Prize in Literature. Why did the three-piece suits take this long to agree with 4R?)

Later, we approached Shakespeare via a movie. We discussed the effects of media and advertising on our consumer choices. We enlisted the help of Vance Packard, starting with *The Hidden Persuaders* and others in the series.

Soon, I needed a source of short films to show an alternative form of expression. I discovered the State Film Centre, which had thousands of short films, and Ed 'Scheff' Schefferle, who worked there. Over the next few years, we became firm friends. I especially liked films by Canada's National Film Board, as did the students.

I only taught 4R, but word spread and students came up to me on the school grounds wanting to learn the same stuff as 4R. The head of English often questioned me about my 'innovation', but several other English teachers joined me and I taught them how to operate a 16mm projector. Dawn, working with the education department's Curriculum and Research (C&R) unit, also came to some classes. At the end of the year, I received A$1000 from C&R for a 'class set' of the new super 8 cameras – a huge boon to my fledgling course that also gave it credibility.

At the end of 1969, Bert Butler at the Film, Photography and TV department at Monash Teachers' College asked me to train pre-service media teachers. Two years after that, I was sent to Technical Teachers' College (now Hawthorn Institute of Education), where I lectured about film, photography, animation and video to keen graduates of art and English. I did that until 1978, when I became an educational media advisor in Indonesia for the Department of Foreign Affairs.

Most of the pioneers of *Metro* and ATOM will have died, especially those I worked closely with from 1965 to 1978: Ed, Dawn, Wayne, Richard Franklin. People had different reasons for joining our association, and each brought a range of skills and subject expertise. Some of the early members may have also had their own agendas – educational, commercial and/or philosophical – but we coexisted. For example, in the mid 1960s, some purists argued against including filmmaking in media education, but my argument was simple: you can appreciate film better if you've made one.

We all had different journeys through and with our beloved association. My own journey arose out of needs and insights. I credit 4R and Dandenong High as catalysts for my new career path. Without them, I might never have stepped outside the sacred boundaries of the English curriculum and into the realms of innovation.

**Above, L–R:** *Film Appreciation Newsletter* vol. 1, no. 8; *M*39, with *Kojak* on the cover

The Victorian education department's curriculum unit seconded me to develop and publish curricula for students in Years 5 to 12, who comprised around 60 per cent of the entire student population. They winked at my work editing *Metro*, even though it was published by an independent association of teachers. Warren Thomas, a visionary administrator in the department's audiovisual branch, led a successful parallel and supportive effort to promote film and media in the curriculum.

We reformatted *Metro* for offset printing: our ambition was to become a national, advertiser- and subscriber-supported quarterly. The 1970s TV series *Kojak* was featured on our first offset cover (*M*39). The format upgrade and expanded operations were supported by another Whitlam Era gift: repeating annual grants administered by Lachlan Shaw at the Australian Film Commission, Screen Australia's predecessor.

Throughout my tenure, *Metro* remained loyal to Whitlam's social-democratic mission, despite the Labor government's dismissal in November 1975. We regarded language competence as a key launching pad for personal and social advancement. We tried to inspire willing teachers at all levels to use popular culture to help their students express themselves as researchers, writers, photographers, filmmakers and video storytellers. As Whitlamism receded into memory, Australia's conversation about education became less about empowerment through literacy. The new focus was on 'academic excellence' and admission to elite universities. A movement of teachers began advocating for *Metro* to reverse our democratic course: they wanted to narrow our editorial mission to supporting Year 12 media studies programs. Others lobbied for *Metro* to promote the introduction of semiotics and other schools of academic film criticism into the Year 12 curriculum.

I passed the baton of *Metro*'s editorship to Helen Kon, and landed in New York just as the chainsaw of Reaganism began slashing any American educational program that could even remotely be described as 'Whitlamist'.

\*

My career has never been more fulfilled than when I worked on *Metro*. As well as those mentioned above, I'd like to remember and thank: Dawn Brown, Ivan Gaal, Wayne Levy, Daphne Merry, John Sergeant, Eric Scherer, Neville Stanley, Peter Yewers, Diana Crunden, Jim Fyfe, Neil Bell, Dr Ian Gordon, John Doig, Harold Dover, Barbara Anderson, Peter Hourigan, Maria Triaca/Harris, Ken and Annette Berryman, and Peter Westfield. My apologies to the many other important contributors who have slipped from my memory.

# A brief history of *Metro*

» WAYNE LEVY
Committee member, ATFAV

*This excerpt has been reprinted from* Metro's *100th issue (Summer 1995) with minor adjustments. In memory of Wayne Levy (1944–2003).*

Little did a small group of educators / film enthusiasts sitting around drinking coffee in Ed Schefferle's office at the State Film Centre in 1963 imagine that the Association of Teachers of Film Appreciation (ATFA) quarterly newsletter we were planning would still be published and read thirty years down the track.

A roneoed publication of eighteen pages was surreptitiously printed and distributed by Schefferle as a 'semi-official' SFC publication. The newsletter was mostly written and edited by John Murray from Coburg Teachers' College […]

I was a student teacher at Mercer House Teachers' College. Being deaf in one ear, I couldn't get a studentship to Coburg Teachers' College and one of my lecturers at Mercer House, Lesley Cunningham, introduced me to Ed and John.

I think I was the first student-teacher to join ATFA. Cunningham was a frustrated filmmaker. The only person I knew at that time to have her own 16mm H16 Bolex movie camera. She had the personality to inspire study of film in her students. I remember that, being a poor student from the wrong side of the Yarra, at a private teachers' college, and all my earned money going towards fees, Lesley actually paid ATFA my first $1.25 student joining fee. The membership fees were $2.50 for individuals and $5 for schools and libraries.

The first few newsletters were distributed to about thirty interested persons in July 1963. We were ecstatic when by 1964 the membership had grown to around fifty members and the budget for the quarterly newsletter was $30. Postage and envelopes were 'fiddled' through the State Film Centre by Ed.

The *Film Appreciation Newsletter* contained such interesting articles as 'Cinema Technique: The Shot'; 'What's Happening on Television', a discussion of *Naked City*, *The Defenders* and *Dr Kildare*. The newsletter finished off with a few film 'appraisals'. An incredible contrast to the recent articles in *Metro* like 'The Age of Innocence: A Bloodless Feast' (*M*97); 'Scorsese's Constraints of Desire' (*M*97); and 'Recent Thrillers: Postmodern Play and Anti-Feminism' (*M*97).

I suppose Ed had garnered the covers from the State Printing Office; perhaps it was used as a cover for some of Henry Bolte's reports to Parliament. Anyway as we got these coloured covers 'free' we used them. Another cover, a photograph of a dead Bonnie, from actual photographs of *Bonnie & Clyde*, appeared and we used this for three issues, and another cover which I always thought of as our 'Easter Bunny' cover was used for a further two issues.

During the 1970s subscriptions picked up as film studies began to expand in schools and universities, and with a publishing grant from the Film and Television Board of the Australia Council for the Arts, through the efforts of Dawn Brown, the newsletter went to a series of black-and-white covers, and later single-colour covers.

When it was merely stapled down the spine my wife Marilyn and I saved ATFA money by collating it ourselves, with pages spread around the lounge-room. This probably explains many doubled up pages and the odd missing page in early editions of the newsletter. Sorry!

It was not until the 1980s and 90s with a membership of over 2000 and with publishing grants from the Australian Film Commission and Film Victoria that the superb graphic colour covers began to appear around No. 90 and beyond. With the artistic endeavours of the present designer and editors of *Metro*, using desktop publishing techniques, it has become as professional as any film and media magazine on the market.

# The bridge

» LISA FRENCH (RMIT UNIVERSITY)
Associate Editor, *Metro* (2010–present)
Contributor, *Metro* (1997–present)

Reaching deeply into both academia and industry, *Metro* has been a bridge between the two for more than fifty years. It provides a unique and extremely important cultural record that, since 1963, has authoritatively documented the shifts and changes in Australian screen culture (which includes all the activities in the sector from production, exhibition and distribution through to critical commentary and industry perspectives).

I first encountered *Metro* when I was a media student at Rusden State College. My lecturer, Peter Greenaway, was centrally involved in ATOM. He was the most significant figure in media education in Australia, and had a huge influence on the path media education took. He was on the ATOM board and, like many who served, gave hours of his time to the organisation – which, for decades, has run 'on the smell of an oily rag'. Greenaway's influence can still be seen in ATOM's previous logo.

Much later, I joined the ATOM board myself and, more than twenty-five years ago, spent three years as coordinator of the ATOM Awards (a highly successful program that was then documented in the pages of *Metro*). My favourite thing about the ATOM Awards was running the children's judging panel, and those were always the awards the industry valued. While I was the awards coordinator, I worked with the wonderful editors of *Metro*: Sheila Allison, Paul Kalina and the incredible Peter Tapp. Peter deserves an Oscar not just for what he has achieved for *Metro*, but also for the scope and depth of ATOM activity across a range of fronts – from film study guides through to the monograph series *The Moving Image*, which has produced books on John Hughes, the Australian Film Institute (AFI), Giorgio Mangiamele and *The Story of the Kelly Gang* (Charles Tait, 1906), among others. Long-serving board members such as Roger Dunscombe also deserve accolades; Peter, in particular, connected me with UNESCO because of ATOM's reach into global media education and gender.

I have written for *Metro* over many years and also proudly hold a post as associate editor. The distinguished names of associate editors are a testament to the esteem in which the magazine has been held by

Back around 1974 it was Dawn who suggested a name change from ATFA to ATFAV, the Association of Teachers of Film and Video […] However, I was horrified when Dawn went on to suggest that our magazine be renamed *Metro*. A quite heated discussion ensued and being a member of the old guard I argued that the ATFA 'newsletter' had gained a place in schools and was read by teachers and students and that a name change would throw everybody into confusion. I remember being outvoted about twelve to one. How wrong I was!

Dawn argued that the name *Metro* had connotations with the 'Paris Metro' (is this a movie theatre?), 'metra' (womb), 'metropolis' (mother city – Dawn was certainly a feminist ahead of her time!), 'metronome' (a device to mark time) and good old MGM. What this had to do with us in film studies here in Australia I never quite worked out! However, in hindsight, I do agree now, Dawn's idea of the name change was a stroke of genius.

*Metro* has developed further than I think any of that first committee ever envisaged. Its stature has kept pace with the times with articles from filmmakers and academics making it required reading by all of us teachers who work in schools, TAFEs and universities and those filmmakers who have put pen to paper and given time for interviews and discussion about their work.

At one stage, I published an index for the newsletter from No. 1 to No. 32. Being the proud owner of a full set of *Metro*s it is fascinating to leaf through them noting the people who have written articles and essays for the magazine over the past thirty years. Sitting here contemplating this collector's delight, I reckon I might just index the remaining numbers in my retirement! There is a wealth of terrific information amassed here in my *Metro*s and the mere act of caressing such a bibliophile's collection is a delight!

*Metro* predates *Cinema Papers*, which recently published its hundredth issue, and we are very well served by both magazines, but I think at times *Metro* might consider some of the old style of article about how to look at such and such film or how to use it in the classroom, or hints for teachers and students in film and video production. *Metro* must not forget its beginnings! I wish to congratulate Peter Tapp and the present committee on the superb presentation of the publication we receive today. I hope I'm around for *Metro* 200 to add to my beloved magazine collection.

**From top:**
*M*100;
*M*97; *Film Appreciation Newsletter* vol. 2, no. 7

academics here and abroad. The authors for each issue further substantiate this, and the magazine itself has welcomed important critical attention for documentary and films from the Asia-Pacific region. Additionally, in 1994, I wrote for a small publication called 'Supplement to *Metro*' with an article documenting a 'Women Applying to Film School' course that I organised for Women in Film and Television (WIFT). That publication quickly grew and became *Metro Education*, and is now *Screen Education*.

*Metro* is held in high regard by the industry, whose screen adventures have turned up in its pages. In particular, I was on the board of the AFI for nine years and, during that time, wrote articles in *Metro* based on the institute's 'Conversations on Film' events. This enabled insightful industry talks to be captured and, through publication in the magazine, their expertise was shared, along with the key debates that were raging at the time. Among them were industry luminaries like Jill Bilcock, Richard Flanagan, Samantha Lang, Pamela Rabe, Sigrid Thornton, Alison Tilson, and Mandy Walker.

In my view, *Metro*'s most significant contribution has been as an archive for Australian (and, arguably, New Zealand as well) cinema and a resource for the teaching of it. That is its greatest legacy. It also forms a unique photographic record of that cinema, and it has a voluminous stable of key writers in the field. As such, it is therefore an invaluable cultural resource – and not just that, it is a great read. Happy 200th issue, *Metro*!

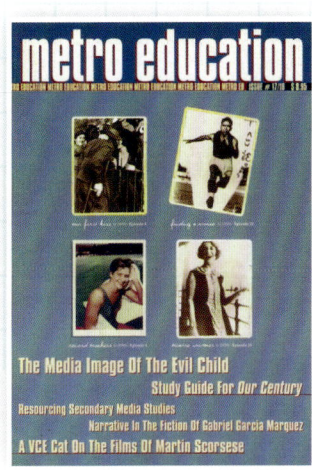

**Above:** Issue 17/18 of *Metro Education*

# Letter from the editors

» GRETA PARRY
Subeditor, *Metro* (2008–2017)
Editor, *Screen Education* (2013–2017)

*Metro* has long held an esteemed place in the Australian screen industries, as it is one of the only publications that devotes significant attention to local releases at every level. Less obvious, but just as important, is the contribution *Metro* makes to the local publishing world. What sets it apart from so many other film publications isn't only its commitment to long-form film criticism, but also its almost stubborn refusal to cut editorial resources or standards: it continues to maintain the highest quality, attracting brilliant editors and some of the best film writers in the country.

I worked as a subeditor on *Metro* from 2008 to 2017 (excluding a short hiatus), and I worked under the three editors I interviewed for this piece. I have seen the magazine evolve with the unique insight, background and passion that each editor brought to the publication; the contributions of each have remained long after their proponent's departure, culminating in the title that we know today.

Natalie Book, who helmed the magazine from 2007 to 2010, says she was attracted to the role because 'there wasn't really anything else like *Metro* around'. When she came on board, she felt that Australian cinema was going through a difficult period: 'In 2008, I think, only one local film, Baz Luhrmann's *Australia*, made more than A$3 million at the domestic box office […] I wanted to make sure we were documenting all of it, looking carefully at why a film worked or didn't – both critically and commercially.' In addition to exploring the state of the national industry, Book introduced regular sections on formats that didn't get much media coverage – short narrative film, short-form and long-form documentary – and revived the games section.

When it came time for Book to move on, she suggested that then-subeditor John Marnell be considered as her replacement. After assuming the role, Marnell worked hard to cultivate more pieces that 'were trying to situate an analysis within the broader culture of Australia', which he felt was one of *Metro*'s strengths. It was a strength of Marnell's, too – his background was in cultural analysis rather than film, specifically, and he had previously worked at esteemed literary journal *Overland*. This experience with sociocultural analysis led Marnell to curate sections based on thematic links 'rather than just whatever the release schedule was'; he recalls, for example, looking at 'both Indigenous filmmaking and documentary as social-justice vehicles'.

Nick Tapper had recently completed a postgraduate degree in publishing when he took over from Marnell in 2011. Tapper, who had previously edited art and film writing, was interested in the unique space *Metro* occupied 'between the film industry, critics and academia – trying to stimulate a discussion that encompassed all three'. Tapper saw the magazine as a means of considering 'what Australian films are trying to do with intellectual rigour while understanding how the industry works and why particular kinds of films get made, for good or ill', something that he continued to foster. He was also keen to 'push the possibility of *Metro* as a space for literary writing within film criticism – elevating film criticism as an artform in a way that is only rarely practised in Australia'.

When I ask Tapper to reflect on the achievement he was most proud of at *Metro*, he recalls that he was pleased to have started the regular Scope screen-industry columns, which remain today, as well as having contributed to *Metro*'s ever-expanding pool of writers. Indeed, just as each editorial lead guided the magazine's general direction and thematic preoccupations, the writers they nurtured or recruited during their tenures had as significant an impact: without great writers, there is no magazine, but without great editorial guidance, there are no great writers.

Book gushes over veteran film writer and long-time *Metro* contributor Brian McFarlane – 'Brian is a national treasure. I don't know what else to say. I can't imagine that there is anyone who knows more about cinema than he does' – and Asian film expert Mike Walsh, whose missives on Asian cinema she remembers as 'incredibly smart, accessible and entertaining'. In keeping with his own background, Marnell brought several non-film writers on board, including some from his connections at *Overland* and other literary spaces, broadening the magazine's scope and reach.

Tapper singles out noted writer and filmmaker Sarinah Masukor as a particularly pleasing addition to the roster during his editorship. Like many other writers, Masukor began contributing to *Metro* relatively early in her career. While the magazine's commitment to long-form analysis has always attracted established writers looking to engage in extended critique rather than straightforward review, *Metro* has also consistently published emerging writers. The editorial staff's dedication to, and enthusiasm for, new voices in writing is, in fact, an extension of ATOM's admirable support for editors early in *their* careers.

The three editors I speak to all took up the position before they had turned thirty, and each has gone on to a prolific career in publishing: Book, until recently, worked as deputy editor for Melbourne-based politics and culture magazine *The Monthly*; Marnell founded a book imprint, MaThoko's Books, in South Africa and is now a researcher with the African Centre for Migration & Society at the University of the Witwatersrand in Johannesburg; and Tapper is now commissioning editor at literary publisher Giramondo in Sydney. Their experience with *Metro* was instrumental in setting them up for such accomplishments. Book explains that working on the various article forms 'gave [her] a great grounding in sensitive editing and rigorous fact-checking – and pretty much every aspect of the magazine-production process'; Tapper 'learned a lot about working with and commissioning writers' during his time at *Metro* – skills that are critical in his current role.

Marnell is especially thankful for the trust ATOM showed him at such an early point in his career: 'I was really given the privilege and the freedom to make substantial decisions about how content was developed, how the magazines were curated and what we were trying to do with the broader ATOM project.' The magazine's commitment to supporting the publishing industry, in addition to the monumental support it offers the screen industries, cements *Metro*'s place as a precious fixture in the national arts landscape.

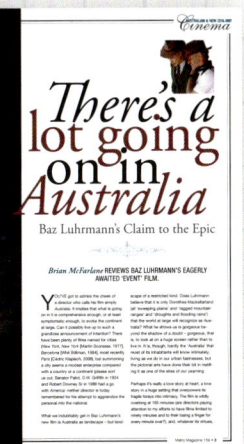

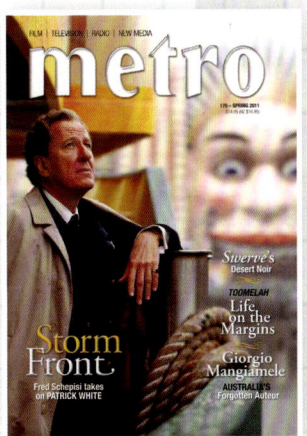

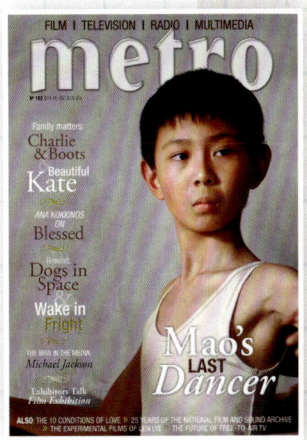

**Row 1, L–R:** *M*153, Book's first issue; Masukor's article in *M*170; *M*166, Marnell's inaugural edition  **Row 2, L–R:** *M*159; a *M*170 piece by *Overland*'s Jacinda Woodhead
**Row 3, L–R:** *M*170, Tapper's debut; *M*157, the first issue Parry subedited; a piece written by Parry for *M*192  **Row 4, L–R:** *M*162; the first Scope, published in *M*173; *M*156

# METRO HITS 200
## BIG SCREEN

L–R: *M*44; *M*181

# Indigenous representations on screen and in print

» GREG DOLGOPOLOV (UNSW)
Associate Editor, *Metro* (2015–present)
Contributor, *Metro* (2003–present)

Australian Indigenous cinema has come a long way over the past sixty years, and there are multiple factors behind the transformation. These include the emergence of immense creative and technical talent, education, recognition, institutional support and funding, and various forms of critical discourse, discussion and support. The history of mainstream recognition and the popularisation of Indigenous cinemas is one yet to be written, but it is safe to say that the work done by *Metro* over some forty years has been instrumental in promoting, discussing and celebrating the incredible achievements in this field.

Indigenous cinematic representations have moved from an absence in Australian feature films (save for a few trustworthy sidekicks of bushranging heroes), to, now, continually dominating the awards roster at a range of major international film festivals. Indigenous cinema has not just come of age – it dominates Australian cinematic representations abroad. Naturally, critical commentary, analysis and reviews have grown alongside these developments. As we celebrate *Metro*'s 200th issue, it is worth examining the role of critical commentary in shaping policy, popular perceptions, education and mainstream views, and how that has positioned Indigenous cinema politically and culturally.

A plausible assumption sitting behind the warm glow of contemporary achievements would be to expect that material written in the 1970s and 1980s

– before the glorious illumination of such scholars as Marcia Langton, Ross Gibson, Jane Jacobs and many others – was, at best, naive or, at worst, bigoted in its representation of Indigenous actors and stories. Sadly, I can take little pleasure in exposing the foibles of the past in cinema writings. In my investigation into the last 200 issues of *Metro*, I can only critique the journal for a lack of early recognition and more rigorous pursuit of locally produced material such as the TV skit show *Basically Black* and Nigel Buesst's university-slacker boxing drama *Come Out Fighting* – both of which came out in 1973 – or, indeed, *Walkabout* (Nicolas Roeg, 1971). *Storm Boy* (Henri Safran, 1976), at least, received some prominent attention in 1977 as a cover story, albeit approached from an educational standpoint (*M*40). Similarly, with the benefit of hindsight, we could criticise the journal for not pre-empting the huge new wave of Indigenous cinemas; however, by the late 1990s, *Metro* was regularly shaping critical and policy debates around Indigenous representation. In celebration of this special issue, I would like to briefly revisit some highlights and examine our industry's trajectory and oscillations in examining Indigenous cinemas.

Arguably the first true long-form critical essay on Indigenous representations in Australian cinema was one written in 1977 by Andrew Pike for *Meanjin*, subsequently reprinted the year after in issue 44 of *Metro*. A measured and detailed overview of the politics of erasing Aboriginal characters from feature films – even those set in the bush – it argued that 'the absence reflects a lack of awareness and comprehension of Aboriginal existence that is perhaps common to most urban Australians'. The article offered a largely ethnographic survey of fiction films featuring Indigenous characters from their first appearances in the bushranging genre until 1912, and posited an explanation for Aboriginal characters' absence, particularly through prolific director Ken G Hall, who, as Pike put it, 'was unable to make them credible as villains for Australian audiences' (*M*44). This latter point is worth pondering given what we now know of the frontier wars and state-sponsored massacres.

Writing in 1988, Jo Dougal and Rod Lucas presented a lucid account of the history of stereotypes, the power of colonially controlled images and then-new opportunities for Indigenous representations. 'The burgeoning of Aboriginal history, autobiography, visual arts, video and film can be seen, in part, as a move to regain control of those things which seek to present themselves as "Aboriginal",' they argued. Aboriginal creatives 'are seeking to establish Aboriginal voices, Aboriginal images and Aboriginal viewpoints different

**Right, from top:** *M*77; *M*96; *M*131/132; *M*190

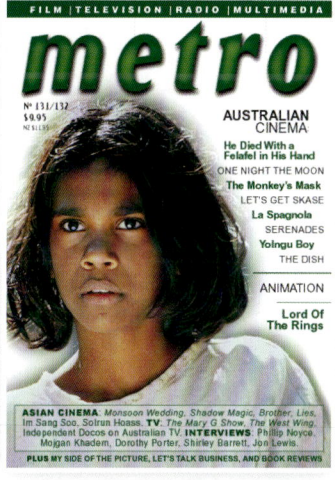

from those (mostly non-Aboriginal) which have sought to represent them in the past' (*M*77). Dougal and Lucas captured that moment of transformation when Indigenous artists began to wrest control over their own image production and dissemination.

By the 2000s, much had changed at *Metro* in terms of the regularity and engagement of its writings on Indigenous cinema, with greater focus put on individual films that were 'unashamedly populist while still managing to be tongue-in-cheek political' (*M*164). An influential 2002 paper by Dave Palmer and Garry Gillard highlighted the power of ambivalence in reshaping representations of Indigenous people by 'constantly threaten[ing] to make non-Aboriginal endorsement of colonialism unsteady. The presence of [Aboriginal Australians] in film problematizes the position, the national consciousness and identities of settler Australians' (*M*134). These instances of ambivalence in Australian cinema, they argued, transforms our way of seeing and our sense of home.

Reflecting on the sustained success of Indigenous films at the box office and at prestigious film festivals around the world, celebrated filmmaker Rachel Perkins struck a conciliatory and pragmatic tone in a 2010 interview with *The Sydney Morning Herald*'s Jim Schembri: 'I've always thought that Indigenous films could cross over into the mainstream and that it was the content that was making them not do that […] Cinema is about entertainment'. The challenges for *Metro* into the future are to maintain the critical and educational interest in Indigenous cinemas that it has thus far encouraged, and to introduce new voices and engage new audiences. Above all, it must continue reminding readers that Indigenous cinema has always been inseparable from our broader understanding of Australian cinema.

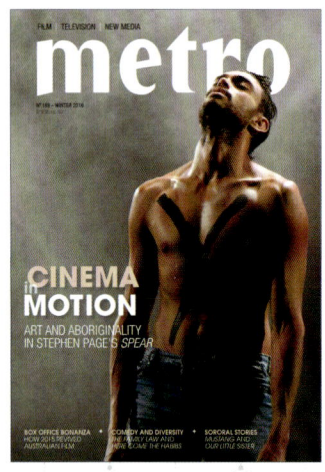

**Clockwise from top left:** *M*189; *M*77; *M*149; *M*195

Clockwise from top left:
*M*184; *M*185; *M*175; *M*172

# Classic takes: the NFSA essays

» BRIAN MCFARLANE

Series Editor, NFSA essay series (2007–present)
Contributor, *Metro* (1993–present)

The original aim of the essays in *Metro*'s National Film and Sound Archive of Australia (NFSA) series was to provide definitive accounts of Australian films that were important during the 'revival' of the 1970s and 1980s, but it has now gone well beyond any such parameter. The series was set in train after Kodak and Atlab issued remastered prints of the films in the early 2000s; since its beginnings in *Metro* 152, forty-four titles have been explored to date. The standard of the essays has been consistently high: thorough in research, written in prose that makes them accessible to a wide readership and providing a first port of call for anyone wanting to pursue any of the films discussed or the work of their makers.

As editor of the series, I only required that each piece cover production history, an examination of the film text itself and the reception of the film by the public and critics. How the individual authors went about approaching these matters was up to them, and the result has been a pleasing variety of methods and attitudes. Some have been concerned with situating their film in the broader context of Australian filmmaking of the period; others, in the context of the director's filmography.

The range of films chosen reflects some of the main trends of the originally designated period. One of the rare films to date outside the 1970s and 1980s was Charles Chauvel's *Jedda* (1955; *M*184) – on many counts one of Australia's most significant films. Indeed, an overall objective for the series was that of striking a balance between the obviously key films,

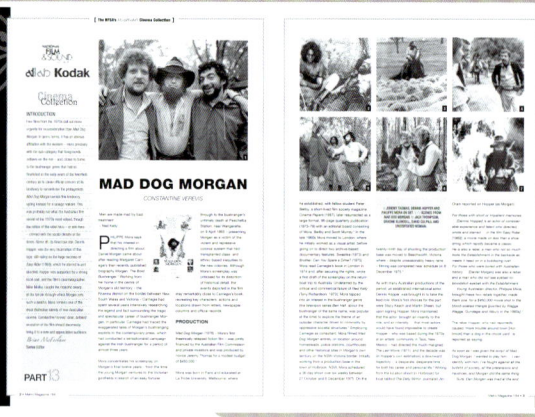

**Clockwise from top left:**
M164; M182; M186; M183

whether from commercial or critical viewpoints, and those that appeared to cry out for resuscitation, films that seemed to have fallen out of the public memory. In this respect, one might draw a contrast between *Crocodile Dundee* (Peter Faiman, 1986; M185), still perhaps the most popular Australian film, and *Night Cries: A Rural Tragedy* (Tracey Moffatt, 1990; M183), a valuable study of aspects of Indigenous cultures but by no means as widely seen as it might have deserved. Again, while the prestigious literary adaptations were commanding critical attention in the first decade of the revival – and thus we have a study of *The Getting of Wisdom* (Bruce Beresford, 1977; M175) – there have also been essays on genre pieces like the thriller *Money Movers* (Beresford, 1978; M161) and social-realist studies of urban lives as in *The FJ Holden* (Michael Thornhill, 1977; M155).

I wanted to see some of the well-known films of the period reappraised, so came an essay on *Sunday Too Far Away* (Ken Hannam, 1975; M158), a crucial title in the business of getting the New Australian Cinema moving. As well, though, it was felt salutary to bring to light again films that, while being very much of their time, seemed to have slipped out of sight – hence the essays on *Mad Dog Morgan* (Philippe Mora, 1976; M164) or *Pure Shit* (Bert Deling, 1975; M165). How would these titles survive critical scrutiny thirty-odd years on? And what about the 'surfing film' phenomenon: would films such as *Crystal Voyager* (David Elfick, 1973; M182) prove to have claims on attention for viewers other than the zealots of the waves?

The kind of research that has gone into each of the essays is important in placing the films in a variety of contexts: historical, generic and industrial, for instance.

**Clockwise from top left:**
*M*191; *M*155; *M*198; *M*180

'Historical' can refer not just to how the film belonged to the period of its making, but also to what it may have meant in terms of, say, a director's career. As to 'generic', these noteworthy Australian works tackled a wider range of film types than might have seemed the case at the time when the big prestige titles (such as Peter Weir's 1975 *Picnic at Hanging Rock*; *M*35, *M*149, *M*193) were more apt to be regarded as works sui generis, so it seemed important to investigate again what made a heist thriller such as *Money Movers* work – or an action-adventure like *The Man from Hong Kong* (Brian Trenchard-Smith, 1975; *M*180) or a war film like *The Odd Angry Shot* (Tom Jeffrey, 1979; *M*156). By 'industrial', I refer to the kinds of problems, obstacles and encouragement that lay behind getting this or that film not just onto the screen, but onto the sound stage – or wherever filming began. It always has to be remembered that film is not just art; it is an industrial product as well, and one of the strengths of the essays in this series lies in how they suggest the interweaving of these two disparate strands of influence.

As series editor, I have been grateful to the film scholars and critics who have been responsible for maintaining the collection's high standard of analysis and readability. Film is a popular artform, and there needs to be some writing about it that takes this into account so that it is made accessible to a reading public beyond those who are already steeped in screen culture. In bringing famous films to new appraisal or bringing less famous ones to light again several decades later, the series has offered the pleasures of recognition or of new insight for anyone who is interested in Australian cinema from whatever stance, whether as film scholar or film enthusiast.

# The changing face of genre

» OLIVER PFEIFFER
Contributor, *Metro* (2013–present)

As highlighted throughout Mark Hartley's entertaining, exhaustive documentary *Not Quite Hollywood: The Wild, Untold Story of Ozploitation!* (2008; *M*158), Australian genre films faced substantial prejudice during their rise in the 1970s and 1980s. After all, they had the misfortune of being released around the same time as such celebrated Australian New Wave titles as *Picnic at Hanging Rock* (Peter Weir, 1975; *M*35, *M*149, *M*193) and *My Brilliant Career* (Gillian Armstrong, 1979; *M*157). In the documentary, critic and social commentator Phillip Adams even admits: 'Most of us were very snobby about genre films – there's no question about it. You didn't approve of them.'

This would perhaps explain *Metro*'s meagre coverage of genre during this period. Significantly, pre-eminent existential shocker *Wake in Fright* (Ted Kotcheff, 1971) didn't receive analysis until almost a decade after its release – though it's perhaps also worth mentioning that the film's original print was lost for forty years. In this particular piece from 1980, however, Dennis Bowers regarded it as 'undoubtedly one of the best films to have been made in Australia', applauding how it extended on its overemphatic source novel to skilfully conjure subtle ambiguity that invited the viewer to draw their own interpretations (*M*51). Decades later, a 2009 analysis would shower similar praise on the now-recognised classic, with Dave Hoskin suggesting that the initial neglect of the film was justified by how too close for comfort its depiction of aggressive Aussie hospitality was for local cinema-goers of the time (*M*162). And, in 2017, Gabrielle O'Brien acknowledged how *Wake in Fright* profoundly reshaped our national cinema outlook and actually inspired the budding auteurs of the Australian renaissance (*M*193).

In 1999, the essence of a cinematic 'Australianness' was discussed in an extensive interview with George Miller, who reflected on his original *Mad Max* series (1979–1985) and how it projected a quintessential alternative to the sanitised sense of national identity presented in those renowned 1970s period films (*M*123). In a similar vein, delving deep into the production history and hostile critical reception of the notorious *Turkey Shoot* (Brian Trenchard-Smith, 1982), a 2009 piece considered how, by that point in Australian cultural history, the Ozploitation period had become heralded as a golden age of local cinema (*M*162). This is arguably due to not just Hartley's aforementioned eye-opening documentary, but also the success of homegrown genre products like *Wolf Creek* (Greg McLean, 2005; *M*145, *M*148, *M*150).

The point is that we've come a long way since the critical snobbery of the 1970s. In 2009, *Metro* published a two-part 'Beyond the Cringe: Ozploitation and Australian Paracinema' special feature (*M*161, *M*162). And, in 2014, the magazine dedicated close to half of its 180th issue to a one-off 'Horror Down Under' section, which paid serious attention to contemporary films like *Wolf Creek 2* (McLean, 2013), *The Babadook* (Jennifer Kent, 2014) and Hartley's own 2013 remake of Richard Franklin's Ozploitation classic *Patrick* (1978). It also shed light on a slew of underappreciated 1980s genre films that were overlooked even in *Not Quite Hollywood* itself, and offered insights into horror distribution, reception and success both locally and overseas.

A spiritual successor to 'Horror Down Under' was 2018's 'Spotlight on Genre Film' special-feature in issue 195, headlined by Warwick Thornton's acclaimed western *Sweet Country* (2017). It also included, among other things, discussions on the rich cinematic world of Aussie sci-fi *OtherLife* (Ben C Lucas, 2017), the 'quintessentially Australian' zombie flick *Cargo* (Yolanda Ramke & Ben Howling, 2017), Albanian–Australian co-production horror title *Bloodlands* (Steven Kastrissios, 2017) and Canberra-shot sci-fi *Blue World Order* (Ché Baker & Dallas Bland, 2016), along with a retrospective essay on noir classic *Dark City* (Alex Proyas, 1998).

And it's personally rewarding for this Queenslander to see that the reach of Australian genre has broadened, with the emergence of productions set in Brisbane and the Gold Coast over the past decade. These have seen accompanying attention in the pages of *Metro*: from an appreciative analysis of the inventively original world building of vampire flick *Daybreakers* (The Spierig Brothers, 2009; *M*164) to an interview with the director behind Chinese-box-office success story *Bait* (Kimble Rendall, 2012), which called for an increase in Aussie genre film-making to attract foreign markets and boost our industry (*M*175).

Fortunately, emerging filmmakers have been listening – and enthusiasm for the wild, untold stories of Aussie genre films shows no signs of dying soon.

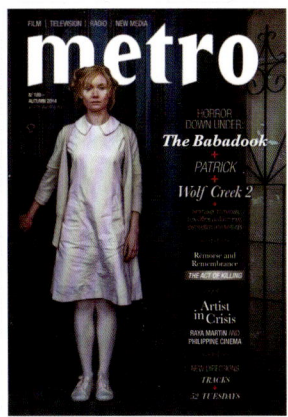

**From top:** The cover of *M*180, the horror issue; *M*193; *M*195; *M*164; *M*180; *M*175; the cover of *M*195, the genre issue

# Old journal, new media

» DAN GOLDING
Contributing Editor, *Metro* (2014–present)

You couldn't have chosen a better date to start a magazine about media than 1963. If chronicling revolutionary shifts in media technology and culture was the goal, then the 1960s was the date to begin. When *Metro* (under its previous title, *Film Appreciation Newsletter*) was founded, digital technology was taking its first steps towards the transition from high-tech Cold War curio to believable part of everyday culture. Cassette tapes – used for transporting then-huge amounts of data, not 1980s pop songs – were around a year old, and ASCII, the standard that underpins how text could be shown on computer screens, had just been developed. The impact that such fledgling technologies would have on media, and daily life, was still the stuff of science fiction. Popular videogames were still a decade away; further still was the advent of home computers, the internet, social media, streaming video and everything else.

Any look back at *Metro*'s history is therefore, unavoidably, a narrative of perhaps the most significant technological revolutions in media.

Videogames were an early fascination for *Metro* writers, who were quick to notice their appeal to children as well as the presence they had in school discussions and, later, in classrooms themselves. To this day, *Metro* has run some coverage of games, and the earliest I can find is the hugely influential puzzle adventure game *Myst*, reviewed presciently in 1994 by Joseph Brabet as 'a milestone in computer games' – though his breathless praise for the 'photo-realistic computer generated renderings at a resolution of 640 x 480 pixels' (*M*98) only reveals the ever-increasing standards of computer imagery and the often-not-affordable technology needed to power them.

Another thing that, in particular, the educators writing for *Metro* have been quick to focus on are the social, ethical and regulatory aspects of videogames. Somewhat fatefully, all the way back in 1985, Paul Gathercoal highlighted the tricky gender dynamics that young computer-game players were exposed to:

[A suburb] is not the sort of area you would expect to find a six year old child crying and running to his mother, screaning [sic], 'Rhonda is raping me again'! It seems hard to believe that such a thing might actually happen. All because Rhonda's little brother had just lost another game on their new interactive joy-stick controlled computer games system (*M*67).

Generally, videogame historians suggest that such language largely didn't become an (unfortunate) part of game culture until the 1990s. That Gathercoal then goes on to claim that 'clerics' and 'cultural watchdogs' will call for the regulation of videogames as a result of this kind of play – something that really only gained any sort of force in the next decade – makes his contribution even more prophetic. Indeed, the regulation of videogames has been a constant topic in *Metro*'s history, from the introduction of a new classification regime in 1994 (*M*99) to culture wars over the medium in the 2000s (*M*143, *M*149, *M*164), and frequently in industry columns – 'Short Cuts', as they were once known, and 'Scope', as they are today – including many of my own contributions.

There are surprises in the back issues. Curiously, a common point of discussion in the 1980s was computer interface design, either in videogames or otherwise (see: several articles drawing out of a 'Filmmaker and Multimedia Conference' – *M*103, *M*108). This reveals something of the lost history of what is today called 'UX' (user interface), which was thought of as a sort of 'walled science', and how it was once considered an exciting convergence of visual arts, image composition and computing.

Of course, the digital revolution didn't just create the fields of videogames and computer software: it changed pre-existing media fields, too. In 1984, Sue Robinson profiled composer Iva Davies – then-singer of the band Icehouse and, later, composer for films like *Master and Commander: The Far Side of the World* (Peter Weir, 2003) – and his use of a brand-new Australian synthesiser, the Fairlight. The Fairlight allowed users to record sounds and alter them – in fact, the 'orchestral hit' sound, ubiquitous to pop music of the 1980s, came from this machine and from Australia – and Robinson's profile preludes the debates around autotune in the 2000s: 'Why have a good performer when you can have a pretty one and make him or her sound good?' (*M*64).

Of course, the internet itself has been ever present in *Metro*'s pages from the 1990s on – becoming, from the mid 2000s, less of a specialist topic and more of an all-consuming entity. That really means that most of the fascinating analyses come from the 1990s – when the internet was just being introduced, and before social media and smartphones made it perhaps the most quotidian media force in history – offering glimpses into alternative histories of the present.

*Metro* published almost everything imaginable on the subject in those early years, even including simple instructions such as those from Elizabeth Reid and Vincent O'Donnell in 1994, who told us all about 'How to read the header text of "e-mail" and "usenet" messages' (*M*100). In 1995, Lisa Gye (a former colleague of mine) gives *Metro* its fullest early examination of the internet, exploring the newfangled linguistics of 'surfing' the web and what it

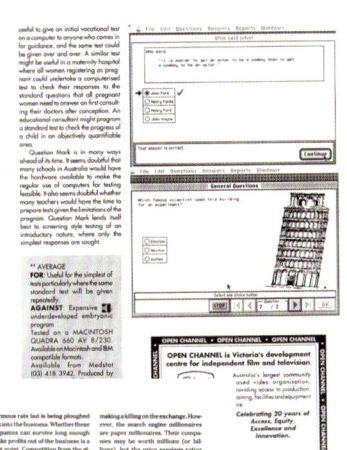

**From top:** *M*98; *M*108; *M*149

might mean for how we, as users and creators, think of it: 'What happens when we close off the way in which we imagine an apparatus?' she asks, presciently (*M*101). Everything from using the internet for business (*M*108), internet censorship (*M*108), the internet and television (*M*106), and the internet and pornography (*M*105) would follow, all the way up to a 'Web Guide' section in 2003 that included advice on something called 'viral marketing' (*M*137).

Of course, digital technology today is so ubiquitous in the media landscape as to be almost invisible except in its most extreme incarnations, like the present-day fad of virtual-reality devices. But looking back over *Metro*'s history – even just from the crucial period of the 1990s to the 2000s, when personal computing, the internet and videogames all went from niche to cultural forces – reveals the scale to which media of all stripes have been transformed under the magazine's watch.

# Sydney and the small screen

» LIZ GIUFFRE
Contributing Editor, *Metro* (2011–present)
Contributor, *Metro* (2010–present)

One of the things I love, as a Sydney-based screen fan and analyst, is seeing how the negotiation between place, media form and content has played out over the time *Metro* has been in existence. Sydney has at times been a leader, at other times a follower, and at other times again merely one place in a chain contributing to a larger screen landscape.

In 1985, *Metro* ran an interview by John Hill with Ian Muir, who had written a Master's thesis at UNSW on the changing role of Sydney television. Hill, himself an academic at the University of Newcastle at the time, asked about how television in a region like Sydney attracted and maintained viewers across different stations and with different interests; Muir responded: 'In Sydney, where we have three commercial stations competing, if you did a content analysis at the end of the week you would find they offered pretty much the same range of things' (*M*67). Sydney in the mid 1980s could be anywhere in Australia in the 2010s, it seems. Similarly interesting is a 1990 study of the media coverage of the Sydney Hilton Hotel bombing from about a decade earlier, which explored the relationship between media forms and the factual discrepancies that arise between them when apparently reporting on the same event and evidence bases (*M*81). The real losers are, of course, the people of Sydney: which reports are to be trusted, and which tell a whole story? Again, a prescient argument to be mindful of in the contemporary era of 'fake news'.

By the 1990s, *Metro*'s role in providing coverage about a local industry under threat – from the publication of documentary maker Dennis O'Rourke's address at the Sydney Film Festival in 1993 (*M*92) to Barbra Luby's piece 'Sydney Film Festival 1997: Addressing the Challenge?' (*M*112) – had become invaluable. Whereas, in 1983, Andrew Vial waxed lyrical about 'our own Sydney Film Festival', which 'is one of the oldest and most successful' of the 'other film festivals' (*M*60) – that is, those other than Cannes – Luby's piece gave a frank account of a festival under financial pressure. She recalled how the 1996 event had 'recorded a loss of approximately [A]$78,000, which, coming after several successive years of small but accumulated losses, meant that it was a situation that had to be reversed'. Yet this pessimistic 'snapshot' also allowed for an opportunity to track progress as the festival turned around again. By

**Clockwise from top left:**
*M*67; *M*60; *M*133; *M*92

1999, Luby was able to report on a Sydney Film Festival that was in much better health, able to serve its city and its medium so that '[t]he cultural needs of Sydney's film community, in a climate where the multiplexes are taking over vital alternative exhibition venues, can only be nurtured' (*M120*).

By the 2000s, important events like the screening of Sydney to the world during the 2000 Olympics were also covered by *Metro*. Helen Wilson's piece on the local Seven Network broadcast of the games included details that would have otherwise been lost to history. Of particular fascination was the commodification of individuals and the broadcast deals done around them: '[S]wimming champion Ian Thorpe continues to be under contract to Seven following the Olympics,' Wilson pointed out, while 'Nine had the broadcast rights to the World Championships in Perth in August 2001, at which Thorpe broke even more world records.' This fact becomes all the more noteworthy when it is revealed that 'Seven intervened to enforce Thorpe's contractual obligations and stop him from appearing with the entire Australian swimming team on Nine's *A Current Affair* shortly afterwards' (*M133*). If looked at without this context in the future (say, by a media student investigating the identity politics of the time), Thorpe's absence may be interpreted as a political or cultural gesture. Instead, Wilson's report shows this to be the simple result of industrial quirks – an aspect of the media we still fail to consider in enough detail.

In only a few short years, screen media would be revolutionised by digital, on-demand and online content creation and dissemination, and *Metro* has been there to cover all of these, too. From Marissa Cooke's 2007 coverage of the launch of ABC2 (*M153*, *M154*) to Stephen Byrne's consideration of the changes in commercial television in the late 2000s (*M163*), the magazine has documented industry changes from production hubs like Sydney and beyond.

I've been proud to have also contributed, even if only in a small way, to this reportage; I've been examining television and new media as part of *Metro*'s Scope columns since 2011 and even long-form articles from time to time before that. In that time, I've covered, among other things, the rise of the 'second screen' (what we now think of as the near-compulsory Twitter feed for live TV), talk shows, and the establishment and rise to prominence of Netflix and other on-demand services in Australia. It's been interesting, from where I work and watch in Sydney, to see how little location can mean sometimes when it comes to audience trends and creative receptions.

Happy 200th issue, *Metro* – thank you for the opportunities as a reader, writer and fan. Here's to a few hundred more!

**Clockwise from top left:** *M154*; Giuffre's feature articles in *M178* and *M185*; *M163*

**Clockwise from bottom right:** Dunks' pieces in *M*190 and *M*197; *M*186, the queer issue

# Penning with pride

» GLENN DUNKS

Contributor, *Metro* (2013–present)

I don't know who said it first, but there is a popular self-help meme that says you are a writer as long as you write. It doesn't matter whether you're afforded the opportunity to write what you wish to write for a living, or whether you partake as nothing more than a hobby or on the side. Fictional novels, investigative journalism, personal blog or whatever other form, it doesn't matter as you sit down at your keyboard or notebook – you are a writer as long as you write.

However, what if what you want to write is film criticism on Australian cinema? And, even further down the cinematic family tree, Australian *queer* cinema at that? It's hard to paint a rosy picture when you audience is one for whom the discourse is often around what's wrong with the industry rather than on the films themselves, when multiple online archives of queer arts culture have been unceremoniously dumped from the internet without even so much as a warning, and when much of the discussion around queer entertainment is often left to the fringes of film coverage or packaged with lazy brand awareness for easier clicks.

'Top Ten Gay Sex Scenes Since *Brokeback Mountain* [Ang Lee, 2005]!'

'Celebrate Mardi Gras with These Eight Queer Movies on Netflix!'

In my relatively brief time as a professional film critic (a decade), I have definitely seen the way queer work is covered in the media change quite dramatically: from the sorts of titles given the space to be talked about, to the types of voices offered the opportunity to discuss and the ideas they are granted the space and freedom to put forward. And, of course, the dichotomy is not lost on me that queer arts coverage struggles at a time when there is more of it than ever before. It's easy to be discouraged. To write is one thing, but to be read and appreciated is another.

Although today's podcasts and specialty outlets can afford writers interested in works with queer themes and aimed at LGBTQIA+ audiences a space in which to engage, it's particularly important to acknowledge the consistent and longstanding history of *Metro* in this space. Not to completely toot the horn of the magazine I have been granted the opportunity to write for – except we're totally going to toot that horn; we're not savages – but it's true that *Metro* offers a place for increasingly-little-seen long-form critical assessments of queer art that do not have a home anywhere else.

Since my first review in *Metro* six years ago, I have covered a variety of queer film and television titles – right up until the magazine's recent coverage of the ABC's *Riot* (Jeffrey Walker, 2018; *M*197), about the gay-rights movement in 1970s Australia. With the Mardi Gras celebrations inspired by those titular riots seeing more and more corporate trappings, and with detailed reviews of products like *Riot* sadly in short supply, having my words on these topics appear in print have made each of my endeavours worth it.

Certainly, it's been hard to come by similar takes on films like *Teenage Kicks* (Craig Boreham, 2016; *M*190), a movie that I did not like, but which offered me – and, I hope, the reader – a portal into coming-of-age stories about Aussie-born queers. Likewise, the trance-like documentary *Ecco Homo* (Richard Lowenstein & Lynn-Maree Milburn, 2015), which obviously had minimal commercial prospects (it never received a traditional theatrical release), was relegated mostly to capsule reviews on the back of its local festival screenings. So I took on this film rich in potential themes for anyone interested in its subject, Melbourne's own queer underground rock muse Peter Vanessa 'Troy' Davies (*M*187).

And how rare and exciting it was to be a part of *Metro*'s powerful 186th issue built around the evolving portrayals of queer stories on screen across the Asia-Pacific region – undoubtedly a rare endeavour demonstrating *Metro*'s ongoing commitment to the causes of representation and discourse. My own contribution revolved around Australia's LGBTQIA+ products upon the twenty-first birthday of *The Adventures of Priscilla, Queen of the Desert* (Stephan Elliott, 1994). Titled 'After *Priscilla*: Queer Cinema Twenty-one Years On', it dove into a litany of works from arthouse gem *Head On* (Ana Kokkinos, 1998) and TV soap *Home and Away* to sequin-studded biopic *Carlotta* (Samantha Lang, 2014). The piece holds a particular significance for me because it allowed me to not only immerse myself in the breadth of Australian queer content in all of its forms, but also be among an edition that highlighted such worthy takes on queer subject matter – the likes of which all too often go ignored.

In *Metro*, at least, journalistic drive and critical insight into queer film and television aren't just novelties but requirements, because to lack them is to miss out on some of the most interesting cinematic works being produced. For this writer, the magazine is a reminder that, even if we pick up the (metaphorical) pen only on the rare occasion, our words are still valued and championed – and, moreover, that queer filmmakers' visions remain a vital asset to our culture and are worth exploring.

**L–R:** 1990s queer coverage in *M*101; Dunks' 2010s survey of queer representation in *M*186

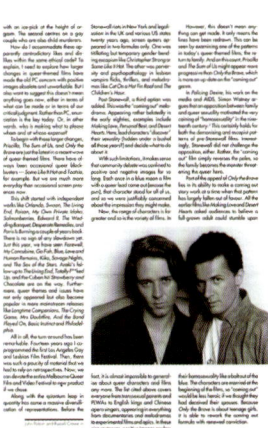

# METRO HITS 200
## BEYOND THE CURTAIN

L–R: A documentary piece by Schenkel from *M*197; Hegedus' essay in *M*181

# Advocacy meets analysis: *Metro* and documentary

» HANNA SCHENKEL

Contributor, *Metro* (2014–present)

'Critic' is not a descriptor inherently laden with goodwill in many circles. There remains a pervasive stereotype of the failed artist, the bitter miser who would rather tear down than build up. Whenever a work is shunned by critics yet popular with audiences, questions arise about what the point of critics really is: *what do they know, anyway?*

Of course, good film criticism reaches far beyond what is popular, and a good critic will never approach their work with the goal of finding fault. In fact, long-form criticism is often far less about assigning value, and more about exploring a filmmaker's approach to a particular subject or genre, or the film's context in cinematic history. It's a search for the hidden meanings and themes only deduced by the kind of close watching usually engaged in primarily by fans and critics.

I have been privileged to be counted among the regular contributors to *Metro* and its sister publication, *Screen Education*, over the past five years, examining documentaries dealing with some of the most important issues of our time: genocide, racism, the refugee crisis, sexual violence and child abuse, among many others. These films have often come to exist only through the great risks and sacrifices of those involved – filmmakers who may be putting their lives and livelihoods on the line to tell a story they deem urgent, subjects who expose their most intimate and traumatic memories and experiences to a global audience.

For documentary critics, it's impossible not to be cognisant of this, and, as such, reviewing these films becomes a delicate balancing act between advocacy and criticism. In the current sparse funding environment for documentary, rare is the film that makes it onto the screen without truly profound subject matter at its heart. When reviewing such titles, it's easy to be swept up into a discussion of content over craft – a trap I myself have undoubtedly fallen into at times.

But a worthwhile story does not necessarily equal a *well-crafted* story, and the kind of documentary criticism featured in *Metro* often serves a dual role. On the one hand, it amplifies important subjects and gives those who tackle them avenues to do so effectively; on the other, it holds up a mirror to documentary makers, challenging them to use the form to its fullest potential.

Which of these roles takes precedence depends on who you ask. While researching for this article, I had the opportunity to speak to another documentary critic who has written for *Metro* over the years. Julia Scott-Stevenson has been reading the magazine since her undergraduate days and contributed to numerous editions since 2011. As a former programmer and impact producer for the Antenna Documentary Film Festival, she also knows firsthand how the coverage provided by publications like *Metro* can bolster a film's long-term success:

*As a festival programmer, I think general coverage and criticism is immensely important to the run of a film, and a publication like* Metro *really comes into its own in the contemporary era that sees a diversity of types of film distribution […] From an impact perspective, inclusion of some of the critical analysis in a study guide, for example, can be really useful.*

Most documentaries are produced with a life beyond the festival circuit in mind, and, increasingly, tailored impact campaigns run by marketing and distribution experts have been bringing these films to where they truly matter – into the hands of teachers, social workers, politicians and those who are affected by, or have power to affect, the topics depicted on screen. This protracted life cycle and aspiration to effect meaningful change make documentaries particularly well suited to *Metro*'s quarterly schedule, partially academic readership and comprehensive style, according to Scott-Stevenson: 'The long-form pieces involving deeper analysis, coupled with the potentially longer life of a film and thus opportunities to share the analysis, really complement each other.'

As the magazine is published by ATOM, a substantial proportion of its readership is made up of educators and academics. A third major segment – filmmakers – was represented by another passionate reader and occasional contributor I spoke to. Peter Hegedus started making documentaries in 1999. His documentary credits include *My America* (2011) and *Inheritance: A Fisherman's Story* (2003), which was shortlisted for an Academy Award.

Hegedus says he 'grew up' with *Metro*, which, for him, was an important source of industry knowledge: 'Especially before the internet came to dominate our lives, I received a great deal of my screen news and information from *Metro*.' The filmmaker also saw his own work critiqued in the magazine, which he took as a sign of success: 'News about my work over the years did appear in *Metro*, and it was always reassuring to be recognised in such a reputable film magazine.'

To Hegedus, a documentary critic's role does not differ much from that of a fiction-film critic, with both acting as crucial gatekeepers in the industry.

*Documentary criticism holds us filmmakers accountable in some way and is therefore pivotal in the process of dissecting, analysing and understanding the work that claims to have observed, explored or uncovered a particular kind of truth.*

After all, it is a desire to portray truth that unites fiction and documentary, be that truth emotional or historical in nature. Indeed, contrary to what disgruntled fans or shunned artists may suspect, most critics are not just deeply passionate advocates for the screen industries, but also driven by this same hunt for truth that inspires filmmakers and documentarians. As such, good criticism forms a vital step in the ongoing evolution of how we tell stories – real and imagined – on screen, and should reach far beyond whether the critic 'liked' what they saw. As Hegedus puts it: 'I believe we must question at all times, to keep us filmmakers and our work honest.'

**Clockwise from top left:** *M*150; *M*145; *M*121/122; a piece by Scott-Stevenson from *M*183

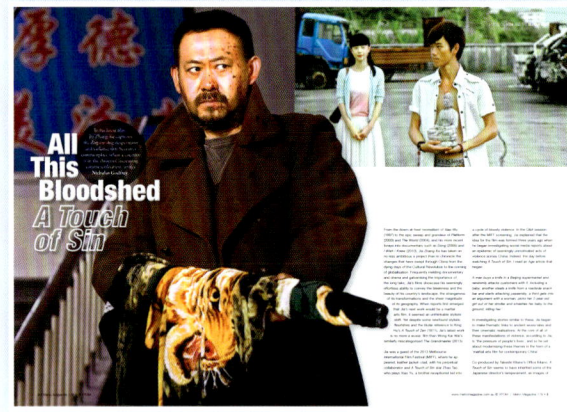

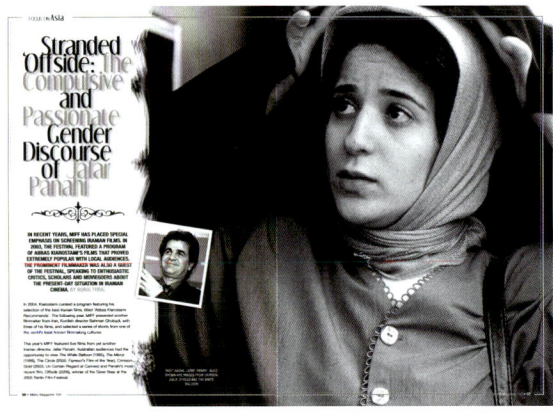
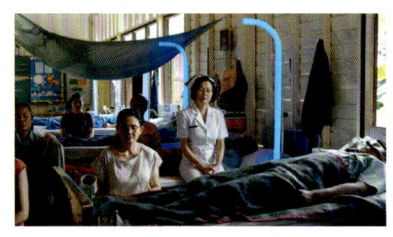

**Clockwise from top left:** A festival overview by Walsh from *M*167; *M*179; *M*176; *M*188; *M*146; *M*183; *M*150; *M*182

# Three paths to Asian cinema

» MIKE WALSH
(FLINDERS UNIVERSITY)

Associate Editor, *Metro* (1998–present)
Contributor, *Metro* (1997–present)

As I work my way through each new edition of *Metro*, I see the contents grouped first into articles on Australian cinema and then into a focus on Asia. This suggests some sort of intellectual urgency or specificity of interest for Australians – a claim that Asian cinema ranks, or should rank, high on our cultural agenda. Given this auspicious occasion for *Metro*, it is appropriate to pause and examine that assumption.

The major pathway many Australians have taken to Asian cinema has been the fan route. Martial arts, anime and hero-gangster films have long led young moviegoers to seek out protagonists with big eyes and heroes who can kick their adversaries in the chest or mow down an army without reloading their automatic pistols. I remember the lights coming up after my first John Woo film and being amazed that all films were not like this. Suddenly, there were movies that *moved*, unfettered by restraint or considerations of good taste or pious moralism. There was a freedom here in which stylistic flourish and daring athleticism could find free rein.

The industrial effects of these films should not be sneezed at by Australians, either. The Madman distribution company grew out of Chinatown Video, a label set up to release VHS versions of Jackie Chan and Jet Li films. The business continues to be anchored on the demand for anime.

A second path to Asian cinema has been the arthouse, which, since the 1960s, has recognised a handful of major auteurs such as Akira Kurosawa and Satyajit Ray. Since 2000, I have followed Asian cinema through festivals around Australia but also in Hong Kong, Busan and Tokyo, reporting on them in the pages of *Metro*. Festivals not only group films so that you can grasp the general trends that are emerging, but also give you a reason to go places. While more and more people are content to have their movies come to them in their homes and on their tiny little devices, I am thankful that the pages of *Metro* remain open to those perverse enough to still want to go to movies – even when it involves a plane trip.

But festival films are also examples of casting off restraint. If Hong Kong's Woo took up Sergei Eisenstein's mantle in furthering the affective possibilities of montage, directors like Taiwan's Hou Hsaio-hsien and Tsai Ming-liang have appeared at the other end of this spectrum, boldly exploring the potential of minimalism and long takes. Other major figures such as Hirokazu Koreeda, Jia Zhang-Ke and Apichatpong Weerasethakul have appeared in Japan, China and Thailand, respectively. While Japan has constituted one of the world's great national cinemas for almost a century, other countries in East Asia have routinely shown a willingness to experiment that has been singularly lacking in this country. Asia has been marked by its embrace of the new. This seems fitting, given that there is nowhere in the world that has undergone such ferocious change in the last few decades as East Asia.

And, finally, there is a third pathway to Asian cinema that has only emerged strongly in Australia in the past few years: the surge in popular Asian cinema for diasporic and student audiences. As Motion Picture Distributors Association of Australia box-office figures show, Indian films of a variety of languages, along with Chinese and Korean films, now constitute fully one-third of all the films released commercially in this country. One-third! If we count among them co-productions such as *The Meg* (Jon Turteltaub, 2018) and *Crazy Rich Asians* (Jon M Chu, 2018), they account for almost 7 per cent of the Australian box office – significantly more than Australian films! To take up the rhetoric of Screen Australia: who is really telling our stories here?

As immigration from an array of countries increases, and as Australian tertiary education becomes more oriented towards a service provided for Asian students, our cinema-distribution landscape is being remade. Companies such as Mind Blowing Films, Southern Star, TangRen and China Lion release about five films each week, yet we rarely see any of them reviewed in the English-language press. These films don't hang around in cinemas, and only a handful make it onto pay-TV or streaming services, but they are an undeniable part of Australian cinema; to pretend otherwise is to deny that the Asian communities of Australia are as Australian now as anyone else.

Certainly, challenges lie in the way of an integration of Asian films into Australian cinema. These are challenges that distributors, exhibitors, audiences and the press will need to face. And they are challenges that I will be keen to follow in *Metro*'s next 200 issues.

L–R: *M*173; *M*171

# Melbourne plays itself

» ANTHONY CAREW

Contributor, *Metro* (2011–present)

Three minutes into *Now Sound: Melbourne's Listening* (Tobias Willis, 2018), I saw myself – unexpectedly – on screen. It was both a little unnerving and not entirely surprising: this was, after all, a documentary about Melbourne's music scene, a film filled with friends and foes and fellow Triple R broadcasters, in which my face was certainly not out of place. This is a very personal example of representation, especially as it reflects on Australia's film industry: people being able to see their stories, their culture, their town reflected back at them. The presence of *Metro* in Melbourne has added another, important layer to that experience: not just seeing your town on screen, but having films set therein thoughtfully, critically discussed – the relationship between local cinema and this publication's coverage being long interwoven.

Melbourne's music community has been perennially chronicled on screen – and, in turn, in this publication's pages – from recent films like *Now Sound* and *Persecution Blues: The Battle for The Tote* (Natalie van den Dungen, 2011; *M*173) to Richard Lowenstein's accounts of the city's post-punk scene: *Dogs in Space* (1986; *M*162), *We're Livin' on Dog Food* (2009; *M*162) and *Autoluminescent: Rowland S. Howard* (co-directed with Lynn-Maree Milburn, 2011; *M*171). As well as capturing the jams and the people, these films are also about places: The Tote is both mythical and tangible, a dive bar on the corner of Wellington and Johnston streets in Collingwood; and *Dogs in Space* was filmed at a sharehouse – 18 Berry Street in Richmond – that Lowenstein had lived in.

At a time when every street corner is the site of a CCTV camera and every cafe has turned into an Instagram photoshoot, the idea of the power of having your landscape documented seems quotidian, quaint. But the arrival of the first ever Hollywood pic

**36** • Metro Magazine 200  |  © ATOM

**Clockwise from top right:** M165; M92; M141

shot on Port Phillip shores, On the Beach (Stanley Kramer, 1959), was, back then, a major event for an isolated island nation. That idea's brought home in Fallout (Lawrence Johnston, 2013; M180), a doc chronicling the production, with its contemporaneous 1950s newsreel footage showing streets – tree-lined Royal Parade, the grid of the CBD – that're both recognisable and un-, lain in the same place but completely, utterly empty. They betray the big-country-town feel of mid-twentieth-century Melbourne (perhaps the source of the apocryphal Ava Gardner quote that it was 'the perfect place to make a film about the end of the world'), which is antithetical to the current cashed-up, cacophonous, teeming-with-peeps vibe of contempo Melbz.

In an internationalist era – of information, culture and film production – it's no surprise that the city's done time as the anonymous metropolis of genre dystopia, local landmarks popping up in entertainment products like Queen of the Damned (Michael Rymer, 2002), Ghost Rider (Mark Steven Johnson, 2007) and Upgrade (Leigh Whannell, 2018; M198). But it's more fun following films through recognisable landscapes, especially if they pass the Thom Andersen test: respecting local geography over mismatched locations. Those wanting to parse drama for fidelity to reality can compare Holding the Man (Neil Armfield, 2015; M186) to Remembering the Man (Nickolas Bird & Eleanor Sharpe, 2015; M189), and modest economic-disenfranchisement / male-angst dramas Tom White (Alkinos Tsilimidos, 2004; M141, M145) and Three Dollars (Robert Connolly, 2005; M144) are made far more interesting if you recognise the streets they (sometimes incongruously) walk.

Melbourne's nocturnal landscape was a stage upon which iconic 1990s angst played out: Romper Stomper (Geoffrey Wright, 1992; M92, M117, M141, M178), Only the Brave (Ana Kokkinos, 1994) and Head On (Kokkinos, 1998; M118, M165) turning familiar locales into veritable mean streets; Animal

**Clockwise from top right:** Articles by Carew from *M*175 and *M*180; *M*189

*Kingdom* (David Michôd, 2010; *M*165), in its own Scorsesean fashion, setting criminal activity against suburban banality. Some of the best depictions of Melbourne's street life have been captured in vérité by the city's most interesting new-millennial filmmaker, Amiel Courtin-Wilson, from his short *Melbourne 2:36AM* (2001) to features *Bastardy* (2008; *M*163) and *Hail* (2011; *M*175).

Courtin-Wilson has had a career-long relationship not just with *Metro* – which profiled him as early as 2001 (*M*134) and covered his more recent works *Ruin* (co-directed with Michael Cody, 2013; *M*182) and *The Silent Eye* (2016; *M*196) – but also with the Melbourne International Film Festival (MIFF). The country's definitive cinematic event is so huge that it can serve as both a passport unto the world and an incubator of local talent/production. MIFF, too, is where *Now Sound* premiered to a local, parochial crowd, so many of whom also saw themselves on screen. One of the key figures in the film is, of course, Courtney Barnett, the Melbourne-based singer/songwriter whose success has found her lyrics, littered with local landmarks, taken to a global audience.

Similarly, I remember, in my distant youth, when *Love and Other Catastrophes* (Emma-Kate Croghan, 1996) earnt international buzz during the indie-movie frenzy of the mid-'90s, wondering what foreign audiences would make of a film so of its time/place that there's a running storyline about then–*Age* film critic (and long-running *Metro* contributor!) Adrian Martin. The specificity is, of course, part of the charm; what cinephile hasn't felt a tinge of the uncanny upon arriving in Paris or New York or Los Angeles, seeing the landmarks made oh-so-familiar by filmed entertainments?

The rising stature of *Metro*'s hometown – culturally, cinematically, musically – has given Melbourne its own such status, this a place routinely seen on screens, with these representations critically parsed, in these pages, by people who, often, live and work (and maybe are on iconic community-radio stations) here. The old cultural cringe has fallen away, the familiar no longer breeding contempt, but something closer to pride. In cinema, the delight always comes in the details, which speaks to that old writer's truism that, paradoxically, the more specific a story is, the more universal it becomes. Meaning: you can never get too local – indeed, too Melburnian.

# The reel south: Adelaide and Metro

» NICHOLAS GODFREY
Contributor, *Metro* (2011–present)

The past achievements of the South Australian film industry have long burdened, and threatened to occlude, its present. Writing in *Metro* in 2006 of 1970s premier Don Dunstan's 'Medici-like inspiration' in establishing the South Australian Film Corporation (SAFC), Russell Porter mused that, 'we didn't realize it at the time, but the people drawn to the SAFC in the mid-seventies were to become among the most influential in the following decades of the Australian film and television industries' (M150). From *Picnic at Hanging Rock* (Peter Weir, 1975; M35, M149, M193) to *Breaker Morant* (Bruce Beresford, 1980; M51, M159), the early SAFC films have exerted considerable legacies.

Over the years, *Metro* has reappraised and recontextualised these films with carefully historicised evaluations. Belinda Smaill analysed Gillian Armstrong's documentaries charting the changing lives of three Adelaide women, beginning with 1976's *Smokes and Lollies*. Smaill examined 'the intricate links between the spectacle of time passing, temporality within the documentary form and changing gender identity', suggesting that 'a historical politics of feminism haunts the series and its reception in a number of ways' (M167). Elsewhere, Adrian Danks revisited *Sunday Too Far Away* (Ken Hannam, 1975), discussing the film in relation to earlier 'runaway' productions that took advantage of outback South Australia, like *The Sundowners* (Fred Zinnemann, 1960), and the 'ocker' films of the early 1970s that 'provided a partial commercial model for [*Sunday*] to follow' (M158).

Indigenous perspectives have long been central to South Australian cinema. Writing on Ned Lander's documentary–fiction hybrid film *Wrong Side of the Road* (1981), Arnold Zable – employing language that reflected the political sensitivities of the time – remarked of its power as

one of the very few films about contemporary urban aboriginal life that gives a clear glimpse of some of the problems and aspirations of the Australian aborigine in our cities. It is a complex view, showing both the continuing forms of harassment and discrimination that form part of the daily pattern of aboriginal life, as well as some of the humour and vitality growing within some aboriginal communities (M58).

And, if the 1980s and early 1990s produced relatively slim pickings for the South Australian film industry, that changed with Scott Hicks' *Shine* (1996). Noel Purdon interviewed the

From top: *M*167; *M*158; *M*58; *M*107

director in the aftermath of the film's international breakthrough, with Hicks pointing out that he had grappled with the tension between the local and the global, musing that 'a film can be Australian, without being narrowly so. It can also be international in its presence, or for that matter in its declaration of presence' (*M*107). Almost two decades later, such a scenario played out with the release of *The Babadook* (Jennifer Kent, 2014), the first film shot at the then-new Adelaide Studios, and which was only validated in its home country after international acclaim. Nonetheless, according to Briony Kidd, the film 'vindicates the recent investment in nurturing new talent in South Australia' (*M*180).

*The Babadook* joins some of South Australia's most notorious exports that probe the darkness at the heart of suburban Adelaide: *Bad Boy Bubby* (Rolf de Heer, 1993; *M*140), *Snowtown* (Justin Kurzel, 2011; *M*169, *M*178) and, moving further out of the city, *Wolf Creek* (Greg McLean, 2005; *M*145, *M*148, *M*150). Dmetri Kamki took aim at the last of these, labelling its success 'the clearest evidence we have of the triumph of mediocrity, and of the lamentable state of film criticism' (*M*148).

But critical favour could be found elsewhere, with the Adelaide Film Festival (AFF) Investment Fund having produced a series of enduring successes: de Heer's ongoing collaborations with David Gulpilil and sound recordist James Currie, the bravura *Boxing Day* (Kriv Stenders, 2007; *M*152) and the idiosyncratic *Look Both Ways* (Sarah Watt, 2005; *M*146, *M*149). Warwick Thornton's *Samson & Delilah* (2009) is the crowning achievement of AFF's financing initiative – and, with it, Tom Redwood announced Thornton as 'the new hope of Australian cinema' (*M*160).

On the eve of her first festival in 2003, AFF director Katrina Sedgwick spoke to *Metro* about the role that a festival plays in the life of a city, stating that Adelaide 'can be transformed by a festival in a way larger cities can't' (*M*135). In 2019, AFF enters an uncertain phase of existence, returning to a biennial format for 2020 after briefly experimenting with an annual format. Adelaide's exhibition culture is further impoverished by the recent closure of DIY cinema Sax & Violins, while iconoclastic new-kids-on-the-block Allison Chhorn and Mike Retter toil at independent digital filmmaking without institutional support. South Australian politicians, bureaucrats and arts administrators alike would do well to heed Sedgwick's words, and evaluate the present, rather than the received glories of the past. Ever-parochial Adelaide would be considerably more impoverished without its cinema – and without the platforms provided by outlets like *Metro*.

**From top:** *M*180; *M*160; *Picnic at Hanging Rock*

**Clockwise from top left:** *M*140; *M*169; *M*152; *M*146; *Wolf Creek*; *Samson & Delilah*

  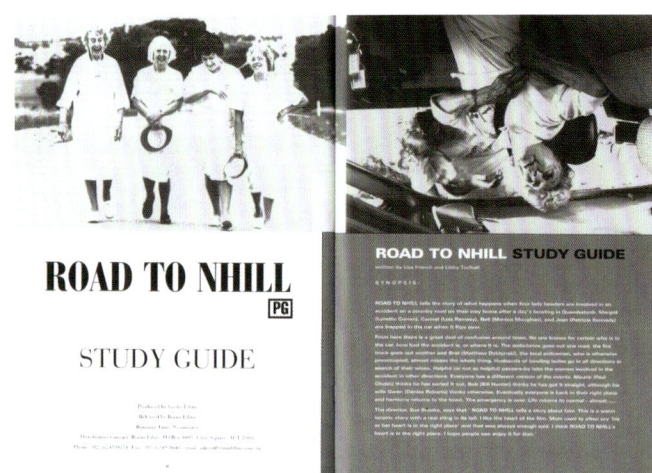

**L–R**: Pike's reflection on Ronin's *Shine* campaign in *M*192; *Metro Education* 15

# Enabling a screen ecology

» ANDREW PIKE (RONIN FILMS)

Long-time supporter of ATOM

The education market for films is traditionally not the place for gala openings, red carpets, glitz and champagne. It's a market that focuses on function, content and access, not media hype, and it often operates below the radar of the mainstream industry. It's often ignored when industry reviews or assessments are undertaken, or when marketing workshops are conducted by government agencies. In some countries, it is not even recognised as a market at all, but rather lumped in broadly with 'non-theatrical' or home entertainment.

ATOM – in all of its activities, including the publication of *Metro* and its antecedent journal, *Film Appreciation Newsletter* – has fought valiantly to encourage and facilitate the informed and appropriate use of films in educational contexts (at all levels) and in scholarly research. The ATOM Awards are almost quixotic in their brilliant effort to stand side-by-side with mainstream industry celebrations, and one can only applaud the courage and vision of ATOM's leadership in doing the work it has done for so long.

*Metro* has, from its very beginning, been an integral part of ATOM's mission and its achievements. The journal has been vital in consistently and steadfastly building greater awareness in the education sector of what the mainstream industry offers, but from a different, scholarly perspective. *Metro*'s voice has always been refreshingly independent and often unpredictable in its approach, frequently emphasising aspects of the production industry that the mainstream itself overlooks. *Metro* has given a platform for new approaches to well-known films and, even more importantly, has championed the work of fresh new voices in the production sector, with interviews and critical essays investigating the work of emerging independent filmmakers.

Through the quality of its work, and the perspectives it promotes, *Metro* has become a vital bridge between the screen industries' education-focused sectors and the more generalist areas of the production industry.

Today, most of a producer's revenue to be earned from the education sector comes from Screenrights and the cluster of off-air copying agencies such as EnhanceTV. Some producers, in Ronin's experience, don't even know about Screenrights' existence, let alone understand how it works. Others may welcome their periodic royalty payments, but see Screenrights essentially as an extension of a TV sale. It is, in fact, much more than that: it is a creature of the education domain, and those people who understand it and choose to work with ATOM's resources, including the scholarly and critical input of *Metro*, can enhance the chance of a greater result. It's a great example of the education market operating by its own subterranean practices, unknown and mysterious to many in the mainstream industry, but delivering a significant financial benefit to producers.

Ronin has been active in the film industry since 1974, and the education market has served us well throughout, with delivery formats ranging initially from 16mm film prints and VHS tapes, to DVD, streaming and downloading platforms, and, now, Screenrights. For as long as I can remember, ATOM, its study guides and its publications, especially *Metro* and later *Screen Education*, have been an essential part of our work, historically and in the present day. We could not have done what we have done, nor survived as long, without ATOM's stimulus and connectivity with the education sector – much of it in every issue of *Metro*. So bravo, *Metro*, for achieving the landmark of 200 issues!

# BACK ISSUES

## Metro has something for everyone

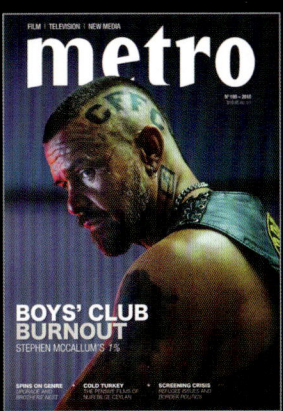

▲ **ISSUE 198**

1%. Upgrade. Brothers' Nest. West of Sunshine. The films of Nuri Bilge Ceylan. Women in North Korea. Border Politics. BackTrack Boys. Midnight Oil: 1984. I Used to Be Normal. [Censored]. Terror Nullius. Australia's early variety shows. Monkey Grip.*

▲ **ISSUE 197**

Breath. Strange Colours. Youth on the March. Winchester. Picnic at Hanging Rock, Wake in Fright and Romper Stomper TV reboots. Riot. Homecoming Queens. 24 Frames. Foxtrot. Human Flow. Gurrumul. Jill Bilcock. Storm Boy.* Sound in Warwick Thornton's films.

▲ **ISSUE 196**

Swinging Safari. Three Summers. Angels Wear White. A Man of Integrity. Claire's Camera. On the Beach at Night Alone. Blade of the Immortal. Westwind: Djalu's Legacy. After the Apology. Blue. The Piano & Top of the Lake: China Girl. Manifesto. The Silent Eye.

▲ **ISSUE 195**

Genre special-feature: *Sweet Country, Cargo, OtherLife, Better Watch Out, Jungle, Dark City. Australian Survivor. Pop Aye. The Challenge. The Song Keepers. Namatjira Project. Spookers. The Picture Show Man.* VOD programming. Co-productions.

**Pick up a copy of Australia's oldest and most respected screen magazine.**

Whether you're an avid film fan or a seasoned theorist, you will find pieces that pique your interest in *Metro*.

Every issue features long-form reviews, interviews and essays on film, television and media – new and old – from Australia, New Zealand and the Asia-Pacific region.

◄ **ISSUE 199**

The *Storm Boy* reboot. *Ladies in Black. Acute Misfortune. Celeste. Jirga. The Merger. Nanette. Dead Lucky. Vitamania. Shoplifters* and *The Third Murder. Mirai. Ash Is Purest White. Island of the Hungry Ghosts. Journey Beyond Fear. RocKabul. Ghosthunter. Dying to Live.* Virtual-reality documentaries. The Karrabing Film Collective. *Shame.**

* Part of the NFSA Restores Collection

**TO PURCHASE:** Visit The Education Shop at <http://theeducationshop.com.au>.
Issues are $19.95 plus P&H (inc. GST).

Individual articles from back issues are also available as PDF downloads from The Education Shop.

AUSTRALIAN AND
NEW ZEALAND CINEMA

# Terror, Tragedy, Truth

## ANTHONY MARAS' *HOTEL MUMBAI*

IN HIS GRIPPING DEBUT FEATURE, ANTHONY MARAS INTERWEAVES MASTERFUL PORTRAYALS BY AN ENSEMBLE CAST WITH REAL-LIFE ACCOUNTS AND ARCHIVAL MATERIAL TO RECOUNT THE GRUESOME EVENTS OF THE NOVEMBER 2008 TERRORIST ATTACKS IN MUMBAI. BY FOREGROUNDING – AND REMAINING FAITHFUL TO – THE STORIES OF ACTUAL PEOPLE WHO LIVED THROUGH THE SIEGE, THE FILM FULFILS THE TWIN DUTIES OF OFFERING TESTIMONY AND TELLING AN ENGAGING STORY, WRITES **FELICITY FORD**.

**Opposite:** Taj Mahal Palace Hotel waiter Arjun (Dev Patel)

**Above, from top:** Eddie (Angus McLaren); Eddie with Bree (Natasha Liu Bordizzo); David (Armie Hammer)
**Opposite, from top:** Chef Hemant Oberoi (Anupam Kher); Sally (Tilda Cobham-Hervey), a nanny employed by David

I was due to arrive at Chhatrapati Shivaji Maharaj International Airport in Mumbai, India, at 6pm on 26 November 2008. I am able to remember the exact date more than a decade later because, on the very same day, the city was wracked by coordinated terrorist actions that escalated into a three-day siege. A few months earlier, the effects of the global financial crisis had culminated in widespread economic instability on both macro and micro levels, with unemployment at an all-time high. Rattled by these troubling developments and concerned about my own precarious employment situation, I made the decision to cancel my flight and instead remain in London. I can distinctly recall the special BBC announcement that fateful Wednesday, interrupting the broadcast to report on the attacks: around 9.30pm, two men armed with AK-47 rifles had opened fire in the passenger hall of the Chhatrapati Shivaji Terminus railway station, killing fifty-eight people and injuring another 104. The incident at the station was the first of twelve carried out by ten men from the terrorist group Lashkar-e-Taiba: one of the largest Islamic terrorist organisations in South Asia, estimated to have several thousand members. Over the course of four days, approximately 174 people were killed (including nine of the assailants) and more than 300 were wounded.[1]

The horrific events of 26/11 are the subject of Greek-Australian director Anthony Maras' debut feature, *Hotel Mumbai*, which premiered at the 2018 Toronto Film Festival and had its general release in Australia in March this year. The film is Maras' second project to be based on real-life events; his critically acclaimed short film *The Palace* (2011) follows a family seeking refuge during the 1974 invasion of Cyprus, and shares emotional resonance with *Hotel Mumbai*. While the real-life attacks occurred all over the titular city, Maras focuses primarily on what unfolded in the iconic Taj Mahal Palace Hotel, a five-star luxury hotel in the heart of Mumbai. The film's diverse ensemble cast includes Indian-British actor Dev Patel as Arjun, a waiter from an extremely impoverished background with a young family at home; Iranian-British Nazanin Boniadi and American Armie Hammer as Zahra and David, a wealthy couple with a newborn baby; and Australian actress Tilda Cobham-Hervey as their nanny, Sally. Some of the characters directly reference real-life figures, such as Anupam Kher's chef Hemant Oberoi, whom Maras interviewed in preparation for co-writing the film alongside John Collee.[2] Additionally, Jason Isaacs' portrayal of Vasili, a playboy businessman with special-forces training, takes after several different people involved in the incident at the Taj Mahal Palace Hotel.[3]

*Hotel Mumbai* is a well-crafted dramatisation, skilfully balancing the attacks' complex chronology with economic pacing and exposition. The film opens with the arrival of the gunmen (played by Raunakk Bhnder, Ishan Khanna, Harjeet Singh and Nitin Dhiman) at a fishing village and follows them as they move through the city to carry out carefully planned assaults on the station, nearby cafes and hotels. In 2008, many of the people in these areas fled to the Taj Mahal Palace Hotel seeking refuge. While Maras' film also makes reference to attacks

in surrounding areas through news reports and conversations between characters, the narrative is firmly located within the hotel. The establishing shots of the train station, the hotel and Arjun's home provide a visual and aural guide to the different spaces and people that the ensuing narrative will revolve around. The use of time and pacing is masterful, with short but strong scenes – Arjun kissing his wife before leaving for work, or a young Australian tourist querying his order at the restaurant moments before the attacks – conveying a considerable amount of detail and providing emotional anchors for the audience. By coupling these ordinary moments with horrifically extraordinary events, the film delivers something of the trauma that an unexpected siege would have on a city.

Enhancing this impact is Maras' careful unravelling of the story. While there is, of course, a lot of bloodshed in the film, it is not so much the type of violence but rather the way in which it is deployed that is most horrifying. Or, rather, it is the *shock* of the attacks, along with the unpredictability of the gunmen, that is most affecting: characters are killed at random with little warning, thereby giving viewers no space or opportunity for comprehension or vicarious grieving. Restricting *Hotel Mumbai*'s narrative to the hotel gives the audience a fixed access point to the events. On a practical level, the incidents at the building act as a representative case study for the broader narratives of survival happening in the surrounding areas. Moreover, the hotel's reputation as a symbol of opulence creates a jarring dissonance whereby merciless acts of violence are carried out against a backdrop of expansive dining halls, elaborate floral displays and chandelier-lined hallways.

As the establishment remains fully functional, the production team had very limited access and were not able to shoot any of its interior spaces; instead, several of these scenes were filmed in a studio in Adelaide and accompanied by more footage taken at another five-star hotel in Mumbai. In addition, the film features extensive shots of the exterior of the real Taj Mahal Palace Hotel, which contributes to the setting's verisimilitude. Maraj then juxtaposes these exterior shots with actual news footage from the time[4] – an approach that proves particularly effective, as it blends the depicted drama with the lived experiences of those who suffered through the attacks. In a key scene, several characters are held hostage by the gunmen; David, Zahra and Vasili are among those detained. As they are made to lie face-down with their hands tied behind their backs, the film deftly cuts between them and harrowing news footage of the hotel surrounded by rescue teams, police, and reporters. Also featured are detailed personal accounts, CCTV footage and dialogue between the gunmen and their leaders, sourced from Victoria Midwinter Pitt's documentary *Surviving Mumbai* (2009), which inspired *Hotel Mumbai*.[5] By reproducing exchanges verbatim – including conversations with the Lashkar-e-Taiba leader known only as 'Brother Bull', intercepted from mobile-phone records – the film adds a sense of veracity to a situation that could otherwise inspire disbelief.

Films such as *Hotel Mumbai* that are adapted from real-life events embody a curious duality, straddling dramatic feature and documentary. Critical discussion of such works often focuses on where they sit along that continuum: *Is it entertaining enough? Is this what really happened?* The line between fact and fiction creates a tension that is inherently tied to expectations about what the final product should 'be' and what it should achieve. Indeed, *Hotel Mumbai* is a suspenseful drama with well-rounded characters and a clear narrative trajectory. However, it is also an account of a very specific historical event, and is thus burdened by an immense amount of responsibility to the traumatic past it is depicting. This task is not simply to honour those killed during the attacks, the survivors living in their aftermath, and the families, communities and businesses affected by this loss, along with all the special services and support staff who were pulled into the conflict. The responsibility also encompasses how this event is remembered in the collective memory of the public and whether the filmic representation accurately attends to the complexity of the situation, the contributing factors that brought it into being, and the depth and extensiveness of heartbreak. This is an exceptionally difficult brief for a film to satisfy – and it is clear that Maras and his team have given much thought as to how best to approach considerations such as historical accuracy, public grief and the personal anguish experienced on both individual and societal levels.

Most notably, Maras prioritised establishing a strong base from which to develop the film, conducting extensive research, interviews and site visits prior to shooting. Over the course of a year, Maras and Collee interviewed survivors, hotel guests, police and staff to unpack the complex stories surrounding the tragedy. Many of these interactions informed their creative decisions around characterisation and plot development – Arjun's character, for instance, was inspired by conversations with different hotel staff, many of whom are living in extreme poverty.[6] Watching Arjun prepare for work, transfer the care of his daughter to his wife at her workplace and then rush to the hotel, only to be dismissed for wearing the wrong shoes, not only invites us into his day-to-day life but also, more broadly, acknowledges the experiential disparities between patrons of the hotel and those residing in lower-socio-economic housing. This disparity in wealth also surfaces when David is held hostage by one of the terrorists in a hotel room. Having been badly wounded, the gunman calls his family to check whether Brother Bull has paid them. The money that was promised has not been received, and, while the family remain optimistic that the figurehead will keep his word, the recruit is unconvinced. This simple exchange – witnessed by David, who remains a silent observer – gestures towards some of the complex networks of vulnerability, faith and financial hardship that might encourage young, angry and impressionable men to become involved in organised-terrorism factions.

In several brief moments, Maras offers the viewer insights into the terrorists themselves. Often, these take the form of interactions that emphasise the men's youthfulness, such as when one eats something from an abandoned food

**Above, L–R:** Arjun; David's wife, Zahra (Nazanin Boniadi); Vasili (Jason Isaacs) **Opposite:** David and Sally being welcomed by hotel staff

**FILMS SUCH AS *HOTEL MUMBAI* THAT ARE ADAPTED FROM REAL-LIFE EVENTS EMBODY A CURIOUS DUALITY ... THE LINE BETWEEN FACT AND FICTION CREATES A TENSION THAT IS INHERENTLY TIED TO EXPECTATIONS ABOUT WHAT THE FINAL PRODUCT SHOULD 'BE' AND WHAT IT SHOULD ACHIEVE.**

cart and a fellow recruit tricks him into believing that he has eaten pork. Scenes showing their ability to socialise and joke powerfully generate cognitive dissonance, as we know of the immense bloodshed they have inflicted; at the same time, such images serve to humanise the men. In another scene, Arjun and two policemen, having gained access to black-and-white CCTV footage from hotel security, watch as the gunmen stalk down a hallway, their lithe bodies dwarfed by their assault rifles, the high ceilings and the expansive hallway. Unable to pair this vision with the magnitude of destruction, a policeman say, as if in disbelief: 'They're just boys.' Indeed, the age of the gunmen was something that Maras sought to underline when creating the film: 'The perpetrators were all young men, barely out of their teens.'[7] In humanising the gunmen rather than casting them as faceless villains, *Hotel Mumbai* captures the senselessness of situations in which vulnerable young men are radicalised by extremist leaders and turned into agents of terror.

*Hotel Mumbai* is an ambitious endeavour. Whenever a film's subject is a historical event with real-life victims and survivors, there is an expectation that the work will faithfully represent the events and stories of all of those involved. Of course this is an impossible aim: the 'truth' is an unwieldy and changeable thing. But a notable strength of what Maras has created is the way he has used several key characters to act as representatives for broader and more complex truths. While, during weaker points, these characters sometimes drift into stereotype – the sleazy businessman, the racist older woman, the selfless waiter – ultimately, there is an integrity to *Hotel Mumbai*'s engagement with these disparate stories and complex narratives. This, I think, is largely owing to how it has been anchored to primary sources such as interviews, news footage and recorded audio from the siege. And it is precisely these voices, images and words that remind us of the extraordinary tragedy of 26/11.

https://www.iconmovies.com.au/movies/hotel-mumbai

*Felicity Ford is a PhD candidate in screen and cultural studies at the University of Melbourne. Her research explores disruptions to cinematic form in relation to sound, vision, movement and time. She is secretary of the Melbourne Cinémathèque and a sessional tutor and lecturer in screen, gender, media and cultural studies.*

**m**

Endnotes

[1] For more on the 2008 Mumbai attacks, see '26/11 Mumbai Terror Attack Anniversary: Here Is How the Tragedy Unfolded', *India Today*, 26 November 2018, <https://www.indiatoday.in/education-today/gk-current-affairs/story/26-11-mumbai-terror-attack-anniversary-here-is-how-the-tragedy-unfolded-1396307-2018-11-26>; and Shanthie Mariet D'Souza, 'Mumbai Terrorist Attacks of 2008', *Encyclopædia Britannica*, <https://www.britannica.com/event/Mumbai-terrorist-attacks-of-2008>. For more on the terrorist organisation responsible, see 'Lashkar-e-Taiba', *Mapping Militant Organizations*, Stanford University, <http://web.stanford.edu/group/mappingmilitants/cgi-bin/groups/view/79>, all accessed 7 March 2019.
[2] Icon Films, *Hotel Mumbai* press kit, 2018, p. 5.
[3] ibid., p. 9.
[4] ibid., p. 11.
[5] ibid., p. 22.
[6] ibid., pp. 5–7.
[7] Anthony Maras, quoted in ibid., p. 9.

**This spread, L–R:** Claire (Laura Gordon); Angie (Olivia DeJonge)

AUSTRALIAN AND
NEW ZEALAND CINEMA

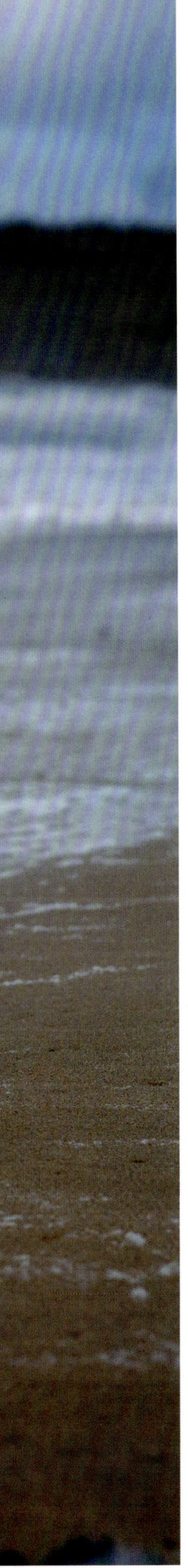

# Breaching Bounds

## THE CONFRONTING BODY IN MIRANDA NATION'S *UNDERTOW*

*UNDERTOW* CHALLENGES TABOO AND FILM TRADITION IN ITS PORTRAYALS OF THE TROUBLED – AND TROUBLING – RELATIONSHIP BETWEEN TWO WOMEN BOTH TOUCHED BY RECENT PREGNANCY. IN CONVERSATION WITH WRITER/DIRECTOR MIRANDA NATION, **ELIZABETH FLUX** EXPLORES THE TRANSGRESSIVE DEPICTIONS AND DRAMATIC NARRATIVE TURNS OF THIS INTENSE DEBUT FEATURE.

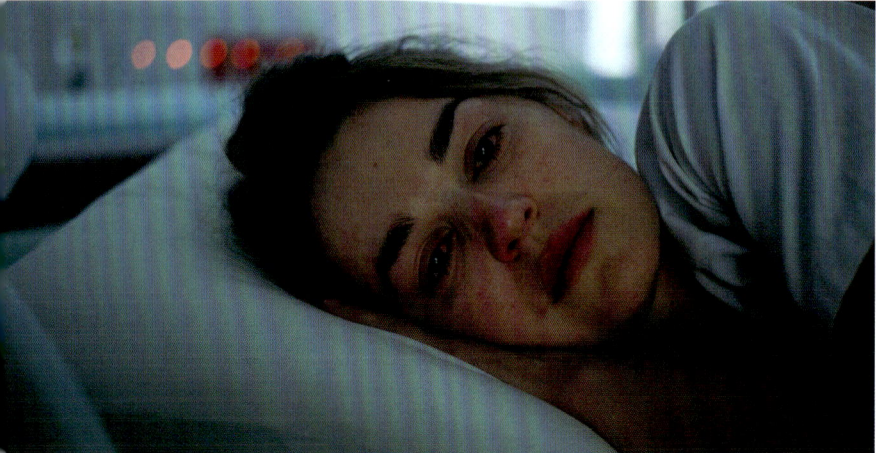

**This spread, L–R:** Claire; Angie

Films are surrounded by invisible walls. They're the categorisations, the genres, the ratings; they exist to keep things orderly and to help shape audience expectations. The walls help us know what is contained within, to compare and contrast with other filmic cities we've visited before. These barriers have value, sure – but then are they too constricting? And with films being an extension of society itself, is the existence of filmic barriers stifling growth, stifling art?

*Undertow* (2018), written and directed by Miranda Nation, tells the story of Claire (Laura Gordon), a married woman who has recently had a late-term miscarriage. The film takes pains to ensure that we, as viewers, experience this trial alongside her: in a key scene, we see her naked, heavily pregnant body lowering itself into a bath, then the water turning red with blood. The fallout from this event plays out quietly: we are shown what the pregnancy has done to her body, the impact it has on her relationship with her loving but perhaps overly protective husband, Dan (Rob Collins), and, most significantly, how it eventually drives her interactions with Angie (Olivia DeJonge), a younger woman who comes into her life at her most vulnerable moment.

Nation explains that, in its simplest form, the film is 'about a woman who has suffered a loss of a baby and becomes obsessed with a young woman who's pregnant, [then] starts to project her unresolved grief and desire onto this young woman and her baby'. The writer/director was initially inspired to write the screenplay after performing in a production of Jean Genet's *The Maids*. 'I was just really fascinated by the complex, love–hate relationship between the two sisters,' she tells me.

*So I really wanted to write something that had this central relationship between two women [...] Not a romantic or sexual relationship – even though I think there are elements of that in [*Undertow*] – but just these two women who, on the surface, are very different and seemingly quite polar opposites, but are two sides of the same coin.*

With *Undertow*, Nation has succeeded in creating something unusual and complex: the relationship between Angie and Claire is in turns sinister and fleetingly tender, with a tension that gradually builds the further into the film we get. We watch as Claire, suspecting an affair, starts to follow her husband. Then our heart rates quicken as Claire initiates contact with Angie, posing as a professional photographer and pretending she is interested in the young woman as a subject. Over the course of the film, Claire grows more and more erratic, and Angie increasingly goes off the rails; we witness

> 'I REALLY WANTED TO WRITE SOMETHING THAT HAD THIS CENTRAL RELATIONSHIP BETWEEN TWO WOMEN ... WHO, ON THE SURFACE, ARE VERY DIFFERENT AND SEEMINGLY QUITE POLAR OPPOSITES, BUT ARE TWO SIDES OF THE SAME COIN.'
>
> —MIRANDA NATION

them descending together, step by step, into the dark. Angie, feeling rejected by everyone around her, and carrying an unwanted baby, shows up to cause a dramatic scene at a black-tie function the football club is throwing. It's a half-hearted protest but a full-blooded scream at society, yelling in every way other than words about how she has been mistreated and used. At the same function, Claire throws all caution to the wind – quite literally in some ways, as she allows herself to become dangerously intoxicated, then heads off first to the beach and then into the sea with her husband's best friend, Brett (Josh Helman): a football bad boy and Angie's on-again, off-again boyfriend.

We also see scenes between Claire and Angie – there's a violent altercation, and there's a conversation at the beach in the aftermath of the black-tie function. Yet, while these encounters between the two women are central to the story, there are times when we're not quite sure whether what we're watching is 'truth', as Claire proves to be an unreliable narrator.

Paralleling this ambiguity, it's difficult to pin down exactly what *Undertow* is on genre terms. It's been described as a 'psychological thriller',[1] a 'character study'[2] and a 'drama'.[3] It contains elements of body horror, of regular horror. In light of this, I ask Nation whether she felt that trying to make her film fit within a genre limited what she had sought out to do, and she responds that they 'were pushed towards genre'. Nation explains further: 'I think [*Undertow*'s] more of a drama with some heightened elements.' She shares, however, that 'during development, nobody wanted to hear that word: "drama"'.

*It's like no-one knows how to sell a drama. Everyone wants a marketing hook, and genre gives them that hook – you've got this supposed target audience that wants to see that type of film.*

*Even though the script that I took to [producer] Lyn [Norfor] in the first place definitely had these heightened elements – which were glimpses into the protagonist's subconscious – I wouldn't have necessarily called it genre. And then people really wanted us to […] call it a psychological thriller, but I still don't think it really is.*

Ultimately, Nation agrees that a preoccupation with genre labels can 'really limit the scope':

*I'm more interested in exploring the subconscious in a way that is quite poetic and visually symbolic, but not necessarily in a genre film […] You just want to create a film that is what it is. You don't necessarily need to tick the boxes.*

Genre isn't the only invisible wall to contend with; there are also taboos and cultural expectations. The pressure to make your story conform to certain societal ideals is nothing new: *Veronica Mars* showrunner Rob Thomas had to fight to keep the sexual-assault storyline in his pilot episode, despite being told it was too dark, as he felt it was necessary to Veronica's (Kristen Bell) characterisation.[4] Joe Wright's 2005 adaptation of *Pride and Prejudice* features a saccharine, overtly romantic ending in its US release but not its British one – the result of a negative response to a pre-release test screening in the UK.[5] Prior to its acceptance into the Universal fold, *Back to the Future* (Robert Zemeckis, 1985) was rejected by Disney in outrage about the 'incest' storyline between Marty McFly (Michael J Fox) and his mother.[6]

**Above, from top:** Angie; Claire with her husband, Dan (Rob Collins)

> 'THERE'S A SENSE OF BETRAYAL, THAT YOUR BODY HAS LET YOU DOWN … [CLAIRE] SEES HER BODY AS THIS BARREN WASTELAND THAT'S KILLED THE BABY INSIDE HER, AND I WAS REALLY INTERESTED IN TRYING TO EXPLORE ALL THAT IN TERMS OF HER SUBCONSCIOUS AND THE WAY SHE FEELS ABOUT IT.'
> 
> —MIRANDA NATION

In the case of *Undertow*, the primary way the film pushes against expectation is its presentation of nudity – particularly through depictions of the pregnant body and non-sexualised explorations of Claire's mindset through the bare physical form. While, traditionally, the pregnant body in film is often framed as a wondrous thing, this isn't always the case in *Undertow*, which appropriates body-horror conventions in its confronting portrayals of Angie's growing belly and Claire's post-miscarriage body, stretch marks and all. These juxtapositions align with Nation's description of the pair as existing within a duality: Claire is desperately grieving the pregnancy she's lost and Angie is trying to ignore one she doesn't want.

*Undertow* pushes the pregnant form further than what we are used to seeing. It's unsettling to watch a pregnant woman binge-drink the way that Angie does; Nation knows this and uses it to skilfully give us insights into Angie's growing despair. There are also moments when Claire stares at her post-pregnancy body – in the bathroom mirror, or after stripping naked after a run. There is a sense of sacrifice in these images, of giving of yourself physically in order to have a child – and so seeing the markers of this on Claire's body without the 'reward' then makes her loss that much more painful.

'I just really wanted to represent the body authentically,' Nation says, explaining the careful, strategic use of nudity in her film. 'But then again, I love nudity in films,' she adds, with a laugh. 'I love all those European films where it's just part of the fabric of the story, and it's not thought of as being risqué or anything. It's just part of life – we all have bodies.' In *Undertow*, nudity is used thoughtfully and purposefully – it demonstrates the natural comfort Claire and her husband have around each other, it underscores awkward moments, and it is also used to explore the ideas and feelings surrounding pregnancy and miscarriage.

Nation points to her own experience of having a child in her late thirties as well as to those of other women she knows who are trying to get pregnant. 'Some of them can't […] And there's that real sense of grief and loss at something that you wanted and couldn't have.' The nudity in *Undertow* is essential to our understanding of this feeling of defeat. 'Often, there's a sense of betrayal, that your body has let you down,' Nation explains.

*[Claire] sees her body as this barren wasteland that's killed the baby inside her, and I was really interested in trying to explore all that in terms of her subconscious and the way she feels about it.*

According to the filmmaker, including nudity in such an unglamorous way meant walking a fine line. 'In Australia and America, we do have a bit of a stigma around nudity,' she says.

*You often see female nudity in a really gratuitous way – women are portrayed as sex objects – so it was really important to us that we never did that. It was something that served the story and really spoke to that exploration of our relationships with our bodies.*

Beyond the formal strictures of classification, filmmakers face the unwritten constraints imposed by viewers, particularly those sectors of the audience with paternalistic attitudes about what we 'should' be exposed to. However, the less that audiences are exposed to ideas or images that push boundaries and challenge preconceptions, the less likely they are to tolerate the few that do – which can only lead to artistic stagnation and homogenisation in the screen industries. One constraint that Nation specifically points out is male nudity. 'I am a bit disappointed there is no male nudity [in *Undertow*] just to balance it out,' she says. 'Because of taboos in the industry, it's much harder to have male nudity on screen.' The impact of this inclusion on *Undertow* would have been subtle, but, to Nation, it could have nevertheless assisted in making the film more 'authentic and gender-balanced'.

Much like the relationship between its central pair of protagonists, *Undertow* is difficult to define. Yet, in deliberately pushing the boundaries of genre and taboo to explore complex themes, it proves itself an accomplished piece of filmmaking. This achievement, of course, largely comes from the commitment of its creator. When I ask Nation about the film's journey, she responds:

*I think the biggest lesson is how to hold on to your vision throughout such a long process with so many different voices and collaborators. And just trying to stay true to your vision but also allowing it to evolve in the ways that it needs to through collaboration.*

*Elizabeth Flux is an award-winning freelance writer and editor. She is an editor for* Reading Victoria *and a past editor of* Voiceworks*. Her fiction has appeared in multiple anthologies and publications, and her nonfiction has been widely published and includes essays on cinema, pop culture, feminism and identity as well as interviews and feature articles.* **m**

Endnotes

[1] See, for example, Sarah Ward, '*Undertow*: Melbourne Review', *Screen Daily*, 10 August 2018, <https://www.screendaily.com/reviews/undertow-melbourne-review/5131593.article>, accessed 5 March 2019.

[2] See, for example, Mitch Ziems, '*Undertow* Is a Compelling Character Study Elevated by Its Feminine Perspective', *The 8 Percent*, 17 August 2018, <https://the8percent.com/undertow-review/>, accessed 5 March 2019.

[3] See, for example, Luke Buckmaster, '*Undertow* Review – Intensely Gripping Female-led Australian Drama', *The Guardian*, 10 August 2018, <https://www.theguardian.com/film/2018/aug/10/undertow-review-intensely-gripping-female-led-australian-drama>, accessed 5 March 2019.

[4] See Sadie Gennis, 'Investigating *Veronica Mars*: Creator Rob Thomas on the Show's Enduring Legacy 10 Years Later', *TV Guide*, 20 September 2014, <https://www.tvguide.com/news/veronica-mars-rob-thomas-anniversary-1087321/>, accessed 5 March 2019.

[5] See Alessandra Stanley, 'Oh, Mr. Darcy … Yes, I Said Yes!', *The New York Times*, 20 November 2005, <https://www.nytimes.com/2005/11/20/weekinreview/oh-mr-darcy-yes-i-said-yes.html>, accessed 5 March 2019.

[6] See David Konow, 'How *Back to the Future* Almost Didn't Get Made', *Esquire*, 9 June 2015, <https://www.esquire.com/entertainment/movies/a35559/back-to-the-future-production/>, accessed 5 March 2019.

AUSTRALIAN AND
NEW ZEALAND CINEMA

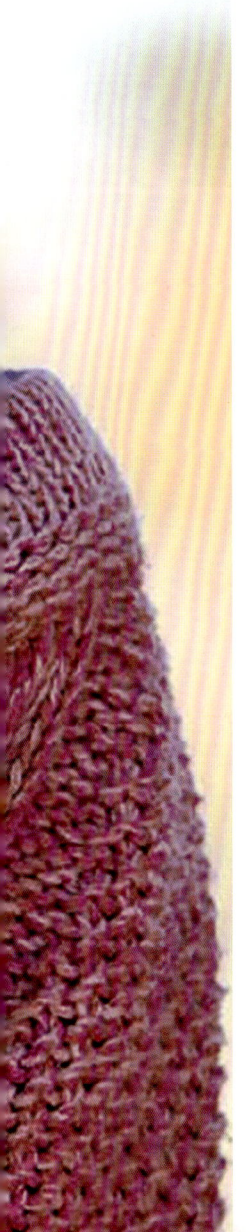

# Bird's-eye View

## CHILDHOOD, GRIEF AND COMMUNITY IN *EMU RUNNER*

IMOGEN THOMAS' STIRRING, IF SENTIMENTAL, FILM CENTRES ON A YOUNG GIRL WHO'S LOST HER MOTHER, THE BIRD SHE BEFRIENDS TO COPE WITH THIS LOSS, AND THE FAMILY AND COMMUNITY THAT RALLY AROUND HER. WHILE *EMU RUNNER* QUITE OVERTLY BUILDS ON ITS MYRIAD CINEMATIC ANTECEDENTS, IT'S ALSO NOTABLE FOR ITS FOCUS ON AN ABORIGINAL STORY – ONE CRAFTED WITH THE LOCAL COMMUNITY'S INVOLVEMENT, WRITES **AIMEE KNIGHT**.

**Previous spread and above:** Gem (Rhae-Kye Waites)

'Never work with children or animals,' goes the old movie-industry adage.[1] Disregarding this 'advice' entirely, Australian director Imogen Thomas sought the talent of kids and birds for her sweet, sentimental debut feature, *Emu Runner* (2018), which draws on the coming-of-age and social-realist traditions to tell a story about family, girlhood and grief. Shot on location in Brewarrina, New South Wales, this quiet achiever also dramatises urgent political and cultural issues affecting isolated Indigenous communities across the country.

Nine-year-old Gem (Brewarrina local Rhae-Kye Waites) lives in a regional town near the banks of the Barwon River. After spending a day fishing with her mum, Darlene (Maurial Spearim), and sister, Valerie (Letisha Boney),

Gem befriends a wild emu – her mother's totem animal – until the unintended consequences of doing so cause far more harm than healing.[2] In this way, *Emu Runner* ruminates on the role of matriarchs and maternal stand-ins for little women missing their biological mothers. This is particularly pertinent in the context of Brewarrina's Ngemba people. Like many Australian Indigenous communities, they are matriarchal[3] and therefore, in many ways, at odds with the patriarchal structure of European colonisation.

The figure of the motherless daughter is common in coming-of-age stories, as seen in on-screen precedents such as *Pretty in Pink* (Howard Deutch, 1986), *Clueless* (Amy Heckerling, 1995), *Sydney White* (Joe Nussbaum,

> *EMU RUNNER* RUMINATES ON THE ROLE OF MATRIARCHS AND MATERNAL STAND-INS FOR LITTLE WOMEN MISSING THEIR BIOLOGICAL MOTHERS. THIS IS PARTICULARLY PERTINENT IN THE CONTEXT OF BREWARRINA'S NGEMBA PEOPLE. LIKE MANY AUSTRALIAN INDIGENOUS COMMUNITIES, THEY ARE MATRIARCHAL.

she witnesses Darlene's untimely death. The child and her family are understandably distraught. Soon enough, the adults in Gem's life feel the pressure to start moving on, but the pre-teen struggles to articulate her enduring grief and sorrow. Yearning for comfort and connection,

2007) and, most recently, *To All the Boys I've Loved Before* (Susan Johnson, 2018) and *Eighth Grade* (Bo Burnham, 2018). These films explore the minefield of father–daughter relationships exacerbated by hormones, heartbreak and the hole left by the loss of a mum. It's a

relatable, important topic, one that *Emu Runner* embraces and builds on by virtue of some key differences. For instance, Gem is a few years younger than her counterparts in the aforementioned films. She's also battling a separate set of emotional, psychological and cultural – all the other films are American – hurdles.

Seeking to fill the void left by Darlene is Gem's dad, Jay Jay (played by writer, director and performer Wayne Blair, who appears alongside a largely untrained cast and brings affection, gravitas and tenderness to the role). Like a male emu responsible for raising its hatchlings,[4] the grief-stricken widower takes it upon himself to keep his family together. Despite his wider community's distrust regarding his abilities, he's fiercely protective of his brood. When Gem steals food for the emu, Jay Jay does his best to discipline her without driving her further into social withdrawal. He also sticks by his son, Ecka (Rodney McHughes), when the young man's alcohol and drug use – in part, a response to losing his mum – makes him a target of racial prejudice in their small town.

## Social realism and community engagement

Touching on themes such as stereotyping, forced child removal, substance reliance and premature death in First Nations communities, *Emu Runner* can be considered a contemporary addition to the cinematic canon of social realism. Films in this genre examine the sociopolitical conditions experienced by working-class people in order to critique the power structures that create systemic oppression. While it has roots in Italian neorealism – see, for example, Vittorio De Sica's *Bicycle Thieves* (1948) as well as Roberto Rossellini's *Stromboli* (1950) and *Europe '51* (1952) – social realism is most commonly associated

**This page, clockwise from below:** Gem with her grandmother Daphne (Mary Waites) and sister Valerie (Letisha Boney); Daphne talking to a neighbour; Gem and Valerie with their mother, Darlene (Maurial Spearim)

*EMU RUNNER* REINFORCES THE NOTION THAT KINSHIP CARE IS BEST, WHEREVER POSSIBLE. THIS ASSERTION IS NOTABLE IN THE CONTEXT OF AUSTRALIAN CINEMA, AND OUR WIDER MEDIA LANDSCAPE, WHICH FREQUENTLY VIEWS ABORIGINAL FAMILIES WITH A PATRONISING, IMPOSING WHITE LENS.

with the cinema of Britain, where the genre boomed after World War II.[5]

British social realism, like Italian neorealism before it, strives for verisimilitude – or the closest approximation of reality that cinema can logistically muster. It uses techniques that evoke the documentary form, such as filming on location and casting actors with little to no formal training, to tell authentic stories embedded within the communities and cultures they portray.[6] This is the case with *Emu Runner*, which makes good use of Brewarrina's natural and human-made infrastructure for sets and scenery. Moreover, its cast largely consists of the town's residents, including Waites, her cousin Boney, and her grandmother and grandfather, alongside the other schoolchildren and townspeople featured.

Thomas wrote *Emu Runner* in consultation with local Ngemba woman Frayne Barker, director of the Gainmara Birrilee Preschool. The two women met while Thomas was involved with an arts initiative at Ourgunya Women's Safe House in 2003. During that time, Thomas also met many women and children from the Brewarrina area. Their stories helped her develop an informed understanding of the issues affecting their community.[7] This led to Thomas and Barker's first collaboration, the short film *Mixed Bag* (2008), in which a white woman visiting a regional town confronts her racial biases. Ten years later, after a persuasive visit from Waites' grandmother, Thomas committed to making *Emu Runner*.[8] Barker came on board as Indigenous script consultant – and staunch supporter – from the very start. She describes the experience as 'empowering' for everyone on set, and notes that the film had broadened people's horizons.[9]

Also key to the project were established actors Blair and Logie Award winner Rob Carlton, whose prior screen experience bolstered the performances of their non-professional counterparts. While Blair's convincing turn as the primary carer of Gem and her siblings sees him offering a proverbial fatherly blanket to his on-screen family, Carlton's concerned cop Stan – alongside city-slickin' social worker Heidi (Georgia Blizzard) – is a pitch-perfect portrayal of how well-meaning authority figures can enact a condescending and ignorant paternalism. Clear outsiders encroaching on the Ngemba mob, and even the white working-class Brewarrina residents, Stan and Heidi move through life informed by innately different frameworks of living, being and grieving. Their trust in 'the system' drives Heidi to take Gem from her family during the film's tense emotional climax. This exemplifies the very real, enduring practice of forced child removal that has ruptured Indigenous communities across Australia for decades.

Rightfully, though, Gem is eventually returned to her family; here, *Emu Runner* reinforces the notion that kinship care is best, wherever possible. This assertion is notable in the context of Australian cinema, and our wider media landscape, which frequently views Aboriginal families with a patronising, imposing white lens that is similar to Heidi's.[10]

## Precursors and life lessons

Thomas cites titles like *The Fallen Idol* (Carol Reed, 1948), *Forbidden Games* (René Clément, 1952), *Paper Moon* (Peter Bogdanovich, 1973) and *The Kid with a Bike* (Jean-Pierre & Luc Dardenne, 2011) as thematic and visual influences on her film.[11] Much like *Emu Runner*, each of these stories places a child in a situation they are not emotionally equipped to process: witnessing a murder, adjusting to life as a wartime orphan, running scams during the Great Depression and being intentionally abandoned by a parent, respectively. While the first three are shot in black-and-white, *Emu Runner* is in colour, capturing the naturally soft, low-contrast pastel palette of places (and people) that seem to have been left behind by society at large.

Noticeably, shades of pink tinge everything Gem touches, from her clothes and bedsheets to the bathroom walls, the peeling paint on her family's fibro house and the dusty

**Above, L–R:** Social worker Heidi (Georgia Blizzard) checks in on Gem; Gem's father, Jay Jay (Wayne Blair), and brother, Ecka (Rodney McHughes)

sunsets that wash her skies in rose-gold light. Lots of long, warm, wistful shots linger on the scenery: traditional lands of the Ngemba, Murrawarri, Ualari, Weilwan and Baranbinja peoples.[12] The cinematography meditates on the trees, plains, seasons and creatures – both native and introduced – that have reshaped the landscape over millennia. A close-up of the emu's face reveals his smooth skin, stumpy feathers, little smirk; he looks surprisingly human. And, while the prevalence of pink is unlikely to be a direct homage to Deutch's *Pretty in Pink*, it at least illustrates Gem's present girlhood innocence; after all, we in the West associate the colour with young women. She's still at an age in which she hasn't yet had to choose between liking 'girly' things (her floral wardrobe and bed linen, for instance) and 'tomboy' things (like sport – Gem is a natural runner). It's also a constant visual reminder of the major feminine presence that has been ripped from her world.

Told squarely from Gem's point of view, *Emu Runner* is thus more likely to resonate with children than with adults. Jaded and curmudgeonly grown-ups may not have the patience for its awkward line readings and overtly earnest tone, whereas younger audiences (and those young at heart) may look past the modest performances and meagre production value to reap emotional reward from the poignant story.

The films *Emu Runner* most closely resembles – 'parrots', even – are those depicting child–animal bonds. Back in the day, they were found in droves throughout Blockbuster's 'Family' section – think: *Old Yeller* (Robert Stevenson, 1957), *The Black Stallion* (Carroll Ballard, 1979), *Free Willy* (Simon Wincer, 1993) et al. Within this subgenre of kids flicks, there's a flock of 'child and bird' titles, such as *Kes* (Ken Loach, 1969), *Storm Boy* (Henri Safran, 1976) and *Fly Away Home* (Ballard, 1996).[13] Many of these films were based on already popular books, suggesting that the moral values and messages contained in stories about kids and animals bear repeating. These 'empathy generator' coming-of-age narratives teach us about unconditional love and the fragility of life. They create secure yet ephemeral spaces to vicariously feel grief, maybe for the first time. And, for kid viewers experiencing separation, loss or death in their real lives, these melancholy movies can validate sorrow, anxiety, anger and confusion. They can provide guidance – however glossy and Hollywood-ified – as to how life can begin again.

\*

Given that a heap of forerunner films have been mentioned, it's worth reiterating that *Emu Runner* does extend on these existing coming-of-age, social-realist and human–animal filmographies. The vast majority of the texts referenced above feature white (and, often, male) protagonists. In contrast, *Emu Runner* increases Aboriginal representation in Australian cinema – particularly in the sphere of kids' films – in the form of its principal and supporting cast, an achievement only strengthened by the fact that its lead is female. Beyond this, as a consequence of the production team's consultation with the Aboriginal community in Brewarrina, the film pays respect to the Indigenous customs and lore that ultimately become integral to the unfolding story.

While *Emu Runner* is joyous, optimistic and sweet, it doesn't shy away from depicting fraught sociopolitical issues that are often ignored or distorted in the broader media landscape.

https://www.emurunnerfilm.com

*Aimee Knight is a writer and critic from Kaurna land. She is the small screens editor at* The Big Issue, *and her work appears in* Little White Lies, The Lifted Brow, Kill Your Darlings *and more.* <http://www.aimeeknight.com.au>

m

Endnotes

1. The quote is commonly attributed to comedian and actor WC Fields, but its actual provenance is disputed, according to etymologist Barry Popik. See Popik, '"Never Work with Children or Animals" (Show Business Adage)', *The Big Apple*, 29 January 2012, <https://www.barrypopik.com/index.php/new_york_city/entry/never_work_with_children_or_animals_show_business_adage/>, accessed 18 February 2019.
2. Perhaps it's worth noting here that, in 1932, white soldiers in Western Australia waged a literal war on their local emus. After just a few foolish weeks, the servicemen lost spectacularly, making emus a fitting symbol for Indigenous resilience in the face of colonial violence; see Urvija Banerji, 'In 1932, Australia Declared War on Emus – and Lost', *Atlas Obscura*, 21 March 2016, <https://www.atlasobscura.com/articles/in-1932-australia-declared-war-on-emus-and-lost>, accessed 26 February 2019.
3. As noted by Thomas; see Gillie Collins, 'Imogen Thomas on *Emu Runner*: "The Film Willed Its Way into Existence."', *Seventh Row*, 2 October 2018, <https://seventh-row.com/2018/10/02/imogen-thomas-emu-runner/>, accessed 26 February 2019.
4. See 'Park Notes: Emu', fact sheet, Parks Victoria, <https://parkweb.vic.gov.au/__data/assets/pdf_file/0003/322104/emu4.pdf>, accessed 13 February 2019.
5. See Richard Armstrong, 'Social Realism', *BFI Screenonline*, <http://www.screenonline.org.uk/film/id/1037898/index.html>, accessed 13 February 2019.
6. Samantha Lay, *British Social Realism: From Documentary to Brit-grit*, Wallflower Press, London & New York, 2002, pp. 8–10.
7. 'Inspiration', *Emu Runner* official website, <https://www.emurunnerfilm.com/inspiration/>, accessed 13 February 2019.
8. Kathleen Ferguson & Dugald Saunders, '*Emu Runner* Film Brings Stars and Opportunities to Remote NSW Community of Brewarrina', *ABC News*, 26 September 2017, <https://www.abc.net.au/news/2017-09-26/emu-runner-film-brings-opportunities-to-brewarrina-locals/8989530>, accessed 26 February 2019.
9. Frayne Barker, quoted in ibid.
10. See Jack Latimore, 'The Passive Racism of Australian Media Is Borne of Arrogance, Ignorance, Fear and Fragility', *The Guardian*, 31 January 2019, <https://www.theguardian.com/commentisfree/2019/jan/31/the-passive-racism-of-australian-media-is-borne-of-arrogance-ignorance-fear-and-fragility>, accessed 26 February 2019.
11. 'Visual Style', *Emu Runner* official website, <https://www.emurunnerfilm.com/visual-style/>, accessed 13 February 2019.
12. 'Inspiration', *Emu Runner* official website, op. cit.
13. *Fly Away Home* charts teenage Amy's (Anna Paquin) connection to a gaggle of Canada geese and, moreover, to her estranged father, Tom (Jeff Daniels), in the wake of her mother's sudden death – a plotline that uncannily resembles that of *Emu Runner*.

AUSTRALIAN AND
NEW ZEALAND CINEMA

# Tearing Out a New Leaf

## *BOOK WEEK* AND THE UNLIKEABLE PROTAGONIST

HEATH DAVIS' SOPHOMORE WORK OFFERS VIEWERS A PORTRAIT OF A MAN BURDENED BY FAILED DREAMS – ONES THAT ARE MET WITH INEFFECTIVE COPING MECHANISMS AND DELUSIONS OF GRANDEUR. COUPLED WITH THE FILM'S COARSE COMEDIC TONE AND PREFERENCE FOR AFFECTING WIT OVER BUILDING CHARACTERISATION, WHAT RESULTS IS A FILM THAT ULTIMATELY FAILS TO ENGENDER SYMPATHY FOR ITS PROTAGONIST, WRITES **MEL CAMPBELL**.

Every year since 1945, Australian schools and libraries have celebrated Book Week: a festival intended to instil a love of literature in young people.[1] The climax of the week is a costumed parade in which children, teachers and librarians dress up as their favourite literary characters. In writer/director Heath Davis' dark-comedy film *Book Week* (2018), a disagreeable high school English teacher spends a week masquerading as his favourite literary character – his fantasy of himself as a successful novelist.

Nicholas Cutler (Alan Dukes) was once a bad boy of Australian literature. His breakthrough novel was published to critical acclaim eight years ago, but his drunken antics on the press tour killed his career. Now, he's stuck teaching English at Little Fields High School, somewhere in the Blue Mountains. Nick despises his phone-prodding students because they don't care about literature. His colleagues despise *him* – especially the long-suffering principal (Tiriel Mora). And head teacher Lee (Susan Prior) is seemingly only his lover because she's out of better options.

But Nick has a chance to turn over a new leaf. He's deigned to pen a trashy zombie novel, and his agent, Blake (Rhys Muldoon), has managed to sell it to a pair of braying publishing bros, Rob (Toby Schmitz) and Adam (Khan Chittenden) – on the condition that Nick rewrite it as a vampire novel. If Nick can behave himself for just the week until the contract is signed, a comeback could be his. But, as the Little Fields school community gears up for Book Week, Nick retreats into self-sabotage, evading responsibilities of all sorts.

Davis has produced something similarly evasive. *Book Week* is ambivalent about its antiheroic protagonist: it doesn't really invite sympathy for Nick, but neither does it truly delight in nor condemn his awfulness. Instead, the film unfurls shaggily, like an experiment in the limits of audience empathy, tantalising us with the possibility of Nick's comeuppance but being clear that he does not deserve redemption.

Accordingly, upon *Book Week*'s release late last year, some critics struggled to reconcile Nick's unrelenting unpleasantness with the film's comedic tone. For instance, *The Sydney Morning Herald*'s Sandra Hall argued that while the 'cranky, boorish' teacher's antics 'precipitate one or two pratfalls, his indestructible smugness mean[s] that they produce few laughs'.[2] In a much more scathing review, *Isolated Nation*'s Joshua Peach wrote that the film 'should be lambasted for believing that unlikeability is a substitute for original or interesting. Cutler is an anti-hero in the dullest and most neutered form'.[3]

Can we only tolerate an unlikeable hero when he's young, cool and gorgeous, or perhaps when he pits himself against social rules and niceties that we secretly oppose? Or do we tolerate unlikeability only as a character's starting point on a journey of self-improvement? *Book Club* intertwines these questions with distinctly Australian parodies of two well-worn film motifs: the 'creative man in crisis' and the 'inspirational teacher'.

**Opposite:** Self-sabotaging secondary school teacher Nick Cutler (Alan Dukes)

## Localising the creative man in crisis

While antiheroes have been celebrated on the Australian big screen ever since the nation's first feature, *The Story of the Kelly Gang* (Charles Tait, 1906), these are not often creative professionals. Australian cinema prefers alienated rovers like Max Rockatansky (Mel Gibson in 1979–1985, Tom Hardy in 2015) in George Miller's *Mad Max* cycle or Jay Swan (Aaron Pedersen) in Ivan Sen's *Mystery Road* (2013) and *Goldstone* (2016), or the garrulous murderers of *Chopper* (Andrew Dominik, 2000), *Wolf Creek* (Greg McLean, 2005), *Animal Kingdom* (David Michôd, 2010) and *Snowtown* (Justin Kurzel, 2011).

One of the rare Australian films to follow a creative antihero is *What I Have Written* (John Hughes, 1996), in which a wife discovers a novella manuscript by her comatose husband that tells a shocking parallel story about their marriage. Another is *Bliss* (Ray Lawrence, 1985), adapted from Peter Carey's eponymous novel, which follows an adman's existential crisis. And *Ruben Guthrie* (2015), also set in the world of advertising, is based on writer/director Brendan Cowell's play of the same name, which fictionalises his own drunken bad behaviour.

In contrast, Hollywood has a rich cinematic tradition of the creative man in crisis, from the titular blocked screenwriter in *Barton Fink* (The Coen brothers, 1991) to the neurotic, nostalgic writer-protagonists of Woody Allen films including *Manhattan* (1979), *Deconstructing Harry* (1997), *You Will Meet a Tall Dark Stranger* (2010) and *Midnight in Paris* (2011). In these stories, the male protagonist finds himself at a creative crossroads whereby his self-image based on literary snobbery duels with commercial demands and chaotic personal circumstances. Such films are also driven by the literary myth that writers should be outsiders who succeed because of pure talent and taste. Another beloved myth is that literary reputations require a certain amount of suffering. Hence, male-crisis narratives romanticise authors' self-destructive failure as much as their literary triumphs against the odds.

The early 2000s saw a particular focus on white men's midlife creative neuroses. Michael Douglas played a has-been author and now creative-writing lecturer in *Wonder Boys* (Curtis Hanson, 2000), based on the novel by Michael Chabon. Nicolas Cage had a metatextual turn as struggling screenwriter Charlie Kaufman in *Adaptation.* (Spike Jonze, 2002). Of the titles in this loose subgenre, *Sideways* (Alexander Payne, 2004) is the film *Book Week* most resembles. Having its origins in Rex Pickett's eponymous novel, *Sideways* follows a depressed, alcoholic, middle-aged failed writer turned high school English teacher – who, despite his own failures, is intensely snobbish – over a pivotal week when a publisher is considering his manuscript. Indeed, *Book Week*'s Dukes has a strong physical resemblance and similar acting style to *Sideways* star Paul Giamatti.

Davis originally wrote the role of Nick for Cowell,[4] whose casting would have better aligned with the premise that Nick had been feted as an enfant terrible within the past decade (Cowell's alter ego Ruben Guthrie also seems to have influenced Nick's drunken tendencies). When Cowell became unavailable, the casting of Dukes allowed *Book Week* to evolve into the story of an arrogant blowhard who had *never* really succeeded. As Davis recalls in interview: 'I thought I needed a Paul Giamatti in Australia and I thought "that's Alan"'.[5]

*Book Week* signals Nick's imagined allegiance to the myths of creative crisis by beginning each 'act' with an on-screen quote from a famous author of the blokey, swaggering variety that Nick idolises and emulates. F Scott Fitzgerald, Ernest Hemingway and Charles Bukowski were all inveterate boozers with chaotic personal lives, yet, somehow, they've emerged into posterity with their reputations not just intact, but enhanced. Nick's relationship to books both drives and restrains him: he clings to his snobbery because it allows him the self-respect his other actions have masochistically stripped away. Does he hope a baptism of whiskey will elevate him to the ranks of literary legends? Or is he self-medicating out of avoidance, because he's afraid that, if he looks honestly at himself and his writing abilities, he won't like what he sees?

These questions hang unanswered – but, importantly, the film does not buy into the myths that animate Nick. Instead, it deliberately maximises his unlikeability by taking every opportunity to puncture his image of himself, showing how vain and pathetic he really is. Indeed, the film is full of awfulness: the kind that's stressful to watch because it's not treated as, and hence not able to vicariously become, enjoyable.

Nick is introduced riding his bike to school, smoking a joint, but this vision of a fancy-free rebel quickly evaporates as we see the contempt and exasperation with which just about everyone in his life treats him. In the scorn-filled scenes between Nick and his dad, Ken (Nicholas Hope), we get a brief insight into where Nick's attitude problem might have begun. But, at almost every opportunity, the film returns to its baseline of Nick's selfishness, making no effort to excuse or romanticise his behaviour.

Perhaps this is where *Book Week*'s 'Australianness' lies. Many Hollywood films about creative crisis are resolved – and their antiheroes, rewarded – when these men change their self-destructive habits, or learn to treat others with more kindness and respect. *Book Week* grants Nick only an ambivalent redemption. At the end of the film, he has failed to embody the literary archetypes he previously prized. But he has managed to preserve his key relationships with his family and with Lee, and seems at peace with his life of suburban mediocrity.

## Deconstructing the inspirational teacher

Nick's character is based on Davis' own experiences of teaching after struggling to launch a Hollywood career, as well as his observations of disaffected fellow teachers. 'Some of the smartest, most empathetic people I've met in my life – not all of them but a handful – are teachers,' Davis told *The Sydney Morning Herald* last year.

[B]ut I was pretty depressed from mixing with these people, looking like my dream was going to come true, but teaching on a substitute basis at a public school. For my own sanity, I wrote this film about how bizarre the experience was. It was always going to be a black comedy because I had to keep a sense of humour.[6]

Despite Nick's occupation, *Book Week* is not really about teaching or mentorship. We rarely see him in the classroom. Nor is the film particularly effective in exploiting the comic possibilities of Book Week itself, apart from showing Nick's colleagues wearing literary-themed costumes. On the contrary, Davis goes to great pains to show that most of Nick's students and colleagues despise him. This atmosphere of disaffection permeates the broader setting so that, depending on the viewer's tastes, the film is either off-puttingly cynical or bracingly realistic in the profound disdain it shows for the school environment. Little Fields is not the kind of grim, unruly school depicted in films including *Blackboard Jungle* (Richard Brooks, 1955) and

**Above, L–R:** Nick and student-teacher Sarah (Airlie Dodds); Nick with Tyrell (Thuso Lekwape), one of his students

*Dangerous Minds* (John N Smith, 1995), but it is a place devoid of 'inspiration', where knowledge and personal development are seldom actually imparted.

Nick's chief antagonist is Melanie (Rose Riley), a senior student and aspiring novelist whose function in the story is reminiscent of that of the ambitious, overachieving student politician Tracy Flick (Reese Witherspoon) in *Election* (Payne, 1999). Melanie both detests Nick and craves his approval regarding her manuscript; she's more like him than either of them would admit. Sensing – probably correctly – that Melanie is more talented than him, Nick repeatedly rebuffs her; their expletive-filled encounters are a highlight of the film.

Some of *Book Week*'s other amusing moments come courtesy of Tyrell (Thuso Lekwape), a loveable, permanently stoned student whose illicit antics Davis treats with an affection denied to Nick himself. In particular, Tyrell plays a key role in embarrassing Nick, who has plotted to portray himself flatteringly as a mentor to at-risk youth during an interview with a local magazine. 'Why does he always have to learn the hard way?' Nick sighs about Tyrell.

Tellingly, this patronising comment could just as easily apply to Nick himself, who is in the weird position of being able to see his own downfall but also unable to shrink from it. Part of what makes him unsympathetic is that, despite his nominal role of authority, he never seems in command of a situation. 'Promise me you won't make any more promises,' Lee begs Nick after their tryst in the English department storeroom. She is destined to be prodigiously disappointed, much like Nick's harassed sister, Nadine (Pippa Grandison), who repeatedly begs for her brother's support. This is, in fact, one rather retrograde aspect of the film: it treats these female characters as guardians of responsibility, the poles towards which the unlikeable male antihero must align his moral compass, redeeming himself by earning their forgiveness.

Two other female characters, however, are much more engaging because they see Nick at his most vulnerable, when his bravado is at its thinnest. Samantha (Jolene Anderson), a former student of Nick's, is now the deadpan cop who always seems to bust him in a moment of undignified criminality. 'I actually should arrest you for being a crap teacher,' she says. And Sarah (Airlie Dodds) drunkenly meets Nick in a bar when he's celebrating his book deal, then takes him home for an ill-advised one-night stand. Not only does she call him out on his false claim that he had been doing volunteer work, but, awkwardly, she's also revealed to be a student-teacher whose week-long placement Nick must now supervise. He swiftly recruits her as a protégée, expansively sharing his tips on how to evade the most tiresome aspects of teaching, and she becomes his sidekick in his self-destructive antics.

Sarah is the closest thing Nick has to an ally and confidant. She doesn't despise him, as others around him do, and nor does she hold him to moral standards she already knows he won't meet. Instead, her perspective aligns with that of the film. She observes Nick with the insight he lacks, but she isn't there to make him appear more likeable or to 'inspire' him to be a better writer, teacher or person. Instead, as in other filmic moments of midlife male crisis so familiar as to render them clichés, Sarah is the no-nonsense figure who forces Nick to be honest with himself. She offers the key lesson of this film: that when the familiar stories we tell ourselves aren't working, we can always tear out the page and start a new draft.

*Mel Campbell is a Melbourne-based freelance journalist and cultural critic, and co-author of the romantic comedy novels* The Hot Guy *(Echo Publishing, 2017) and* Nailed It! *(Echo Publishing, 2019).*

**m**

Endnotes

[1] For more information on Book Week, see its official page on the Children's Book Council of Australia website, <https://www.cbca.org.au/cbca-book-week>; and 'Children's Book Week Posters', State Library of South Australia website, <https://digital.collections.slsa.sa.gov.au/nodes/view/2663>, both accessed 26 February 2019.

[2] Sandra Hall, '*Book Week* Review: With a Boorish Teacher as Its Hero, Comedy Struggles for Laughs', *The Sydney Morning Herald*, 23 October 2018, <https://www.smh.com.au/entertainment/movies/book-week-review-with-a-boorish-teacher-as-its-hero-comedy-struggles-for-laughs-20181022-h16yiz.html>, accessed 20 February 2019.

[3] Joshua Peach, 'Film Review: Is *Book Week* Better Left on the Shelf?', *Isolated Nation*, 21 November 2018, <https://isolatednation.com/articles/2018/11/21/book-week-better-left-on-the-shelf>, accessed 20 February 2019.

[4] Don Groves, 'Al Dukes Lands the Lead in Heath Davis' Comedy *Book Week*', *IF.com.au*, 12 January 2018, <https://www.if.com.au/al-dukes-lands-lead-heath-davis-comedy-book-week/>, accessed 20 February 2019.

[5] Heath Davis, quoted in Garry Maddox, 'Lessons in Life: How a Casual Teacher Finally Became a Filmmaker', *The Sydney Morning Herald*, 19 October 2018, <https://www.smh.com.au/entertainment/movies/lessons-in-life-how-a-casual-teacher-finally-became-a-filmmaker-20181010-p508rd.html>, accessed 11 February 2019.

[6] ibid.

# In the Crease

### SELF-REFERENTIAL STORYTELLING IN TED WILSON'S
### *UNDER THE COVER OF CLOUD*

A WITTY CINEMATIC METATEXT THAT REVELS IN AMBIGUITY AND INTERPRETATION, *UNDER THE COVER OF CLOUD* STARS ITS DIRECTOR AS AN AUTHOR IN SEARCH OF BOTH HIS NEXT BIG PROJECT AND AN ALMOST-MYTHOLOGISED HERO. WHAT UNFOLDS IS A SKILFULLY REFLEXIVE PORTRAIT OF A MAN, HIS FAMILY, THEIR BELOVED SPORT AND THE TOWN THEY LIVE IN – PLUS THE ACT OF FILMMAKING ITSELF, WRITES **LEAH JING**.

AUSTRALIAN AND
NEW ZEALAND CINEMA

*Under the Cover of Cloud* (2018) begins with its protagonist returning home on the trusty *Spirit of Tasmania* ferry. Having lost his job, he is on his way to visit his family in Tasmania, in the hope that he might start writing a new book, 'something bigger'. His mellow voiceover notes: 'I want to write something beautiful about cricket – a piece of literary nonfiction. It will, in some sense, be about Tasmanian batsmen, and it will be from the heart.'

Starring writer/director Ted Wilson as himself, and his family as themselves, and Tasmania's cricket legend David Boon as himself, *Under the Cover of Cloud* is a film about itself but also not about itself; it is a film about cricket but not about cricket. It is a fiction that feels almost real, while also functioning as a documentary so neatly sliced up that reality seems *just* outside the screen. So when an audience member asked, during the post-screening Q&A at the 2018 Melbourne International Film Festival (MIFF), where they could find the book that Ted-the-protagonist was ostensibly writing in the film, Wilson-the-director – who is also Wilson-the-writer and, of course, Wilson-the-actor we'd just spent an hour-and-a-half watching both act and not-act as Ted-the-protagonist – broke into a grin.

Though there are a handful of scenes showing Ted solemnly writing into a spiral-bound notebook, sometimes smoking a cigar, it is not Ted's elusive book but rather what we are watching on screen that is the final manifestation of his 'literary nonfiction': the book Ted-the-protagonist is trying to write becomes, instead, the film Wilson-the-director has made.

The nineteen-year-old postmodernism obsessive or perhaps Barth/Barthes/Barthelme[1] fanatic in me swoons. Welcome to the funhouse, yes, but: 'For whom is the funhouse fun?'[2] And so Ted Wilson multiplies, as if Barth's own protagonist, Ambrose, had taken a wrong turn and somehow become lost in Launceston. But there are no mirrors here: just blue-grey mountains, household chickens, a laconic dog and Ted's endearing mother, Colleen, garrulous and kind.

\*

I tell my co-worker, H, that I'm writing an essay about a film that is about writing a book about cricket. H has recently taken up playing cricket; yesterday was cricket practice, and their muscles are sore. I think about the merits of practice, and then how perhaps all documentary filmmaking is practice – but then, what the *real thing* would be, I'm not too sure.

We sit around at work, waiting for something to happen. The mail comes and H signs for it. We open the *New*

**Opposite:** Ted Wilson **Above, from top:** Ted with his mother, Colleen; Ted en route to Tasmania (two images)

SIMILAR TO THE TERM 'LITERARY NONFICTION', WILSON'S NOTION OF A 'DOCUMENTARY PORTRAIT' HOLDS ITS OWN INTERNAL CONTRADICTION. *UNDER THE COVER OF CLOUD* BECOMES AN EXERCISE IN THE EVERYDAY. WILSON RECOGNISES THE UNIVERSALITY THAT UNDERPINS THE COMFORTING BANALITY OF FAMILY RELATIONS.

York Times crossword. 'Five across, five letters: a feeling based on intuition?' We think for a while, then give up. H clicks back to *The Guardian*'s live cricket feed to follow the game. H reads a few lines aloud. It sounds like poetry.

\*

The film poster for *Under the Cover of Cloud* resists generic classification, and perhaps rightly so. Sitting somewhere between a poster, a book cover and an artwork, it bypasses the more literal film still or photograph, instead conveying a sense of the film through an impressionistic painting of gum trees. An impression, indeed. Labelled neither a fiction nor a documentary, *Under the Cover of Cloud* is merely marketed as 'A modern Tasmanian film'.[3]

On Wilson's website, the film is described as being '[d]enuded of narrative fanfare',[4] though some fanfare is found in Ted's own inconsistent voiceovers, which somehow simultaneously dictate narrative structure and emerge as quite pointedly at odds with the final story. He notes: 'As I sat on the couch, my thoughts turned to David Boon […] he was diminutive, pugnacious and famous for his heavy drinking. Boony was truly an unlikely hero […] It was clear to me that I would benefit greatly from being in his presence.' Yet, ultimately, protagonist-Ted's half-hearted mission to find Boon is obscured by director-Wilson's other mission: to create a 'unique documentary portrait of middle Tasmania, rare in its loving commitment to a warm and convivial present'.[5] Wilson pointedly turns plot into subplot, and subplot into plot, and then questions the very concept of 'plot' altogether.

**Above, from top:** Ted having lunch with his family, including his older sister Rebecca (far left) and brother Ben (right); Ted with cricketer David Boon; Ted

Similar to the term 'literary nonfiction', Wilson's notion of a 'documentary portrait' holds its own internal contradiction. *Under the Cover of Cloud* becomes an exercise in the everyday. Wilson recognises the universality that underpins the comforting banality of family relations. Ted begins his visit to Tasmania by seeing his sister Jessie and her husband, and playing with their kids. The Wilson family is pulled into opaque reality, or perhaps framed as a clear fiction. Ted's relationship with his mother soon becomes the focal point of the film.

Wilson's moments with Colleen-his-mother and Colleen-the-actor slide together. He tests limits in four long scenes/interactions with her. An unassumingly brilliant actor, Colleen Wilson holds her own while still appearing like a 'regular' mother, faithfully complying with her son's artistic wishes. One can imagine her sighing, though clearly delighted, and asking, 'Are you sure it needs to be me?' while enlisting Wilson to bring in the laundry, or pull something from the top shelf. Ted's interactions with his mother build from a silly moment during the Wilson family lunch, when Colleen tells the table, '*I* know David Boon!' and then cackles: 'A different David Boon.' Ted's brother Ben remarks, 'That won't work so good for your book, though, Ted, unless your spin was "people who live in Tasmania with the same names as famous athletes".' This reference to multiple identities aside, the persistence of these sweet motherly moments build, layer atop one another, and ultimately subvert the traditional 'quest' narrative that is ostensibly set in motion by Ted at the start of the film. It is through these long moments with Colleen that Ted's 'quest' narrative is instead twisted into a narrative of return: to family, to home, to self.

Throughout the film, shots are close, implying a certain intimacy. But they also waver, underscoring how each shot is mediated through the camera's eye. Wilson-the-director is careful to remind us that the camera is far from inert, nor does it have agency of its own. This mediation becomes quite clearly the result of human intervention. We are looking at what director of photography Joshua Aylett is seeing, and this mediation is never dissolved.

\*

At MIFF, Wilson admitted that the final film was cut from fifteen hours of footage. His editor, James Vaughan, trimmed it down over a month, during a paid drug trial in hospital.[6]

Wilson's disregard for plot is perfectly underscored when Ted, sitting alone, writing and smoking a cigar in his sister's backyard, decides to pick up her dog and drops it among the backyard chickens – a very pointed, failed attempt to create drama. The chickens, of course, are mostly unperturbed, and the dog pauses, then wanders away. Ted looks on, holding his cigar. Of course, this dramatic failure by protagonist-Ted is, simultaneously, also a perfectly executed point by director-Wilson.

But this is not to say there are not moments that appear completely fictional, moments almost too perfect to be real. Take, for example, a scene in which Ted sits alone, looking out

**Above, from top:** Colleen with her youngest daughter, Jessie, at family lunch; Ted with one of Jessie's children

> AS WITH *INFINITE JEST*, WILSON'S METAFICTIVE ACCOUTREMENTS DON'T DETRACT FROM THE TEXT'S IMPACT … *UNDER THE COVER OF CLOUD* IS, PERHAPS, A PERFECT TEXT FOR THE INTERNET AGE. IT DOESN'T MATTER, WILSON SEEMS TO SAY, WHETHER IT'S FACT OR FICTION. ACCEPT THE FACT AS FICTION AND THE FICTION AS FACT.

on the bay. A droll, almost facetious voiceover: 'Why am I here?' As he drinks his coffee, spiral-bound notebook in hand, a dolphin appears in the water.

\*

The film, though invoking (through the veritable plethora of Teds and Wilsons) a postmodernism of sorts, is perhaps more indebted to artists that have succeeded the movement. A comparison might be made with David Foster Wallace's 1996 *Infinite Jest*. In this 1079-page novel, the continual flipping between the body text and its 388 endnotes draws attention to the physical object of the book itself as well as to the act of reading, while also evoking the back-and-forth exchanges that recur in the sport of tennis (a central location in the plot is the Enfield Tennis Academy). However, the narrative is arguably far from obscured by metafictive reference.

In perhaps that same mode, *Under the Cover of Cloud* plods on like a cricket match. And, as with *Infinite Jest*, Wilson's metafictive accoutrements don't detract from the text's impact. Instead, they become passing commentary on the fictionality of life, a recognition of the field we play in. *Under the Cover of Cloud* is, perhaps, a perfect text for the internet age. It doesn't matter, Wilson seems to say, whether it's fact or fiction. Accept the fact as fiction and the fiction as fact. It will occur regardless.

\*

On the beach with his mother, Ted considers his quest to find Boon. 'What I'd get from him, I don't know.'

\*

I meet my parents for lunch, tell Dad I'm writing a piece about 'The Cricket'. His face lights up. I ask him if he's ever met a cricketer. 'I got Dougie Walter's autograph!' he says. 'I was too shy to ask him, so I just stood there with my autograph book and my pen. But he signed it … I think he got the idea.' Dad laughs.

*And Don Bradman – he sold our family a piano. My dad went to school with him. The thing about David Boon, he held the same position as Don Bradman. That's a position of the highest esteem. The job of the opener is to see the shine off the ball. See, when the ball is shiny, it can swing and swerve through the air. But, once the shine has been taken off the ball, the ball loses its movement. So the master craftsman, the top-order batsman, he can come in and dictate the play for the day. That's why you put the best batsman at number three.*

To make the analogy that Wilson spends the film taking the shine off the ball, waiting for the best batsman to appear to hit the film home, would be too easy, and it would be a disservice to the beautiful moments of the everyday that Wilson has painstakingly documented. But the somewhat-sudden appearance of Boon does seem straight out of a dream.

\*

I ask my mother if she remembers David Boon. 'I did! I liked him. I always waited for him to come on. He was chubby, gnarly. A big handlebar moustache.'

Dad adds, 'Compact. A compact style … consistent, you know. Stayed in the crease.'

\*

We're still reading cricket commentary/poetry when another co-worker walks in, peers at the computer screen to see the crossword. H says: 'A feeling based on intuition. Five letters?'

She pauses. Then: '… hunch!'

\*

It would also be a disservice to Wilson to suggest that *Under the Cover of Cloud* is anchored on a hunch. But the film does feel based on intuition; he succeeds in creating moments of stillness that drag and pull. *Under the Cover of Cloud* is far from a simple exposition on the nature of documentary, or the texture of reality. Instead, Wilson reaches beyond postmodern posturing and asks: *What is the power of a story? What is the power of family? What does it mean to create art in today's world?*

At times, the film is an endurance watch. And it is *not* the final appearance of Boon that enables *Under the Cover of Cloud* to sidestep the exhausting and narcissistic recursiveness that typifies postmodernism, but, rather, the poignant scenes featuring Ted and his mother. Ted's (or is it Wilson's?) proposed goal – to create 'a piece of literary nonfiction […] from the heart' – is realised in this stunning depiction of family, which sits in the crease between fiction and fact.

http://www.tedwilsonfilms.com/under-the-cover-of-cloud/

*Leah Jing is the editor of* Liminal *magazine. She is a PhD student in cultural studies at The University of Melbourne, and has been a Wheeler Centre Hot Desk fellow, one of Footscray Community Arts Centre's emerging cultural leaders and a 2019 Victorian Nominee for Young Australian of the Year.* m

Endnotes

[1] Author John Barth, literary theorist Roland Barthes and short-story writer Donald Barthelme, all of whom are frequently associated with postmodernism.

[2] John Barth, 'Lost in the Funhouse', in *Lost in the Funhouse: Fiction for Print, Tape, Live Voice*, Doubleday, New York, 1968.

[3] See '*Under the Cover of Cloud*', Ted Wilson official website, <http://www.tedwilsonfilms.com/under-the-cover-of-cloud/>, accessed 6 February 2019.

[4] ibid.

[5] ibid.

[6] See John Roebuck, 'Review | *Under the Cover of Cloud* (2018)', *ReelGood*, 5 August 2018, <http://reelgood.com.au/reviews/review-cover-cloud-2018/>, accessed 4 February 2019.

# THE PAROCHIAL *Fantastic*

## Australian Television Fantasy in *Bloom* and *Tidelands*

GLOBAL TIDES RESULT IN LOCAL RIPPLES AS AUSTRALIA'S LARGEST STREAMING SERVICES RESPOND TO THE BURGEONING DEMAND FOR GENRE PRODUCTS: FROM NETFLIX COMES THE PULPY *TIDELANDS*, AND STAN OFFERS THE MORE SEDATE AND THOUGHTFUL *BLOOM*. YET, WHILE BOTH CONFIDENTLY EMPLOY FANTASY TROPES, EACH BETRAYS A DISCOMFORT IN SETTING THEM AGAINST A FAMILIAR AUSTRALIAN LANDSCAPE, WRITES **TRAVIS JOHNSON**.

AUSTRALIA ON THE SMALL SCREEN

**Previous spread, L-R:** A 'de-aged' Gwen (Phoebe Tonkin) in *Bloom*; malevolent matriarch Adrielle (Elsa Pataky) in *Tidelands*
**Above, from top:** *Tidelands*' reluctant heroine, Cal (Charlotte Best); Adrielle with henchman/lover Dylan (Marco Pigossi)

> Of the two, *Tidelands* is the more obviously commercial; with its beachside setting and cast of predominantly young and attractive people, it could easily be summarised as '*Home and Away* with mermaids'.

**Above, L–R:** Cal with older brother Augie (Aaron Jakubenko); Adrielle with fellow Tidelander Violca (Madeleine Madden)

For much of Australia's screen history, genre fare has been ghettoised. On the big screen, horror, science fiction, action and the odd pure fantasy have been largely relegated to the 'Ozploitation' rubric – see: *Razorback* (Russell Mulcahy, 1984), *Mad Max* (George Miller, 1979), *The Man from Hong Kong* (Brian Trenchard-Smith, 1975) and *Frog Dreaming* (Trenchard-Smith, 1985), among various others. On television, such offerings – horror aside – have tended to be aimed at children, giving us the likes of *Round the Twist*, *Spellbinder* and *The Girl from Tomorrow*.

Many of these projects attained some measure of critical and commercial success, but generally within their mandated cultural confines. However, recent shifts in cinema and television globally have seen these once-derided genres ascend to a position of prominence. Nowadays, the success of prestige genre series such as HBO's *Game of Thrones*, combined with the box-office clout of Disney's Marvel brand as well as its rivals and imitators, is hard to ignore. Add to that the rise of digital distribution and streaming services, and their demand for content that can be marketed and consumed across cultural borders, and the screen-production sector worldwide has had no choice but to respond.

On local shores, this has resulted in a number of notable small-screen works, including Foxtel's *The Kettering Incident* and the ABC's *Cleverman*. Now, two streaming services with major stakes in the Australian viewing market have gotten into the game, each presenting a small-town fantasy drama, albeit of markedly different flavours: in mid December 2018, Netflix aired *Tidelands*, and only a few weeks later, on 1 January this year, Stan premiered *Bloom*.

## Unfolding genre

Of the two, *Tidelands* is the more obviously commercial; with its beachside setting and cast of predominantly young and attractive people, it could easily be summarised as '*Home and Away* with mermaids'. Created by Stephen M Irwin, Leigh McGrath, Nathan Mayfield and Tracey Robertson, the eight-part series focuses on Calliope 'Cal' McTeer (Charlotte Best), a recent parolee who returns to her fishing-village home of Orphelin Bay after a decade in juvenile detention. The supernatural intrudes on the narrative in the form of a local population of 'Tidelanders', the offspring of human sailors and mythical sirens. Led by matriarch Adrielle (Elsa Pataky), the Tidelanders live in a kind of multicultural, pansexual, polyamorous commune outside of town. To the surprise of no-one paying attention, Cal learns that she is herself a Tidelander by birth, and the show follows her efforts to uncover both her origins and the connections between the Tidelanders and her human family, including her estranged, Machiavellian mother, Rosa (Caroline Brazier), and drug-dealing brother, Augie (Aaron Jakubenko).

By contrast, *Bloom* is a more restrained affair. The magic-realist six-part series explores how the discovery of a mysterious plant that restores youth affects the ageing population of the quiet backwater of Mullan. Created by Glen Dolman, the show centres on retired actress Gwen Reed (Jacki Weaver), who suffers from dementia, and her husband and carer, Ray (Bryan Brown). When Gwen is 'de-aged' by the plant (and subsequently played by Phoebe Tonkin), it seems like a miracle – until it is discovered that the effect is temporary. As the rest of the Mullan townsfolk slowly learn about the

**This spread, L–R:** *Bloom*'s Gwen in old age (Jacki Weaver) with her husband, Ray (Bryan Brown); young Gwen with her former lover Max (Sam Reid), also de-aged; Gwen with the villainous Sam (Ryan Corr)

*Tidelands* seems desperate, at times, to embrace modernity … In *Bloom*, however, modernity itself, as represented by the plant and the youth it brings, is the threat.

mysterious plant, it becomes a precious commodity, with a number of different characters fighting for control of the resource.

While both *Bloom* and *Tidelands* sit comfortably under the 'genre' – or, if you're feeling precious, 'heightened' or 'elevated' genre[1] – umbrella, in terms of tone, they each approach their shared territory from very different angles. *Tidelands* takes its cues from violent pay-TV dramas like *Sons of Anarchy* and *Breaking Bad*, revelling in violence, nudity and crudity. It opens with a scene combining all three, with a young, naked female Tidelander, Leandra (Jet Tranter), murdering a fisherman in a particularly gruesome manner, setting the tone for the rest of the series. The show eventually teases out the mysteries surrounding the origins of the Tidelanders, but its personal rivalries and antagonisms are, for the most part, plain, and would not look out of place in any given subset of the *Underbelly* franchise. Indeed, the main narrative engine is a drug-trafficking arrangement between Augie and the Tidelanders, with the latter providing the former with 'product' to onsell.

'Drugs' play a part in *Bloom* as well, with the unnamed plant standing in for any given substance that might 'plague' a rural Australian town. In fact, in his review of the show for *The Sydney Morning Herald*, Karl Quinn summarises its central conceit as 'a country town consumed by a drug that makes its users feel invincible but which ultimately leaves them, and their loved ones, ravaged. Ice, ice, baby.'[2] But *Bloom* doles out its story slowly. Whereas *Tidelands* sets an aggressive pace, regularly delivering fights, sex and betrayals several times an episode, *Bloom* is elegiac. Its most recognisable genre-mates are the 'cosy catastrophes' of British science fiction literature once derided by author Brian Aldiss: stories, like John Wyndham's *The Day of the Triffids*, in which conservative, middle-class British villagers are menaced by quiet threats beyond their ken.[3]

## The march of time

Matching its up-tempo storytelling, *Tidelands* seems desperate, at times, to embrace modernity. Juggling two genres – fantasy and crime – it revels in the trappings of excess that mark the latter, with a noted preponderance for high fashion and sleek cars. Even the Tidelanders' headquarters are a gorgeous example of postmodernist, eclectic architecture and decor – an odd refuge for an ostensibly ancient race. In *Bloom*, however, modernity itself, as represented by the plant and the youth it brings, is the threat. With its ageing weatherboard houses and grey, weatherworn picket fences, Mullen could be any small Australian town from the last forty years. Rarely do we see a piece of modern digital technology in the storyworld. The sets are decorated with vintage, well-used furniture and fittings, the older cast dressed in age-softened fabrics and out-of-date fashions. The town could almost literally *be* the past.

*Bloom* mistrusts the modern age, and it mistrusts the young. When the de-aged characters – which include not only Gwen but also her former lover Max (John Stanton

**Above, L–R:** *Bloom*'s Ray and young Gwen; *Tidelands*' Adrielle

> *Bloom*, for its part, certainly takes place in a recognisably Australian setting … However, it is mired in a de facto model of the country's past and refuses to engage with the realities and complexities of contemporary Australian life.

in old age / Sam Reid in youth) and nursing-home patient Farida (Usha Cornish / Amali Golden) – realise that the effect of the plant wears off, the extreme measures they take to secure their personal supplies are not just the follies of youth long fled, but evidence of the intrusion of dangerous modernity into safe and soporific Mullen. That modernity is not embodied by anything concrete, but rather the behaviour of the de-aged characters. Narratively, these are still old people, but now in young bodies. However, it is that very youth, the series implies, that makes them a danger.

The recklessness of youth is the essence of modernity; we see this in the way that Gwen and the others embrace chance and possibility over safety and routine, thereby threatening the sedentary status quo. In contrast, the town's sense of morality remains anchored in the staid and empathic Ray, who struggles to deal with the now erratic and impulsive Gwen, who has decided she wants to have a baby – something she was denied as a teenager. Ray, ever cautious, is not keen on the idea, so she takes up with Max instead and proceeds to try to conceive.[4]

This dim depiction of madcap motherhood in *Bloom* is only magnified in *Tidelands*, which seemingly holds matriarchs in absolute contempt. The latter presents us not only with a pair of villainous mums – Pataky's Adrielle and Brazier's Rosa – but with an entire mythology built around abandoned children and absentee parents. We eventually learn that the sea-dwelling sirens that rear the Tidelanders drown each human sailor they seduce; months later, an infant Tidelander is left on the shore, to be cared for and/or shunned by the citizens of Orphelin Bay. As a result of this practice, the women of the town have come to loathe the Tidelanders and their siren-mothers, banding together in a secret coven called the Sea Widows. Rosa herself is a member of this collective, contributing to our understanding of her hostility towards ostensible daughter Cal. In turn, Adrielle uses the Tidelanders' collective lack of identity to position herself as their leader: 'We have no mothers, and so I am your mother,' she says, in one of many portentous pronouncements.

It is not unexpected, then, that *Tidelands* taps into the potential of a young mother to break Adrielle's monopoly on power – an intergenerational conflict that inverts what could be called *Bloom*'s *intra*-generational conflict (in that multiple characters essentially straddle two age groups). As in *Bloom*, youth is a threat to *Tidelands*' status quo. Both in Orphelin Bay and within the commune, it is taken on faith that Tidelanders are sterile crossbreeds. In time, however, the series not only turns up a secretly pregnant Tidelander, Violca (Madeleine Madden), with designs on power, but also heavily hints that Cal is the subject of a rather murky prophecy to similar effect.

### Milieu and mythology

While *Bloom* carefully skirts any concrete explanations for the single fantastical element it contains, *Tidelands* is steeped in a mythology of its own making – replete with prophecies, ancient artefacts,[5] magical powers and more – that runs parallel to and sometimes crosses over with the personal mythologies/histories of the human characters. It is, it must be said, a notably white mythology, which is both disappointing and somewhat inexplicable given the stated in-universe history of the setting: we're told that sirens have preyed on human sailors for hundreds of years. The Tidelanders themselves, at least, are played by a fairly multicultural ensemble – suggesting that the characters, too, are of myriad backgrounds: Pataky has Spanish, Romanian and Hungarian heritage; Dalip Sondhi, who plays Adrielle's right-hand man Lamar, is of Indian descent; Tranter is Asian-Australian; and Madden is a Gadigal woman. Despite this, various flashbacks only ever show the sirens interacting with characters of European descent. Surely they would have encountered the pre-colonial Indigenous inhabitants of – and, later, non-European immigrants to – the locale?

It's particularly striking that an Australian fantasy series dabbling in ancient myths from elsewhere in the world neglects to incorporate those from the cultures of the country in which it's set. *Tidelands*' mythology is imported, a mishmash of Mediterranean legends merely dropped into an Australian setting. Later in the series, one character even makes an explicit comparison between the series' Tidelanders and the *rusalka* of Slavic folklore. No such effort is made to connect the series with any Indigenous mythological creatures, characters or narratives.

What the series *does* do is freely borrow from Australia's colonial past for its own purposes. At one point, a flashback depicts a human raid on a Tidelander camp, with children being dispersed through bushland by mounted militia. At another point, we see a group of nineteenth-century Sea Widows hunting and killing a siren as payback for the deaths of their husbands. Both scenes feel as though they could have been drawn directly from the frontier wars during Australia's early settlement, depicting atrocities committed by the British against Indigenous peoples.

On the whole, though, perhaps because of the deference to the international market that comes with being a Netflix production, *Tidelands* downplays its sense of place. Its mythology is generic. Its characters, both supernatural and mundane, are archetypes familiar to us from any number of similar overseas productions – Cal, the reluctant heroine with hidden power; Adrielle, the sexy despot; Lamar, the conniving sidekick. Specific references to actual Australian locations, such as the cities of Sydney and Melbourne, are kept to an absolute minimum. In striving for universal accessibility, *Tidelands* ultimately avoids commenting on or embodying any specific Australian experience.

*Bloom*, for its part, certainly takes place in a recognisably Australian setting. Its language is more overtly in the Australian colloquial idiom, and its country setting gives it a familiar bushland backdrop; even the presence of iconic actors like Brown and Weaver work to situate it here more concretely. However, it is mired in a de facto model of the country's past and refuses to engage with the realities and complexities of contemporary Australian life. Mullan, with its aged population, antique bric-a-brac and conspicuous lack of modern telecommunications technology, might as well be *A Country Practice*'s Wandin Valley circa 1983. Like *Tidelands*, *Bloom* lacks specificity – although, in this case, the lack is temporal, not geographical or cultural.

Throughout its six episodes, the series looks to yesterday for comfort. The real myth at its heart doesn't revolve around a youth-bestowing magical plant, but rather a simpler and more rustic Australia that, for the vast majority of viewers, simply doesn't exist anymore. Yet the world those viewers live in – and, by extension, those viewers themselves – only intrudes on Mullen metaphorically, in the form of the magical plant/drug that changes, and causes addiction in, its inhabitants. It's hard to believe that the inferred audience of *Bloom* – viewers uncomfortable with the pace and technology of the contemporary world – are the same ones most likely to engage with the series via its chosen tech-savvy platform. That the show peddles this particular brand of conservative nostalgia using digital media is oddly discomfiting.

*Bloom* and *Tidelands* are both ambitious, expensive, well-cast and well-made fantasy productions, of a type not often seen on Australian screens. However, by not engaging directly and specifically with both Australia as it stands today *and* the past that informs our current reality, they both fall short of their obvious potential. Our myths don't have to speak to everyone, but they do have to speak to us.

https://www.stan.com.au/watch/bloom
https://www.netflix.com/au/title/80191239

*Travis Johnson is a freelance critic who has written for* The Guardian, Empire, FilmInk, Flicks.com.au, SBS *and many more.*

Endnotes
1. See J Gideon Sarantinos, 'What Is an "Elevated" Genre?', *Gideon's Screenwriting Tips*, 19 October 2012, <https://gideonsway.wordpress.com/2012/10/19/what-is-an-elevated-genre/>; and Bilge Ebiri, '*Widows, Black Panther, Suspiria*, and the Year of the Elevated Genre Film', *Vulture*, 5 December 2018, <https://www.vulture.com/2018/12/widows-suspiria-and-the-year-of-elevated-genre-films.html>, both accessed 6 March 2019.
2. Karl Quinn, '*Bloom* Is Proof Australian TV Can Be As Bold as Anything from Overseas', *The Sydney Morning Herald*, 27 December 2018, <https://www.smh.com.au/entertainment/tv-and-radio/bloom-is-proof-australian-tv-can-be-as-bold-as-anything-from-overseas-20181224-p50o48.html>, accessed 6 March 2019.
3. See David Barnett, 'The Discreet Charms of "Cosy Catastrophe" Fiction', *The Guardian*, 25 November 2009, <https://www.theguardian.com/books/booksblog/2009/nov/25/cosy-catastrophe-fiction>, accessed 13 March 2019.
4. Gwen is not the only young-again character with their mind set on sex – itinerant criminal Sam (Ryan Corr) seduces local baker Tina (Nikki Shiels) seemingly within minutes of arriving in town. *Bloom* carefully frames the possibility that a child might be conceived by these reckless nouveau youths as particularly troubling.
5. Adrielle uses the drug money she obtains from Augie and co. to fund a worldwide search for shards of lost siren treasure, which she believes will grant her more power.

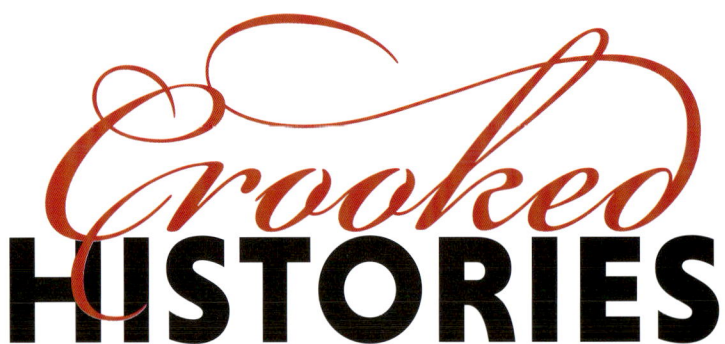

# Crooked HISTORIES

## *Underbelly* and Australian Self-mythologisation

THROUGHOUT ITS SIX SEASONS AND VARIOUS SPIN-OFFS, *UNDERBELLY* HAS TANTALISED AUDIENCES CLAMOURING FOR NARRATIVES ABOUT SCOUNDRELS AND SEEDY ENGAGEMENTS. WITH ITS FAST-PACED STORYTELLING, DEVOTION TO THE HEADLINES, AND SIMULTANEOUS SYMPATHY FOR AND CENSURE OF ITS DEPICTED CRIMINALS, THIS FRANCHISE THAT DRAMATISES CHAPTERS IN OUR CRIMINAL HISTORY HAS ALSO CARVED FOR ITSELF A REPUTATION AS A DISTINCTIVE AUSTRALIAN PRODUCT, WRITES **DAVE CREWE**.

AUSTRALIA ON
THE SMALL SCREEN

**This spread, L–R:** Various characters from Season 1 – shady figures Graham Kinniburgh (Gerard Kennedy), Mario Condello (Martin Sacks) and Alphonse Gangitano (Vince Colosimo); police detective Steven Owen (Rodger Corser); Mick Gatto (Simon Westaway, right) with a bloodied Tony Mokbel (Robert Mammone)

Over a decade on from its first episode, *Underbelly* remains the last scripted piece of Australian television to become a true phenomenon. Even before it aired, the series dominated discussion around Australian popular culture. Its first season, which was broadcast from February to May 2008 and was adapted from John Silvester and Andrew Rule's *Leadbelly: Inside Australia's Underworld Wars*, chronicles the wheeling, dealing and, most of all, killing that occurred between Melbourne's organised crime factions from 1995 to 2004. The success of the franchise – which aired a spin-off miniseries, *Underbelly Files: Chopper*, as recently as last year – is testament both to our baser desires as viewers (with sex and violence ubiquitous throughout) and a distinctively Australian fascination with the darker aspects of our recent history.

What made *Underbelly* especially memorable before a single episode hit the screen was its well-publicised legal controversies. An injunction from the Supreme Court of Victoria meant that the series aired in Victoria months after the other states, with edits imposed to keep those in active criminal trials anonymous.[1] These complications served to both underline the perceived realism of the series – which hewed closely to salacious news reports from only a few years earlier – and further fuel audience interest already stoked by a formidable marketing spend. With the advent of accessible pirating platforms that allowed Victorian viewers to circumvent the injunction,[2] it's not surprising that the show was *everywhere* in Australia.

The legal drama that consumed the drama series speaks not only to the show's popularity, but also, more importantly, to the driving philosophy behind it. Before the series premiered, I recall expecting an Australian take on *The Sopranos*: morally ambiguous protagonists, commentary on the human condition, character studies wrapped in sex and violence. That would've aligned the show with the primary mode of prestige television popular at the time. Instead, *Underbelly* – in all its iterations, with subsequent seasons drilling back into earlier generations of Aussie criminality – is a cruder take on the post-*Sopranos* 'golden age' television model, stringing together a sequence of notable crimes with, often, only a passing interest in characterisation. The bulk of the series adopts a Wikipedia approach to storytelling, dutifully including significant events that would warrant a subheading or dot point on, say, the 'Melbourne Gangland Killings' page. Convicted criminals' exploits are given prime placement, while unsolved crimes – or those too obscure to make headlines – are left to languish on the margins.

While this model is perhaps precautionary (that is, sticking to established facts to mitigate the threat of legal action), I think it's key to understanding the series' appeal. With Australia's past rarely portrayed prominently in pop culture beyond Ned Kelly and Gallipoli, *Underbelly*'s success can be – at least partially – credited to its local audience's desire to see the messier moments of our modern history. And, even if there hasn't really been an Australian series to follow in *Underbelly*'s footsteps, this mode of storytelling has seen more than its fair share of imitators on local television in the years since, from *Hawke* to *Molly*.

As I rewatch *Underbelly* with fresh eyes, what stands out is its flop-sweat anxiousness to be liked by Australian

**Above, L–R:** *Badness*' Anthony 'Rooster' Perish (Jonathan LaPaglia); *A Tale of Two Cities* and *The Golden Mile*'s Dennis Kelly (Paul Tassone); *A Tale of Two Cities*' 'Aussie Bob' Trimbole (Roy Billing) **Opposite, from top:** *Razor*'s May Seckold (Catherine Glavicic), Kate Leigh (Danielle Cormack) and Mona Woods (Pippa Grandison); Season 1's Mokbel, Jason Moran (Les Hill), Gatto, Kinniburgh, Carl Williams (Gyton Grantley), Condello, Gangitano, Mark Moran (Callan Mulvey) and Lewis Moran (Kevin Harrington)

audiences. Unlike its more prestigious American contemporaries, *Underbelly* eschews restraint and ambiguity in favour of attention-grabbing conventions. A blaring soundtrack is filled with contemporary pop songs, and Caroline Craig's narration clarifies narrative specifics while doling out moral judgement. (Case in point: when Jason Moran, played by Les Hill, is released from prison in the eighth episode of Season 1, she explains that he 'finished his sentence for being a vicious, brutal, ugly little turd'.) Each episode is dotted with various incidences of sex, drugs and violence, and any 'boring' stuff (you know, like dialogue) is often underlined with overexposed, fragmentary step printing.[3] Aesthetically, the show strongly evokes the likes of Quentin Tarantino's early films or Kinji Fukasaku's *Battles Without Honour and Humanity* series, except without attaining analogous artistry.

Then there's the nudity. A few years before *Game of Thrones* weaponised gratuitous nudity, *Underbelly* ensured that nearly every episode featured female actors (and, *very* occasionally, male ones) doffing their clothes at the thinnest excuse. Sometimes, it was unnamed extras gyrating in the series' many strip-club or massage-parlour scenes; just as often, main characters showcased their naughty bits to keep audiences' eyes glued to the screen. The most notorious example is surely found in the sixth episode of Season 3, subtitled *The Golden Mile*, in which police officer Debbie Webb (Cheree Cassidy) – whose nakedness would've served no real narrative justification – holds a meeting at a nudist beach. This emphasis on sex appeal aligns *Underbelly* more closely with the more exploitative television shows of the era (think: *Californication* or *Spartacus*) than with prestige series like *Mad Men* or *The Wire*.

Despite this, I'm not convinced that *Underbelly* truly fits in with any of the television shows coming out of the States at the time. It's structurally unusual, for starters: its anthology format, with each season tackling a new era with (mostly) new actors, wasn't popularised in the US until *American Horror Story* circa 2011. Meanwhile, the historical subject matter, while far from exceptional in the context of audiovisual narratives, was distinct at the time in both its currency and detail. There are plenty of historical television series and feature-length biopics, but, until *Underbelly*, few television shows represented recent events in this sort of warts-and-all detail. Indeed, the closest equivalent in American television wouldn't arrive until 2016 series *American Crime Story*, the first season of which focused on OJ Simpson's trial.

Earlier, I mentioned *Underbelly*'s 'Wikipedia storytelling'. That approach is hardly restricted to this show; countless Hollywood biographical/historical films have assumed the same dot-point approach to narrative (Bryan Singer's 2018 *Bohemian Rhapsody*, Morten Tyldum's 2014 *The Imitation Game*, and so on), to varying results. But, when used across up to thirteen episodes in multiple seasons,[4] the strengths and weaknesses of this storytelling style become very apparent.

Let's start with the weaknesses. First, there are the sacrifices to narrative coherence necessitated by the artistic decision to cram in every major crime across the time period depicted. Whether it's the late Season 1 introduction of Keith Faure (Kim Gyngell; the character was unnamed due to the aforementioned injunction), the Les and Brian Kane (Martin Dingle Wall and Tim McCunn) diversion in Season 2, subtitled *A Tale of Two Cities*, or the shift in focus to Michael 'Doc' Kanaan (Ryan Corr) in *The Golden Mile*, the series frequently diverges from established protagonists for quick detours that tick off big headlines but only have a tangential connection to the core storyline.

Unlike its more prestigious American contemporaries, *Underbelly* eschews restraint and ambiguity in favour of attention-grabbing conventions … Each episode is dotted with various incidences of sex, drugs and violence.

Then there's the obligatory tiptoeing around crimes that never produced a conviction. That's most pronounced in the legally fraught first season, particularly in the showdown between Mick Gatto (Simon Westaway) and Andrew 'Benji' Veniamin (Damian Walshe-Howling) that led to the latter's demise and Gatto's being charged with murder, for which he was later acquitted. Veniamin's death is kept off screen, while associated attempts to evoke ambiguity are largely unsuccessful: Gatto comes off as, if not the good guy, then at least innocent.

It's the same story with the portrayal of The Golden Mile's John Ibrahim (Firass Dirani). Initially framed as the protagonist of this season, Ibrahim – who's never been successfully convicted of a crime – floats through the narrative without much agency or purpose. His inclusion in the Kings Cross–centric season is mandated by his notorious profile, but the screenwriters seem adrift when it comes to meaningfully incorporating him into the storyline, splitting the difference by portraying him as both a saint (as when he tries to defuse a violent brawl) and a criminal (as when he dodges conviction for the murder of Talal Assaad, played by Rahel Romahn). This approach to presenting a character as 'multidimensional' speaks to the showrunners' obvious desire for their show to be perceived as authentic; however, for audience members, it's frequently frustrating.

It's not all bad news. While Underbelly's first season particularly suffers from scattershot storytelling, the two subsequent seasons attain a tighter focus despite having expanded the 'core' cast. These prequel seasons – centring on events in Melbourne and Sydney from 1976 to 1987 (*A Tale of Two Cities*) and Kings Cross from 1988 to 1999 (*The Golden Mile*) – did have the luxury of more legal freedom than Season 1, given they're dealing with events from decades, not years, prior. But I'd argue that the real strength of these seasons is that they use the theme of police corruption not only as a narrative throughline (featuring returning actors), but also to examine systemic cultural and logistical issues that allowed organised crime to thrive, rather than being reduced to isolated pockets of greed and vice.

The centrality of such corruption is significant – and rare. As critic Lauren Carroll Harris has argued in *Daily Review*, Aussie crime shows and movies typically offer 'a simplistic, cops-and-robbers, goodies-and-baddies view of the police', with corruption only depicted as 'individual and isolated incidents of illegitimate policing'.[5] Though that dynamic *was* maintained, somewhat implausibly, in *Underbelly*'s first season, both subsequent seasons use findings from the 1995–1997 Royal Commission into the New South Wales

> The second and third seasons credit the success of the criminals featured to neither genius nor dumb luck, but rather the tacit permission of a justice system content to look the other way … for a price.

Police Service (seen in *The Golden Mile*) to present a portrait of a deeply corrupt and misogynistic[6] culture at the core of Australia's justice system.

The second and third seasons credit the success of the criminals featured to neither genius nor dumb luck, but rather the tacit permission of a justice system content to look the other way … for a price. While I'm not completely convinced by the contemporaneous claims that *Underbelly* glamorised crime or violence,[7] the portrayed exploits of the convicted criminals do tend to pale in comparison to the nefariousness of those tasked with stopping them. It's telling that some of the series' most affecting moments involve police officers, whether it's the murder of *A Tale of Two Cities*' corrupt lawyer Brian Alexander (Damian de Montemas) or the sexual assault of *The Golden Mile*'s rookie detective Claudia Campanelli (Megan Drury).

Though reports at the time suggested that the fourth season, *Razor*, would centre on Queensland corruption leading up to the Fitzgerald Inquiry,[8] the eventual angle producers took was notably different, rewinding eight decades to the 'razor gangs' of the 1930s. For me, this is where the series begins to hit diminishing returns. Granted, the particulars are much the same – brawls, boobs and betrayals – but the core of cultural critique impelling the best episodes of the series thus far fades away for a return to empty, historically relevant thrills. While *Underbelly* continued to draw audiences, with *Razor*'s premiere the highest-rating TV drama episode in Australia for 2011,[9] the show's cultural prominence was undeniably fading as its subject matter deviated from recognisable recent figures and headlines.

Digging into these television ratings helps us to understand the legacy of *Underbelly*. Granted, the series hasn't disappeared entirely, as last year's *Chopper* – with Vince Colosimo returning to the role of Alphonse Gangitano for the third time – attests, but it's certainly not the juggernaut it once was. It's also tempting to slot *Underbelly* into the continuum of crime dramas that have aired in Australia across the decades, as Andrew Nette did in his 2015 *Metro* piece 'Crime Pays: *Underbelly*, *Homicide* and *Blue Murder*'.[10] But, with only a passing interest in police-procedural conventions and an emphasis on crime over the investigation of the same, *Underbelly* feels like an outlier in this subgenre.[11] Rather, I'd argue that *Underbelly*'s legacy is found by checking the highest-rating Australian TV drama the year after *Razor*: the miniseries *Howzat! Kerry Packer's War*. Or two years after that, when *Underbelly* spin-off *Fat Tony & Co* was outperformed by the miniseries *Never Tear Us Apart: The Untold Story of INXS*.[12] Such ripped-from-the-headlines dramatisations[13] might diverge sharply from *Underbelly*'s subject matter, but each is intent on depicting episodes from Australia's recent past with the same grit and glitz granted to American history in Hollywood films.

As evidenced by these ratings, this mode of storytelling clearly resonates with Australian audiences. This isn't necessarily a surprise; true-crime and historical/biographical stories have always been broadly popular to a range of audience demographics both here and abroad.[14] But *Underbelly* and the 'Wikipedia' miniseries that followed in its wake feel specifically geared to local audiences. That's in part an obvious consequence of the subject matter; it's hard to imagine international markets being especially interested in the crook culture of Kings Cross or the pitch that Samuel Johnson *is* Molly Meldrum.[15]

More significantly, the forthright mythmaking showcased in *Underbelly* and its ilk caters to a specifically Australian inclination to celebrate – or, at least, express fascination in – the dirtiest corners of our history. Whereas other nations' most enduring historical icons might be war heroes or noble leaders, Australia's is almost certainly Ned Kelly. An outlaw. A 'rebel'. Remembered primarily for that fearsome suit of armour that's indelibly associated with his *inability* to escape capture. His failure, in other words. As much as Australian myth does have a tinge of the jingoistic – cricketer Don Bradman's intimidating batting ability, the so-called Anzac legend, platitudes about mateship – our ingrained tall poppy syndrome ensures that it's the grimier legends that tend to take hold of the public imagination. Bob Hawke remains one of our most popular former politicians, not for any significant policy positions, but arguably for his ability to chug yard glasses (and, perhaps, his notorious infidelity) – which is why he gets to be played by Richard Roxburgh (in Emma Freeman's *Hawke*, 2010) while Robert Menzies remains relegated to history textbooks.

Hollywood biopics may turn to hagiography more often than not, but Australian historical series, miniseries and films tend to centre on our crudeness, our corruption, our – if you're being generous – 'larrikin spirit'. The success of *Underbelly* can partly be credited to Aussie audiences' desire to see our culture, even the seedy stuff, as significant. At the same time, it speaks to a roughness at the core of our character. Colonial Australia did, after all, begin with ships full of convicts; *Underbelly* reminds us that we haven't necessarily travelled all that far.

*Dave Crewe is a secondary school teacher and freelance writer based in Brisbane, Queensland. He is the founder and editor of the website* ccpopculture, *and has been published by* SBS Movies, Screen Education, The Guardian *and* The Big Issue. **m**

### Endnotes

1. See 'Grave Doubts over *Underbelly*: Court', *The Age*, 8 February 2008, <https://www.theage.com.au/national/grave-doubts-over-underbelly-court-20080208-ge6pc2.html>, accessed 25 February 2019.
2. See Nick Miller, 'Pirates Promise *Underbelly* Downloads', *The Age*, 13 February 2008, <https://www.theage.com.au/technology/pirates-promise-underbelly-downloads-20080213-gds0uk.html>, accessed 25 February 2019.
3. A stuttering style of stop-motion most memorably used in Wong Kar Wai's 1994 film *Chungking Express*, employed here for emphasis or to attempt to evoke excitement.
4. The first four seasons each had thirteen episodes, while seasons five and six as well as associated spin-off *Fat Tony & Co* had eight, eight and nine episodes, respectively.
5. Lauren Carroll Harris, 'What Australian Screen Stories Get Wrong About Police, Crime and Brutality', *Daily Review*, 1 December 2016, <https://dailyreview.com.au/australian-screen-stories-get-wrong-police-crime-brutality/53132/>, accessed 25 February 2019.
6. And every other kind of -phobic you could think of. Case in point: the death of *The Golden Mile*'s trans sex worker Wanda (Mitch Bartlett), who is treated with disdain by the officers who discover her body.
7. See Richard Clune & Yoni Bashan, '*Underbelly* Gangster Glamour Wears Off', *The Sunday Telegraph*, 10 January 2010, <https://www.dailytelegraph.com.au/underbelly-gangster-glamour-wears-off/news-story/7f39da23c8aa04c5c2d2a82fa80745e1>, accessed 25 February 2019.
8. 'Fourth Series of *Underbelly* Series to Be Set in Queensland', *Herald Sun*, 25 November 2009, <https://www.heraldsun.com.au/entertainment/television/fourth-series-of-underbelly-series-to-be-set-in-queensland/news-story/e87ae7dcca41babf9af8fdef5661e511>, accessed 25 February 2019.
9. See the entry for 2011 in Screen Australia, 'Top 50 Episodes on Australian Free-to-air Television, 5-city-metro, 2008–2017', 'Top-rating Australian TV Drama – Metro & Regional', <https://www.screenaustralia.gov.au/fact-finders/television/australian-content/top-drama-titles>, accessed 25 February 2019.
10. Andrew Nette, 'Crime Pays: *Underbelly*, *Homicide* and *Blue Murder*', *Metro*, no. 183, Summer 2015, pp. 50–5.
11. Interestingly, despite *Underbelly*'s success, there hasn't really been an Australian series to follow directly in its footsteps in terms of exploiting the 'true crime plus sex plus violence' formula. The closest we've gotten is 2012's *Bikie Wars: Brothers in Arms*, which I'd forgive you for forgetting.
12. See the 2012 and 2014 figures, respectively, in Screen Australia, 'Top 10 Titles on Free-to-air Television, 2008–2018', 'Top-rating First-release Australian Adult TV Drama', <https://www.screenaustralia.gov.au/fact-finders/television/australian-content/top-drama-titles/first-release-series>, accessed 25 February 2019.
13. Though I don't mean to contend that *Underbelly* inspired the production of such miniseries, which have dominated Australian scripted television over the past decade. For example, *The King: The Story of Graham Kennedy* (Matthew Saville, 2007) played on cable television a year before *Underbelly* and garnered significantly high TV ratings at the time.
14. See, respectively, Rob Owen, 'True Crime Tales Are on the Rise Across Broadcast and Cable', *Variety*, 3 August 2017, <https://variety.com/2017/tv/news/manhunt-unabomber-menendez-brothers-the-keepers-unsolved-1202510421/>; and Kat Eschner, 'Why Do We Love Period Dramas So Much?', *Smithsonian.com*, 15 December 2016, <https://www.smithsonianmag.com/smart-news/why-we-love-period-drama-180961474/>, both accessed 27 February 2019.
15. Johnson was 'hand-picked' by Meldrum himself for the role; see Cameron Adams, 'Samuel Johnson Transforms into Molly Meldrum for a New Miniseries', *News.com.au*, 16 February 2015, <https://www.news.com.au/entertainment/tv/samuel-johnson-transforms-into-molly-meldrum-for-a-new-miniseries/news-story/7d08b01a7379e745d3bb5afd5793e7f4>, accessed 27 February 2019.

# QUIET RAGE

## The Fire and Finesse of Lee Chang-dong's Cinema

THE FILMS OF LEE CHANG-DONG OFFER PROVOCATIONS FOR REFLECTING ON THE DANGERS OF VIOLENCE, THE DISEMPOWERMENT WROUGHT BY DISADVANTAGE, THE ENIGMA AND ENNUI OF YOUTH. FROM 1997'S *GREEN FISH* TO LAST YEAR'S WIDELY ACCLAIMED *BURNING*, THE OEUVRE OF THIS KOREAN NOVELIST-TURNED-DIRECTOR QUIETLY BRIMS WITH CEREBRAL RIGOUR AND SUBDUED STYLE, WRITES **ANTHONY CAREW**.

FOCUS ON ASIA AND
THE MIDDLE EAST

**This spread, all images:** *Burning*

What would a president see in *Burning* (Lee Chang-dong, 2018)? When, at the end of 2018, Barack Obama made like any self-respecting cinephile and posted a films-of-the-year list on his socials,[1] he showed plenty of cred, listing acclaimed arthouse and indie movies, like *Burning*, alongside the all-conquering *Black Panther* (Ryan Coogler, 2018). It's interesting to contemplate what a man who once occupied a seat of such supreme power would love in Lee's drifting 148-minute tone poem. Its central device, the disappearance of a young woman, Hae-mi (Jun Jong-seo), is never resolved; instead, it's a mystery that, in staying unsolved, leaves everything about the film mysterious. The thematic subtext of the screenplay, economic inequality, definitely gives it universal resonance. But it was nonetheless surprising, upon scanning the former US president's faves, to see just how universal that resonance is.

There is a president in *Burning*, but it's not Obama. It is, of course, his successor, Donald Trump, a totemic embodiment of economic inequality. Lee could've used a more Korean figure, like Park Geun-hye, the daughter of a former totalitarian leader, who found herself impeached as South Korean president in 2016 and eventually imprisoned in 2018 for collusion, corruption and abuses of power.[2] But Trump, that human sign-o'-the-times, is both more ubiquitous and more specific. In *Burning*, we hear a presidential speech playing on the television owned by Jong-su (Yoo Ah-in), an aspiring writer who's been forced – by his father's legal troubles – to return to his downtrodden hometown and work the family farm. While Trump, in all his grotesque buffoonery, is often deployed as a punchline, here, he's evoked as a more complex figure: he may embody economic inequality, but his appeal transcends it – or, at least, plays to both sides of the crowd. A simpler film would've made him a mirroring symbol for the movie's ostensible antagonist, Ben (Steven Yeun), Jong-su's rival for Hae-mi's affections. Ben is an amoral, aloof, handsome, Americanised, globetrotting rich kid – and possible arsonist and/or murderer – who dwells not in some dust bowl by the Korean border, but in a high-rise in Gangnam. While Trump's tax policies cater to such one-percenters, his rhetoric is aimed at people like Jong-su: rural victims of economic crisis, stewing in inarticulate rage, looking for someone to blame. 'This is a film about anger. I think everyone is angry these days. I think it was also some people's anger that made Trump president,' Lee said, upon *Burning*'s release.[3] 'The two [characters] exist on opposite ends of the spectrum. But a lot of young people today live somewhere between these two poles. Many feel the helplessness that [Jong-su] feels, but they want to live like Ben.'[4]

*Burning* marks, in many ways, Lee's ascension to prominence in the international consciousness. Though he'd previously directed five features of increasing accomplishment – *Green Fish* (1997), *Peppermint Candy* (1999), *Oasis* (2002), *Secret Sunshine* (2007) and *Poetry* (2010) – before *Burning*, he'd never captured the cinematic zeitgeist, was nowhere near as celebrated as peers like Park Chan-wook or Bong Joon-ho. Born in 1954 in Daegu, South Korea, Lee grew up in a theatre household, but always wanted to be a writer. In 1983, his first novel, *Chonri*, was published to much local acclaim. Lee only transitioned to cinema when director Park Kwang-su recruited him to co-write the screenplay for *To the Starry Island* (1993); by then, Lee had been undergoing a midlife crisis, with Korea's increasingly liberal political climate[5] leading him to question his identity as writer. '[W]hat it meant to live and work as a writer in Korea [in the 1980s and early 1990s] was to be an activist,' Lee offered in 1998. 'I felt like I had lost my direction as a writer […] It was at that point that I felt I should turn to making films.'[6]

---

**Lee is still a novelist at heart, his micro stories suggesting macro ideas. Through his depictions of patriarchy, hypocrisy, individualised justice/restitution, corruption, bribery, violence, modernisation and economic disenfranchisement, he's poking at broader social issues.**

**This spread, top and middle:** *Burning* **This spread, bottom, L–R:** *Peppermint Candy*; *Green Fish*

So Lee made Park an offer: he'd write the screenplay, but only if he could be *To the Starry Island*'s assistant director, learning the trade on the job.[7]

After the commercially unremarkable debut of *Green Fish*, Lee's next two films, *Peppermint Candy* and *Oasis*, were solid box-office successes in Korea, giving him the freedom to explore more idiosyncratic ideas. But, following a brief stint as South Korea's culture and tourism minister, Lee worked more slowly, questioning the worth of any new idea. This attitude remains today; of *Burning*, the director muses, '[Jong-su] is trying to be a writer and always asking himself, "What kind of story can I write?" Like [Jong-su], I ask myself that all the time, as if I'm a filmmaker who's just starting his career.'[8] He has also explained: 'I've never made films that [deliver] messages, nor have I ever felt the urge to make such pieces. I just like to ask questions.'[9]

Lee's questions usually interrogate Korean society. While he has particular filmmaking fondnesses – meting out classic melodrama over slow-moving works of realism, karaoke, incongruously jaunty music, rivers and trains as symbolic images of the movement of time, characters riding in cars and on buses, depictions of people with disabilities – Lee is still a novelist at heart, his micro stories suggesting macro ideas. Through his depictions of patriarchy, hypocrisy, individualised justice/restitution, corruption, bribery, violence, modernisation and economic disenfranchisement, he's poking at broader social issues. His directorial 'style' is largely unobtrusive, observational – 'I don't want to make a film in which you defraud reality or betray reality through an illusion,' Lee has said[10] – leading him to demand that those in front of the camera inhabit the environment, the moment. 'I am notorious for giving actors a hard time,' shares Lee.[11] 'I often tell my actors "Don't act."'[12]

*Green Fish*, Lee's debut, is his least-accomplished work. But beneath this oft-generic tale of gangsters, violence and male possessiveness is a portrait of a changing Korea, detailing how rapid modernisation and desperate economic development have created a hyper-capitalist mentality of gaining wealth and status at any cost. 'The theme of the film is the nature of violence,' Lee explained, upon its release. 'Of course there is a diversity of violence, from political violence to gangster violence. But I think violence is violence, regardless of who is committing it.'[13]

Having finished his mandatory military service, Mak-dong (Han Suk-kyu) returns to Ilsan, the rural town where he grew up. His childhood memories are of an agrarian idyll – rice paddies, green fields, streams in which they fished – but Ilsan is rapidly changing, now an exurban developmental hub of apartment towers. He ends up working for a gangster in Seoul, torn between his rural morality/naivety/virginity, his immoral work and his infatuation with femme fatale Mi-ae (Shim Hye-jin), a fading nightclub singer and his boss's best girl. *Green Fish* is the tale of a simple country boy corrupted by violence, anger, resentment, lust – something it shares with *Burning*, no matter how radically different their delivery, suggesting the timelessness of the theme of traditional culture lost in the face of ruthless progress.

*Peppermint Candy* is an even more explicit study of an evolving Korea: set at various points throughout recent history, its story mirrors the politico-economic cycles of the nation itself. In a striking gesture – staged a year before Christopher Nolan's famous *Memento* (2000) – the plot is

**Above, from top:** *Peppermint Candy* (two images); *Oasis*

presented backwards, retreating through the past, the episodic narrative broken by reversed footage of a train journey (at one point, people are seen running in rewind, foregrounding the device). '*Peppermint Candy* is a film about a sort of time travel. And so I needed a way to visualize time. That's the train,' Lee explained in 2008. Describing train travel as having altered 'mankind's perception of time', he went on to say: 'Film is, of course, a medium that deals with time, and in that sense, the fact that one of the first films ever made is [the Lumière Brothers'] *Arrival of a Train* [1896] is very symbolic.'[14]

*Peppermint Candy* opens in Spring 1999 with a sad, drunk salaryman, Yong-ho (Sol Kyung-gu), stumbling along a rubbish-strewn riverbank; there, a party of people have gathered to sing karaoke. He climbs up onto the nearby bridge and stands in front of an oncoming train. As it's about to strike him, he yells either – depending on your subtitled translation – 'I want to go back!' or 'I am going back!' From there, we do go back, essentially solving the 'mystery' of why this man was driven to suicide. Moving from 1999 through 1994, 1987, 1984, 1980 and, finally, 1979, the narrative refracts the political situations of the nation at those times: financial collapse, economic boom, police brutality, student protest and military state all at play across one man's life. We see Yong-ho bouncing between two women: his lost love, Sun-im (Moon So-ri), and the wife he never really liked, Hong-ja (Kim Yeo-jin). *Peppermint Candy* is about masculinity and emasculation, and how progressive youths turn into conservative adults when given money and power. The film ends where it began – on that same riverbank, but twenty years earlier – irony instilled through Yong-ho and Sun-im, young and idealistic, meeting among a sun-dappled gathering of students. It's here that the origin of the film's totems – a camera, the titular lollies, trains – is established; it's a moment of innocence, for both character and Korea, that'll soon be shattered.

For *Oasis*, Lee worked again with *Peppermint Candy*'s leads, casting them in challenging roles: Sol plays an ex-con, Jong-du, with a mild mental disability and wild emotional instability; and Moon plays Gong-ju, a woman with cerebral palsy, with whom he undertakes a scandalous affair. The narrative begets a study of social prejudice, hypocrisy, condescension: a pair of outraged extended families refusing to accept the sexual agency of Gong-ju, that she could be anything but a victim. Running counter to this are scenes of fantasy and magic realism in which Gong-ju is unafflicted, a 'normal' woman, free to engage in a regular relationship – scenes that can be read as either Jong-du's dreams or Gong-ju's own self-conception. Arriving in 2002, *Oasis* feels like a corrective to a run of contemporaneous Hollywood films – think: the execrable *The Other Sister* (Garry Marshall, 1999) – that turned characters with mental disabilities into either cute pets or pitiable sufferers; Lee's lead characters are complex, contrary, often difficult-to-like people, prone to as many fits of rage as flights of fantasy.

*Secret Sunshine* arrived five years later, after Lee's ministerial stint, and served as a 'level-up' work for the director. It's a study of faith, willing delusion, Korean Christianity, hypocrisy, small-town gossip and paranoia. While people involved with

> While people involved with the production were worried about how local Christians – a powerful lobby in Korean society – would receive the movie, Lee regarded *Secret Sunshine* as a sincere exploration of belief.

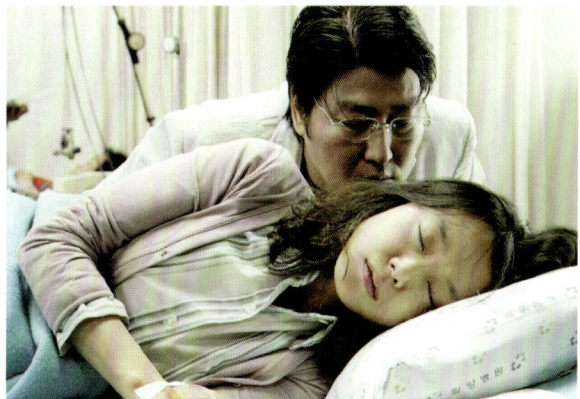

**Above:** *Secret Sunshine* (three images)

the production were worried about how local Christians – a powerful lobby in Korean society – would receive the movie, Lee regarded *Secret Sunshine* as a sincere exploration of belief: 'One of the most important things to me was to find a way to portray things that are not visible to the naked eye, faith being one of them.'[15] It stars Jeon Do-yeon – in a role for which she won Best Actress at Cannes – as Shin-ae, a woman who moves, with her young son, to the hometown of her recently deceased husband in an attempt to put their dreary past behind them. Instead, tragedy strikes again: her son, kidnapped; his body, eventually found by a local river. In her grief and depression, Shin-ae embraces the local religious zealots she'd previously avoided; whether she's prey for cynical recruiters or someone finding faith in dark times is, in that Lee-like way, left open-ended. Her born-again faith is instantly lost, though, when she visits her son's killer in prison and finds that he, too, has found God, enlightenment, absolution.

While *Secret Sunshine* treads bleak emotional terrain, Lee never shies away from absurdity, inserting comic protest, mischievous sabotage, karaoke and macho bluster amid the drama. Song Kang-ho plays Jong-chan, a would-be love interest who's had his affections set on Shin-ae from the start – a puppy-doggish figure of masculine cluelessness and man-child pining. An exchange with a friend who's dismissing Jong-chan's romantic chances feels like greater commentary

**Above, L–R:** *Poetry*; *Burning*

> *Burning*'s own title is taken from an act of destruction that could be either cathartic or meaningless, meaning forever tough to pin down in a picture so open-ended, so slippery, so uninterested in solving its own mysteries.

on the film itself: 'You're like a melodrama, dude, [but] you don't look the part,' the friend says, to which he replies, 'Your view's too narrow. It could be comic melodrama.'

Lee's subsequent work, *Poetry*, feels like a much less comic companion to *Secret Sunshine*: another film about tragedy, crime, punishment and moral reckoning in a gossipy small town. It opens with a close-up of a rushing river, before showing a dead body floating on its current – a body that turns out to be a local schoolgirl who's taken her life by jumping from a traffic bridge. Eventually, it's revealed that she was raped by a gang of schoolmates; Lee has admitted that his 'main motive for making this film' was to address 'a sexual assault committed by a group of juveniles in a small town in South Korea' that had occurred a few years prior.[16]

Abhorring conventional depictions of 'justice' in films,[17] the director sought an unexpected way in to the story. That comes through its principal character, Mi-ja (Yun Jeong-hee), a sixty-something woman who, in the early stages of Alzheimer's, joins a local writing group in the hope of penning her first ever poem. Mi-ja is 'young at heart', prone to flattery, filled with vanity, her elaborate outfits at odds with her downtrodden social station. She's the guardian to her moody, dude-ish grandson Wook (Lee David), who, it turns out, is one of the rapists. Mi-ja learns this when a group of fathers – she's the only woman in their midst – gets together, working out how they're going to 'solve' the shared problem of their criminal kids. Both the school and the family of the victim want to avoid scandal and agree to bought silence, the fathers offering to pay 30 million won in 'restitution' to settle the situation (*Oasis* also highlights this particular form of Korean economic 'justice'). Mi-ja doesn't have her share of the money, but, even as she enacts her own questionable plans to come into the cash, and continues to lovingly feed her grandson at home, she struggles under the moral weight of the pay-off. At the same time, she flounders writing her first poem, only finding 'inspiration', perhaps troublingly, with the discovery of her grandson's guilt and upon meeting the dead girl's family. The uneasy alliance between tragedy and creativity in *Poetry*'s narrative was Lee interrogating himself with '[q]uestions like, why do I write novels and make films; and to what extent my writings or films can affect the world'. He continued: 'Art is a pursuit for beauty and there is the question of how it is related to the filth and vice of the world. The question is similar to what Theodor Adorno had asked: is it possible to write lyric poetry after Auschwitz?'[18]

After *Poetry*, Lee devised three scripts that he 'didn't have the conviction to make' into film, each of which dealt with 'the anger and helplessness of young people today'.[19] He eventually found the right vessel for that theme in a 1983 short story by Haruki Murakami, 'Barn Burning', whose brevity and abstraction – it's a story about telling stories – hardly make it an immediate candidate for adaptation. But Lee was attracted to both its mystery (boy loses girl to rich cad, then girl vanishes without a trace) and its mysteriousness, which 'gave [him] a lot of room to develop and expand into the cinematic medium'.[20]

*Burning*, Lee's grand adaptation, uses this simple story to explore so many of his favourite themes: how social injustice manifests as violence, and economic disenfranchisement as rage; how the individual's pursuit of justice in a corrupt society leads to their own corruption; how Korea's changing society, and the forward march of progress, leaves poor, rural people behind. It's also a film about being young, and the yearning for something beyond your station – whether it be a girl (for Jong-su), freedom and enlightenment through travel (for Hae-mi) or ways to combat the ennui of wealth (for Ben). '[P]roblems are more individualized […] Everyone has their own reasons for being angry,' Lee has said.[21] The greater theme, he offers, is that 'the millennials living in Korea today will be the first generation that are worse off than their parents' generation […] This film is about young people who feel impotent, with rage bottled up inside them.' When working on his various post-*Poetry* screenplays, interrogating this theme, Lee even called this new undertaking 'Project Rage'.[22]

*Burning*'s own title is taken from an act of destruction that could be either cathartic or meaningless, meaning forever tough to pin down in a picture so open-ended, so slippery, so uninterested in solving its own mysteries. Movies lacking resolution aren't usually beloved by audiences – and presidents – but *Burning* charms viewers with the glow of both its handsome cast and its handsome cinematography (by Hong Kyung-pyo, a Bong collaborator with whom Lee had never worked before). The film is largely shot during that glorious photographic time known as 'magic hour' – at dawn and dusk – making it look far more beautiful than his previous pictures. This isn't empty style, though, but rather an approach playing into *Burning*'s mysterious tone and deeper themes, depicting the 'boundary that exists between light and darkness'.[23] Its centrepiece is a scene in which Hae-mi, right before her disappearance, dances her 'dance of the Great Hunger', of yearning, of sexual liberation – a silhouette set against the radiant dusk horizon. She moves along borders: between two men vying for her attention, between South and North Korea, between day and night. This scene, according to Lee, 'reflects the mystery of this movie, the uncertain line between truth and lies, the real and the false'.[24]

For Yeun, a millennial acting in this film about millennials, this mystery resonates with the contemporary moment. 'What realities are we living in? How many masks do we have on? How many versions of ourselves do we have? Are we real, are we not?' he asks,[25] the actor taking his director's cue of raising endless questions. It's no surprise, then, that *Burning* struck a chord in 2018 (and beyond), ending up on all manner of best-of lists, be they by Barry O or no. In its enigma and its rage, we find a tale in which rural Korea evokes the digital dystopia: that global feed wherein the same environmental and presidential horrors are splattered all over the one infinite scroll, uniting a generation of plural identities in singular anger.

*Anthony Carew is a Melbourne-based critic.*      m

Endnotes

1. Post dated 29 December 2018 on Barack Obama's official Facebook page, <https://www.facebook.com/barackobama/posts/10156393283416749>, accessed 27 February 2019.
2. See Choe Sang-Hun, 'Park Geun-hye, South Korea's Ousted President, Gets 24 Years in Prison', *The New York Times*, 6 April 2018, <https://www.nytimes.com/2018/04/06/world/asia/park-geun-hye-south-korea.html>, accessed 27 February 2019.
3. Lee Chang-dong, quoted in Justin Chang, 'Director Lee Chang-dong and Actor Steven Yeun on the Profound Mysteries of *Burning*', *Los Angeles Times*, 27 May 2018, <http://www.latimes.com/entertainment/movies/la-et-mn-burning-lee-chang-dong-steven-yeun-20180527-htmlstory.html>, accessed 27 February 2019.
4. Lee Chang-dong, quoted in Daniel Kasman, 'Mysterious Elements: Lee Chang-dong Discusses *Burning*', *MUBI Notebook*, 29 May 2018, <https://mubi.com/notebook/posts/mysterious-elements-lee-chang-dong-discusses-burning>, accessed 27 February 2019.
5. 1992 saw Kim Young-sam elected as the first civilian president since military rule was imposed in 1961.
6. Lee Chang-dong, quoted in David Walsh, 'Dirt in the Soul', *World Socialist Web Site*, 19 May 1998, <https://www.wsws.org/en/articles/1998/05/fish-m19.html>, accessed 27 February 2019.
7. See Stan Glick, 'ACF 108: Lee Chang-dong E-interview', *AsianCineFest*, 3 May 2008, <http://asiancinefest.blogspot.com/2008/05/acf-108-lee-chang-dong-e-interview.html>, accessed 27 February 2019.
8. Lee Chang-dong, quoted in Dennis Lim, 'Interview: Lee Chang-dong', *Film Comment*, 25 October 2018, <https://www.filmcomment.com/blog/cannes-interview-lee-chang-dong/>, accessed 27 February 2019.
9. Lee Chang-dong, quoted in Yoon Min-sik, 'Lee Chang-dong Throws Questions, Not Messages, with His Films', *The Korea Herald*, 27 May 2018, <http://www.koreaherald.com/view.php?ud=20180527000060>, accessed 27 February 2019.
10. Lee, quoted in Walsh, op. cit.
11. Lee Chang-dong, quoted in Dennis Lim, 'A Portraitist of a Subdued, Literary Korea', *The New York Times*, 30 September 2007, <https://www.nytimes.com/2007/09/30/movies/30lim.html>, accessed 27 February 2019.
12. Lee Chang-dong, quoted in Glick, op. cit.
13. Lee, quoted in Walsh, op. cit.
14. Lee, quoted in Glick, op. cit., emphasis removed.
15. Lee, quoted in Lim, 'A Portraitist of a Subdued, Literary Korea', op. cit.
16. Lee Chang-dong, quoted in David Jenkins, 'The *Poetry* of Lee Chang-dong', *TimeOut* London, <https://www.timeout.com/london/film/the-poetry-of-lee-chang-dong-1>, accessed 27 February 2019.
17. See Sarah Cronin, '*Poetry*: Interview with Lee Chang-dong', *Electric Sheep*, 27 July 2011, <http://www.electricsheepmagazine.co.uk/features/2011/07/27/poetry-interview-with-lee-chang-dong/>, accessed 27 February 2019.
18. Lee Chang-dong, quoted in ibid.
19. Lee, quoted in Lim, 'Interview: Lee Chang-dong', op. cit.
20. Lee, quoted in Kasman, op. cit.
21. Lee Chang-dong, quoted in Karen Han, '*Burning* Is the Angry as Hell Movie We Need Right Now', *VICE*, 27 October 2018, <https://www.vice.com/en_us/article/evwe9a/burning-is-the-angry-as-hell-movie-we-need-right-now>, accessed 27 February 2019.
22. Lee Chang-dong, quoted in Patrick Frater, '*Burning* Director Lee Chang-dong: Still Angry After All These Years', *Variety*, 3 December 2018, <https://variety.com/2018/film/asia/lee-chang-dong-burning-cannes-1202812485/>, accessed 27 February 2019.
23. Lee Chang-dong, quoted in Amir Ganjavie, 'Slow-burn: Director Lee Chang-dong on Storyboarding, Shooting, Lighting, and Scoring *Burning*', *MovieMaker*, 14 November 2018, <https://www.moviemaker.com/archives/moviemaking/directing/interview-with-lee-chang-dong/>, accessed 27 February 2019.
24. Lee, quoted in Lim, 'Interview: Lee Chang-dong', op. cit.
25. Steven Yeun, quoted in Tasha Robinson, 'Steven Yeun on *Burning*, *The Walking Dead*, and Changing Roles for Asian-Americans', *The Verge*, 4 November 2018, <https://www.theverge.com/2018/11/4/18057584/steven-yeun-interview-walking-dead-burning-sorry-to-bother-you-asian-roles-korean-haruki-murakami>, accessed 27 February 2019.

# DARKNESS IN THE SPOTLIGHT

## Binaries and Brutality in Zhang Yimou's *Shadow*

WHILE ZHANG YIMOU'S LATEST *WUXIA* OFFERING BEARS THE HALLMARK ACTION AND MELODRAMA ELEMENTS OF HIS EARLIER WORK, IT STANDS APART IN TERMS OF VISUALS, FEATURING A SUBDUED, LARGELY MONOCHROMATIC PALETTE AND UNFURLING, BRUSHSTROKE-LIKE COMPOSITIONS. WITH THIS CALCULATED STYLISTIC MOVE, THE CHINESE DIRECTOR ALLOWS THE VIOLENCE, CORRUPTION AND CONFLICT AT THE CORE OF HIS HISTORICAL TALE TO STARKLY TAINT EACH FRAME, WRITES **DEBBIE ZHOU**.

FOCUS ON ASIA AND THE MIDDLE EAST

**This spread, clockwise from left:** A Pei Kingdom soldier; Jing (Deng Chao) and Madam (Sun Li) during a tender moment; the King of Pei (Zheng Kai); Madam; Jing

Sword-wielding warriors, lofty, dramatic flights and epic historical backdrops are hallmarks of Chinese director Zhang Yimou's striking *wuxia* films: *Hero* (2002), *House of Flying Daggers* (2004) and *Curse of the Golden Flower* (2006). Building worlds with ornate finesse, these films conjure emotive forces through vibrant, eye-popping colours and heightened choreography. His latest film, *Shadow* (2018), marks a lavish return to form, but he subverts the motifs audiences have come to expect by employing almost monochromatic cinematography and carefully crafted movement. Here, a muted palette instils the film with the elegance of Chinese ink-brush paintings, bringing forth starker depictions of violence that provoke more severe questions about the consequences of a destructive gluttony for power.

*Shadow* opens on a quivering Madam (Sun Li) peering through the keyhole of a high-scaling royal-palace door. An intertitle conveys that she is on the brink of making 'the most difficult choice of her life', though this deliberation is – as revealed later, in a cyclical return to the same shot – a flash-forward. The scene foreshadows *Shadow*'s knotty obsession with royal politics, wherein intrigue and secrets lie behind closed doors and decisions can make or break the status quo.

Set during the Three Kingdoms era, the film soon reveals its master schemer as the King of Pei's (Zheng Kai) supposedly loyal second-in-command, Madam's husband, Commander Yu (Deng Chao). The scene immediately following the flash-forward shows the Commander entering the palace to face the ramifications of his defiant actions, having just bristled tensions with the foreign forces that have occupied the city of Jing. Exiled from their own land, representatives of the Pei Kingdom, headed by their young king, have struck a peace treaty with General Yang (Hu Jun) and his troops. It's a long, detailed set-up of the palace's twisty relations, but the details are crucial: Zhang's adapted script, penned with Li Wei and based on an original screenplay by Zhu Sujin, is another example of the director's propensity for taking history into his own hands. Dismissing any sense of historical accuracy in this film, he has admitted to *Variety*: 'It's no longer a Three Kingdoms story following my adaptation.'[1] Yet the creative licence Zhang has taken has made for a more fascinating tale, with the Commander's Machiavellian scheme reimagining this episode in China's past. Masquerading as an obedient subordinate, the Commander successfully conceals his duplicity deep within the labyrinthine royal residence. In time, we discover that this duplicity takes physical shape in the form of his own doppelganger: a 'shadow' intended to be a body double, ensuring that his position in the aristocratic hierarchy remains secure. The Shadow is Jing (also played by Deng) – kidnapped off the streets by the Commander's father, forced to live in obscurity for twenty years, and named after the very city this double was raised to capture.

The film reveals the Shadow's hideaway through a cut away from the decorative expanses of the royal compound, the camera sliding through a damp cranny and into the palace's underground. In this den, we then see the Commander, long-haired and considerably aged, hanging over the fresh-faced Jing. He pierces Jing's bare chest with a small dagger, the Commander impassive as his double's pained howl echoes through the cave; simply, he says their 'two hearts must beat as one'. We learn that, with the Commander's health deteriorating as a result of his fight with General Yang, Jing has been tasked with assuming the part of his nobleman equivalent. And, through this exchange, Zhang affirms the agony of men with no status when they are reduced to pawns and ruined as the powerful execute exploitative gambits for rank.

This forced duplication of a single identity opens up a personal crisis for Jing, whose sense of self becomes marred with questions about his own individuality. He becomes not only a 'shadow' for the Commander's former younger, more attractive self, but also an object for Madam's deflected affection. During an intimate scene in which Madam applies ointment on his wound, Jing desperately exclaims: 'I am nothing but a servant.' Close-ups of their faces betray their magnetic connection. 'You are you … you yearn to go home,' Madam replies, soft-spoken. Jing's desires and consequent reasons for compliance, unlike those of his double, aren't linked to the royal power struggle; he yearns for Madam's reciprocal attention and a long-awaited reunion with his mother.

Jing's fear of losing himself within the castle's imprisoning walls and among the entangling power plays is captured with subdued lighting, which blankets the film with desaturated gloom. *Shadow* features few artificial lights, though it depicts Jing – scared of the darkness – unable to sleep without his candle, which flickers through the veiled screens of his bedchamber; if he succumbs completely to the darkness, to his role as a shadow, then who really is he? Although cinematographer Zhao Xiaoding (a frequent collaborator of Zhang's, having worked on titles such as *House of Flying Daggers* and 2014's *Coming Home*) captures the muted colours of skin tones and spilt blood, *Shadow*'s primarily black-and-white composition visually represents the dichotomous forces at play in the film. Yet only rarely does light leak into the greyscale frame, such as through crevices between rocks in the underground – streaks of optimism largely drowned out in a world of gloom.

The specific way these colours and textures manifest in *Shadow* give the impression that each frame has been painted with an ink brush, an aesthetic choice that is also illustrative of revisionary history drawn fresh onto a new canvas. The film's lavish production design only brings this inspired approach further to life. A spectacular bird's-eye shot bears witness to the Commander and his Shadow during a practice duel; rain spatters from the heavens onto an enlarged tai chi symbol, the pair standing on opposite sides – one on the yang, the other on the yin. The whooshing of their silk robes punches through the slow-motion choreography, the men moving with grace as though in a flight-like dance. The epic motions of their bodies become more defined through the careful use of contrast and lines, the silky, elaborate aesthetic rendering everything in the frame as though brushstrokes on parchment.

Zhang drenches *Shadow* in a greyscale that matches its ink-brush quality, but the triad of blacks, whites and greys is also tainted by pale skin tones and sickeningly red blood: colourful diversions that steadily pin the film's focal point on the human body. It aligns with Zhang's signature use of colour – in this instance, expressive monochrome and the bleeding-through of singular chromatic schemes – to elucidate characters' emotions as well as larger meanings underpinning narrative events. It's a trademark displayed in his earlier *wuxia* films: in *Hero*, colours come alive to distinguish conflicting versions of events; as director of photography Christopher Doyle described it at the time, 'Every story is colored by personal perception.'[2] Rather than tapping into colours' conventional symbolic associations, however, *Hero* uses them to weave together thematic threads. For instance, pulsing red costuming, brushwork and flags visualise the romance between assassins Broken Sword (Tony Leung Chiu-Wai) and Flying Snow (Maggie Cheung Man-Yuk). In a similar vein, *House of Flying Daggers* utilises colour for extravagant symbolism, with green, in particular, representing the height of conflict. The iconic fight set in a bamboo forest sees Xiao Mei (Zhang Ziyi) wielding a bamboo stick as her weapon, scraping it across lush grass and having it splinter against the soldiers' verdant uniforms. Elsewhere, colour coordination creates a unique ambience that feels both natural and rhapsodic in its beauty, as when silhouettes of green-clad soldiers fly through treetops, contributing to the film's overall sense of grandeur.

Yet Zhang's indulgent, showy aesthetic – which aligns with those of his *wuxia* contemporaries – is not without criticism. As academic Abi Stevens has pointed out, following Ang Lee's *Crouching Tiger, Hidden Dragon* (2000) and Zhang's own *Hero*, the lavish *wuxia* style became particularly attractive to audiences outside of East Asia. But, as the genre rose to global success, so did scrutiny, with this recent iteration of *wuxia* criticised for participating in a form of 'cross-cultural spectatorship' that panders to a transnational audience.[3] Yet, as researcher Stephen Teo writes, 'What is unique about *wuxia* in the contemporary era as the genre entrenches itself in the Chinese Mainland is precisely this juggling of transnationalism and nationalism.'[4]

Such is the case with *Shadow*, which calibrates elements specific to Chinese culture and history (if a little inaccurately) to appeal to an international audience. Here, human movement is not simply deployed for dazzling spectacle, but also to convey the brutal manner in which conflicting forces counter each other. Much like how black and white are juxtaposed, the opposing forces are shown brandishing weapons that correspond with the traditional gender binary. The Pei Kingdom's victory weapon is an umbrella, an object associated with femininity, which contrasts with the Yang forces' more conventional, 'masculine' sword. In the film's climactic clash between the Pei and Yang forces, hundreds of female Pei convicts, waiting in a secret forest location, ambush Jing City. The umbrellas they wield assume another form, now made of glittering silver blades and spinning like windmills. As the umbrellas open, the blades puncture the air and clang against one another; the sound design amplifies the cohort's noisy movement as they slide down a hill as one. Blades fly into human bodies; flesh is slashed; bones are broken. The red blood that spills out stains the almost monochrome frame with a vivid lucidity – a staggering reminder of the fragility of the human body, and of how the ruthlessness of war makes survival a gruelling struggle. The enormity of the body count is writ large.

While the film is largely consumed with the power struggles on the field and within the royal court, it also emphasises the subjugation suffered by women expected to obey their husbands and family members. The Princess (Guan Xiaotong) – sister to the King – laments that the future lies in 'masculine power', her world having no place for women like her and Madam. Although the Princess is amusingly outspoken (she sits behind a translucent screen, throwing jibes at her brother while he orders his men), she is humiliatingly sold as a concubine to General Yang's son, Ping (Leo Wu), to keep the peace between the kingdoms. On the one hand, the Princess is granted some agency – later, disguised as a female convict, she takes control of her own fate in a violent duel. Yet, on the other, she, like Madam, inevitably takes a back seat while this deadly drama plays out; the two women are rendered passive by men who use them as devices to enable impulsive masculine action. Though her kingdom emerges victorious, the Princess dies in her pursuit of justice, and Madam must sit silently as she watches Jing return successfully from battle in the Commander's guise.

The suppression of women under male rule is not a new theme for Zhang, who previously explored it in the operatic *Curse of the Golden Flower*. But, unlike that drama, which portrayed the physically and mentally crippling effects of male-dominated leadership through a woman's eyes, *Shadow* shuffles its women to the sidelines, shifting its focus to an ordinary man who rises to overcome his own subservience. During a Q&A at the 2018 Toronto International Film Festival, Zhang asserted this very wish to spotlight Jing's triumph over aristocracy:

*I decided to make a film about […] an ordinary person and how this commoner struggles for survival while he's caught in the middle of the power play. As a body double, he was able to finally regain control of his own fate and, in the end, he even had a choice: […] Will he become the new king of this old kingdom, or will he just forget all about it and return to his original […] identity as a commoner?*[5]

But perhaps, ultimately, *Shadow* speaks more to the brutal consequences of exploitation and manipulation than to its protagonist's struggle against social hierarchy. At the conclusion of the film, Jing emerges from the palace, bleeding heavily; he communicates to the Pei army waiting outside that an intruder has killed their king. This is all a ruse, of course – in preceding scenes, Jing callously murdered *both* of his masters: the King *and* the Commander. In this moment, Jing is no longer the Shadow; having defeated his oppressors, he now has an identity of his own. Yet it is one that becomes inextricably part of a corrupt cycle that links him to his predecessors' mindless violence.

Zhang drenches *Shadow* in a greyscale that matches its ink-brush quality, but the triad of blacks, whites and greys is also tainted by pale skin tones and sickeningly red blood: colourful diversions that steadily pin the film's focal point on the human body.

As we return to Madam watching through the keyhole, confronted with the 'difficult choice' of whether to reveal Jing's true identity or keep silent, a larger question arises: will it even make a difference? Whereas once she was the Shadow's source of comfort during his darkest days, it is now she who is shut behind closed doors and in need of consolation. As Madam learns, in the struggle for power, there is little room for remorse.

*Debbie Zhou is a Sydney-based freelance arts writer and critic, and a managing editor of online film journal* Rough Cut. *She has also written for* Time Out Sydney, The Guardian, The Big Issue *and* Audrey Journal. **m**

Endnotes
1. Zhang Yimou, quoted in Patrick Frater, 'Zhang Yimou Explores New Ideas in *Shadow*', *Variety*, 5 September 2018, <https://variety.com/2018/film/spotlight/zhang-yimou-shadow-venice-film-festival-1202928306>, accessed 15 February 2019.
2. Christopher Doyle, quoted in Robert Mackey, 'Cracking the Color Code of *Hero*', *The New York Times*, 15 August 2004, <https://www.nytimes.com/2004/08/15/movies/film-cracking-the-color-code-of-hero.html>, accessed 15 February 2019.
3. Abi Stevens, 'Short Guide to the *Wuxia* Film', *Mapping Contemporary Cinema*, 2012, <http://www.mcc.sllf.qmul.ac.uk/?p=1384>, accessed 15 February 2019.
4. Stephen Teo, *Chinese Martial Arts Cinema: The Wuxia Tradition*, Edinburgh University Press, Edinburgh, 2009, p. 180.
5. Zhang Yimou (via translator), in '*Shadow* Director Q&A | TIFF 2018', YouTube, 12 September 2018, <https://www.youtube.com/watch?v=m4cMc0r-pQA>, accessed 15 February 2019.

# FILM À LA MODE

## Juxtaposing East and West in *Yellow Is Forbidden*

IN HER REVELATORY DOCUMENTARY, PIETRA BRETTKELLY CHARTS THE METEORIC RISE OF TALENTED CHINESE HAUTE COUTURIER GUO PEI. BUT THE FILM ALSO GOES BEYOND ITS SUBJECT: THROUGH METICULOUS IMAGES OF RESPLENDENT GOWNS, INTIMATE FOOTAGE AND INSIGHTFUL INTERVIEWS, IT EXPLORES CLASHES BETWEEN CULTURES, CRAFT AND ASPIRATION, AND THE GRUELLING LABOUR BEHIND THE GLAMOUR OF HIGH FASHION, WRITES **REBEKAH BRAMMER**.

FOCUS ON ASIA AND THE MIDDLE EAST

**Above, L–R:** Ensembles from Guo Pei's 2017 *Legend* collection (two images); a gown from Guo's 2012 *Legend of the Dragon* collection

Having made an impact following its world premiere at the Tribeca Film Festival in 2018, Pietra Brettkelly's *Yellow Is Forbidden* cements the New Zealand filmmaker's reputation for taking audiences on fascinating cross-cultural journeys. This documentary is the result of nearly two years spent with Chinese fashion designer Guo Pei across six countries, chronicling the couturier's quest to gain the ultimate respect in the fashion world: an invitation to Paris' Chambre Syndicale de la Haute Couture. As well as being an exquisite visual spectacle that showcases the intricacy and beauty of Guo's creations, the film explores the interactions between Eastern and Western cultures in the world of high fashion. Brettkelly pays respect to her subject's Chinese heritage through explorations of the sociohistorical and cultural references in Guo's work, while allowing us to witness the designer's sometimes-tenuous relationship with the largely Eurocentric fashion world.

The term 'haute couture' is protected under French law, and use of it requires approval by the Chambre Syndicale de la Haute Couture.[1] Its historical and cultural significance remains strong, even in a world of ubiquitous brands and fast fashion, as it is synonymous with handmade, exquisitely designed and, of course, wildly expensive goods. Guo's love of the couture tradition and her almost encyclopedic knowledge of designers (Cristóbal Balenciaga is a favourite) is explored early in the film, and the lofty esteem with which she holds French fashion sets the scene for her journey. She likens haute couture recognition for a designer to an Oscar win for a film director – and, similar to films, each of her collections requires an intensive time commitment and involves an army of workers in the background.

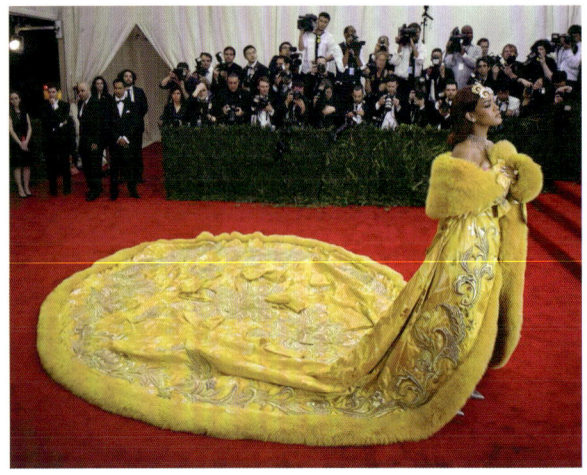

**Above, from top:** Pop star Rihanna wearing the now-famous cape designed by Guo at the 2015 Met Gala; the catwalk for Guo's 2018 *Elysium* collection; Guo with her parents **Opposite:** Octogenarian model Carmen Dell'Orefice at Guo's *Legend* show

The insight that *Yellow Is Forbidden* offers into the creation of each garment is mind-boggling: from design concept to catwalk, a single garment – such as the yellow cape famously worn by singer Rihanna to the 2015 Met Gala – can take up to two years to complete. In the film, we observe Guo visiting an embroidery workshop in China to check the progress of the workers; as the country is synonymous with mass production (and designer knock-offs), it is refreshing to be shown the attention to detail and level of expertise required to embroider one of Guo's gowns. At the same time, as critic Keith Uhlich has pointed out, Brettkelly does not shy away from showing the 'routine tedium' experienced by those who put in those hours, especially in contrast to the more glamorous life of the couturier herself.[2]

Yet Brettkelly does also expose us to the person behind the jetsetter, emphasising the twenty-plus years of hard work that enabled her to achieve the 'overnight' (Western) recognition brought by Rihanna's wearing of her design. In a pre–*Yellow Is Forbidden* article, *The New Yorker*'s Judith Thurman identifies two Guo Peis. The first one designs demi-couture items for her customer base in China, which are quite conservative in style: 'a uniform for women performing an old-fashioned role'.[3] She also makes traditional Chinese wedding dresses and evening gowns that embrace and promote Chinese culture, featuring phoenix and dragon imagery in their embroidery. The film shows Guo with this client base – she refers to them as 'ordinary women', an unusual choice of words for an elite group with so much wealth that they can afford her designs – and we learn that they are indeed the bread and butter of her business: their purchases support her more expensive and time-consuming masterpieces. Her respect for and careful attention to these clients are obvious, but her interactions with them also reveal her complicated attitudes towards the Western fashion world. She candidly comments, 'Even though China is rich in culture, [Western fashion-industry members are] prejudiced against us because we're from the East.' Yet she and her clients also discuss Asian women having plastic surgery to make their features appear more 'European', and she warns the women not to wear traditional cheongsams, presumably for fear of looking too provincial. As Brettkelly has said of her subject, 'Guo Pei doesn't have all the inspirations of the West, but she strives for acceptance there. She treads the line between assimilation and acceptance.'[4]

Guo's family life is shown as an important driver for both grounding her in her culture and achieving professional success; with her sights set on the West, maintaining this connection to her past is important. We are given access to her private life; scenes filmed in her home show her at work in her study, producing drawings of exquisite garments and revealing her quirky personality traits, such as her collection of hundreds of teddy bears. Her husband, Cao Bao Jie, is her main investor, and often acts as her translator. She refers to him as her 'wings' and, as we see throughout the documentary, he is never far from her side. In one of *Yellow Is Forbidden*'s most touching scenes, Guo visits her ageing parents and recounts to them the difficulties of growing up and becoming a designer in an era of extraordinary change in China. She reflects on her grandmother's influence on her choice to pursue the profession and create beautiful works of art. We also learn that it was her grandmother who taught her to embroider, and that the high standard Guo demands of her artisans can be traced back to this desire to honour her family and her country's history. Later, the film

Guo's family life is shown as an important driver for both grounding her in her culture and achieving professional success … the high standard Guo demands of her artisans can be traced back to this desire to honour her family and her country's history.

> Feeling the weight of emerging as one of few Asian designers to be accepted into the haute couture world, Guo states, 'I am not a nation,' asserting her wish to be accepted as a designer first and foremost, rather than as a representative of her culture and country.

introduces us to Guo's daughter; the designer mentions her hopes that her daughter will carry the mantle and become a designer herself someday.

The second Guo that Thurman identifies is the expert couturier that *Yellow Is Forbidden* spends most of its time with. Thurman calls her a 'fabulist of sovereign fancy', whose creations contain both 'fantastical decoration that alludes to her own heritage' and various other historical and artistic references.[5] The collection of Guo's that is presented in the film, spring/summer 2017's *Legend*, takes its cues from a Christian cathedral, a deliberate step away from presenting influences from her Chinese background. Feeling the weight of emerging as one of few Asian designers to be accepted into the haute couture world, Guo states, 'I am not a nation,' asserting her wish to be accepted as a designer first and foremost, rather than as a representative of her culture and country. This is one of the film's most interesting conceptual junctures, pitting East against West, and encourages the audience to ask: do we expect too much from artists in terms of representing their cultural heritage/s? After all, if we are all global citizens in a global economy, surely, artists are free to explore a range of influences?

Even beyond Guo's work, cultural appropriation remains a hot-button topic in a number of artistic fields, including fashion itself. Creative consultant and stylist Megha Kapoor asserts, 'Borrowing from other cultures is inherently a part of the creative process,' describing fashion as a space for the celebration of different cultures.[6] But, as writer Anisha Khopkar points out, this 'becomes problematic when historical context and cultural sensitivities are ignored', citing as examples Gucci's incorporation of turbans, Chanel's sale of a boomerang as an 'accessory' and Victoria's Secret's use of a Native American headdress.[7] Fashion photographer Luca Camaiani, in his review of an exhibition of Guo's work in Canada, recognises that the current political climate may cause some to jump to conclusions regarding cultural appropriation, but feels very strongly that Guo's output balances '[W]estern cultural influence with a clear Asian identity, and by doing so, possibly challenges popular connotations of cultural appropriation'. He invites us to instead question the charges that paint Guo's work as appropriative, contending that it is both respectful of its cultural influences and artistically beautiful.[8] Elsewhere, fashion journalist Osman Ahmed argues, 'Well-intentioned appropriation can be a force for good, creating a cultural exchange and enriching the available vocabulary for designers, artists and image-makers.' Mentioning fusions in cuisine as accepted forms of cultural melding, he asks why fashion can't be free to do the same without fear of criticism, and encourages all designers to look to Guo's work as an example of how culture can be meaningfully explored in their industry.[9] *Yellow Is Forbidden* builds on the conversation around this complex issue, particularly as we are more likely to have discussed Western designers aping Eastern cultural influences in the past, rather than the reverse.

The film culminates in the *Legend* catwalk show, with its accompanying on- and offstage drama. It is here, perhaps, that we get to see all the facets of Guo: the mother strongly bonded to her family, her daughter by her side; the accomplished designer at the helm of an impressive production; the nervous Eastern visitor on the precipice of having her dream of being accepted in the West realised. We see few Asian faces on Guo's catwalk, but, again, is there an obligation to be representative? The spectacular final gown is worn by the then-85-year-old New York model Carmen Dell'Orefice. Again, Guo has defied expectations, choosing to employ an octogenarian Western woman in an industry and from a culture obsessed with youth – arguably a comment on the timeless nature of beauty that she projects in her work.

Interestingly, critics have disagreed on the scope of this documentary's appeal: while *The New Zealand Herald*'s Francesca Rudkin suggests that 'you don't need to be interested in fashion to enjoy this visual feast of a film',[10] *Screen Daily*'s Wendy Ide believes that it 'will struggle to claim much of an audience outside of individuals with a vested interest in fashion'.[11] Yes, an interest in the fashion world is perhaps the major drawcard of *Yellow Is Forbidden*, with its insights into the nature of that bastion of extravagant consumerism that is haute couture. But our aspirational fascination with luxury brands extends well beyond this limited target market: while few of us can ever hope to own a Chanel suit, we might spring for a bottle of N°5 perfume as a treat. Guo herself has also released a range of cosmetics in collaboration with MAC.[12] Haute couture's survival, despite its exclusivity, rests on a broader connection to consumers: its effect on the wider consciousness spans everything from a pop star wearing a desired gown to the availability of more 'affordable' creations.

*Yellow Is Forbidden* was but one significant film about a fashion designer that made the festival rounds last year; two other notable titles were *McQueen* (Ian Bonhôte, 2018) and *Westwood: Punk, Icon, Activist* (Lorna Tucker, 2018). Although Guo may lack the recognition and notoriety of the subjects of these two films, critic Richard Gray believes Brettkelly's film is on par with them in its ability to capture the artist's process.[13] Thanks to Jacob Bryant's cinematography, *Yellow Is Forbidden* is also a visually stunning work that stretches far beyond pretty pictures of pretty clothes. In particular, the use of shadow puppets during narrative exposition and close-ups of both gowns and imagery such as swimming fish adds visual interest while referencing the designer's Eastern roots. Beyond the aforementioned peek

**Above:** A dress from Guo's *Legend* collection

it offers into a specific world (in this case, that of haute couture), the appeal of any fly-on-the-wall documentary sits with its subject; Brettkelly's portrayal of Guo, with all her contradictions, leaves the audience, whether interested in fashion or not, wanting to know more about her.

https://www.madmanfilms.com.au/yellow-is-forbidden/

*Rebekah Brammer teaches English as a Second Language in Brisbane, and has studied drama, film and television, and applied linguistics. She has been contributing to* Metro *and* Screen Education *since 2008.*

m

Endnotes

1. See 'La Haute Couture', Fédération de la Haute Couture et de la Mode website, <https://fhcm.paris/en/the-federation/history/>, accessed 22 February 2019.
2. Keith Uhlich, '*Yellow Is Forbidden*: Film Review | Tribeca 2018', *The Hollywood Reporter*, 23 April 2018, <https://www.hollywoodreporter.com/review/yellow-is-forbidden-review-1104820>, accessed 22 February 2019.
3. Judith Thurman, 'The Empire's New Clothes', *The New Yorker*, 21 March 2016, <https://www.newyorker.com/magazine/2016/03/21/guo-pei-chinas-homegrown-high-fashion-designer>, accessed 22 February 2019.
4. Pietra Brettkelly, quoted in Alice Newbold, '*Yellow Is Forbidden* Is a Celebration of How Remarkable Women Are', *Vogue*, 4 May 2018, <https://www.vogue.co.uk/article/guo-pei-yellow-is-forbidden-pietra-brettkelly>, accessed 22 February 2019.
5. Thurman, op. cit.
6. Megha Kapoor, quoted in Anisha Khopkar, 'We Need to Talk About Cultural Appropriation in Fashion', *ABC Life*, 28 November 2018, <https://www.abc.net.au/life/cultural-appropriation-and-fashion/10501010>, accessed 22 February 2019.
7. Khopkar, ibid.
8. Luca Camaiani, 'Guo Pei, Appropriating Beautifully', *Medium*, 14 November 2018, <https://medium.com/@lucacamaiani/guo-pei-appropriating-beautifully-e6fdb8ef427d>, accessed 22 February 2019.
9. Osman Ahmed, 'Why Fashion Needs Cultural Appropriation', *The Business of Fashion*, 1 June 2017, <https://www.businessoffashion.com/articles/opinion/why-fashion-needs-cultural-appropriation>, accessed 22 February 2019.
10. Francesca Rudkin, 'Movie Review: *Yellow Is Forbidden*', *The New Zealand Herald*, 1 November 2018, <https://www.nzherald.co.nz/entertainment/news/article.cfm?c_id=1501119&objectid=12151242>, accessed 22 February 2019.
11. Wendy Ide, '*Yellow Is Forbidden*: Tribeca Review', *Screen Daily*, 22 April 2018, <https://www.screendaily.com/reviews/yellow-is-forbidden-tribeca-review/5128274.article>, accessed 22 February 2019.
12. See Felicity Kinsella, 'MAC Team Up with Chinese Couture Designer Guo Pei on Capsule Collection', *i-D*, 1 May 2015, <https://i-d.vice.com/en_au/article/ywd3yj/mac-team-up-with-chinese-couture-designer-guo-pei-on-capsule-collection>, accessed 22 February 2019.
13. Richard Gray, 'Westwood, Guo, and McQueen: Cuts of Fashion on Screen', *The Reel Bits*, 18 June 2018, <https://thereelbits.com/2018/06/18/westwood-guo-and-mcqueen-cuts-of-fashion-on-screen/>, accessed 22 February 2019.

**Above:** Children jumping off a crag on the Kimberley Coast

DOCUMENTARY

# THE COST OF COUNTRY

## Capital and Ownership in *Undermined: Tales from the Kimberley*

Nicholas Wrathall's disturbing and illuminating documentary weaves together stories and scenes from the titular region in north-west Australia, offering cinematic testimony on the dislocation and disadvantage afflicting its Aboriginal residents as well as the ongoing threats to the unique natural landscape posed by Big Mining and Big Agriculture. The film offers persuasive evidence that we need to look beyond the simplistic and compromised media portrayals of this region, writes **Rochelle Siemienowicz**.

'How are we, as Australians, letting our country be developed [and for] whose benefit?' This is the question posed in voiceover in the opening sequence of feature documentary *Undermined: Tales from the Kimberley* (Nicholas Wrathall), which premiered at the 2018 Melbourne International Film Festival (MIFF) and was financed by the MIFF Premiere Fund. It's the urgent question at the heart of a complex and complicated collection of stories that are at times inspiring, disturbing and baffling.

An Australian filmmaker who has spent many years living and working in New York, Wrathall is best known for the 2013 political and literary portrait documentary *Gore Vidal: The United States of Amnesia*. He is also a writer and producer on *Undermined*, alongside Stephanie King, an award-winning campaigner around welfare and sustainability. While Wrathall and King are white Australians, the voices showcased in their unashamedly political film are almost exclusively Indigenous. Importantly, young Bardi / Kija / Nyul Nyul activist and musician Albert Wiggan, also a co-producer and adviser on *Undermined*, emerges as the documentary's most compelling character.

The region in question is the Kimberley, located in the north of Western Australia (WA) – a stunningly beautiful and mineral-rich territory roughly three times the size of England. A substantial proportion of its long-term residents are Indigenous, and more than half of them live in around 200 remote Aboriginal communities, comprising anywhere from twenty to 900 people.[1]

But, with the full support of state and federal governments, Big Mining and Big Agriculture are fast moving in, promising jobs but posing serious threats – not just to the local communities, many of which are being pressured to negotiate or shut down, but also to the natural environment, particularly the fragile freshwater supplies of the Fitzroy River.

The opening montage of *Undermined* sets the scene for a vast and complicated series of stories. We see a map of Australia: mostly brown, but with delicate fringes of green. The frame's focus shifts to the top-left-hand corner of the map, so big and bright in its own right. Cut to breathtaking aerial and low-level drone footage of crystal-blue oceans, cresting whales, white-sand beaches and red canyons; there are lush waterfalls, rust-gold sunsets and flocks of cockatoos taking flight. Broome-based director of photography Mark Jones, also a co-producer of the film and a key instigator of the project, obviously knows exactly where to go for those shots of flooded wetlands that mirror the kind of dreamy cloudscapes you only get in the far north.

Tourism WA is not, as far as I can tell, a sponsor of this film, but it would be a rare viewer who does not immediately put the Kimberley on their bucket list. This effect is intentional, for one of the film's key arguments is that cultural and environmental tourism – or the 'forever industries', as one interviewee puts it – offer the best future for the region, as opposed to the short-term, precarious benefits afforded by exploitative mining and agriculture, which will eventually pack up and leave the Australian taxpayer to foot the bill for repatriation.

Interspersed with these early landscape shots are scenes of local Indigenous people going about their everyday lives. There are elderly women fishing in a river, a weathered stockman assessing his cattle, kids in baseball caps watching the bucking antics of a rodeo and Aussie Rules footballers wrestling for a mark. In voiceover, the film's key characters state their cases and concerns. All of them, in different ways, are advocating for Indigenous self-determination and the preservation of the natural environment.

Reading the description above, you might expect *Undermined* to be a simple documentary with a clear throughline. In reality, however, it's a knotty and diverse collection of anecdotes and interviews, case studies and issues. These are all tied together by a palpable love and concern for the region, and a loyalty to the individuals and interest groups who have assisted – or, perhaps, enlisted – the filmmakers to tell the world what's happening up in our country's north-west. This is a place where mainstream media coverage is sketchy at best and racist at worst.[2] Speaking to MIFF last year, Wrathall said the final documentary represents only a small portion of the stories that he and the team collected in the Kimberley over the two years they spent making the film.[3] Reading this, one immediately thinks of the plight of editors Peter O'Donoghue and Andrew Arestides, who were tasked with mining the hundreds of hours of footage for the most compelling storylines, many of which were unfolding in real time and remain unconcluded.

According to Wrathall, the initial impetus for the film came in 2015, when the filmmakers heard stories of the forced closures of Aboriginal communities. The WA government's official position was that they were dysfunctional or unviable, but the real motive, he and the residents contend, was to open up the land for development.[4] As the filmmakers set out to investigate, their findings led them to a dense geopolitical web of issues and stories, from the practicalities of land ownership and native title, to the conflicts between and within Indigenous groups, activists and organisations, as well as the tragedies of youth suicide and rural unemployment. Undoubtedly, the filmmakers' attempts to bring all of these together and make sense of the bigger picture in the region is admirable and necessary. At the same time, the visible challenges of tying so many threads together makes it clear why so many other filmmakers exploring Indigenous stories have chosen to limit themselves to one issue (*After the Apology*, Larissa Behrendt, 2017), one key character (*Gurrumul*, Paul Damien Williams, 2017) or one particular Indigenous community (*Another Country*, Molly Reynolds, 2015).

I have watched *Undermined* several times now and I'm still grappling to get a hold on it. Like the vastness and diversity of the Kimberley landscape itself, the multitude of material presented is sometimes overwhelming, particularly for an ignorant urban viewer far removed from the region and its politics. This ignorance does, of course, proffer the argument that films like *Undermined* need to exist and find an audience within wider Australia, and also that other filmmakers and journalists must dive in and attempt to answer some of the serious questions it poses.

In contrast to the complex array of Indigenous perspectives presented in the film, the government's official positions and policies – showcased in short, locked-off interviews – are worryingly

**Opposite:** Various areas of the Kimberley, Western Australia **Above, from top:** Albert Wiggan; Mervyn Street; Alfie White; Street's Gooniyandi dancers

**Above:** Kevin Oscar

simple, even simplistic. Matt Canavan, the Federal Minister for Resources and Northern Australia, talks about removing 'barriers that stop people from developing the north'. Tony Eyres, of government agency Austrade, talks about the proximity of the region to Asia, whose nations are 'demanding those natural resources', and says with concern that the vast majority of WA is held in native title and that a 'mutually beneficial' conversation needs to happen. To find their motives suspect seems fully justified, especially in light of the nation's history of colonial theft and the ongoing mistreatment of Indigenous peoples and their lands throughout Australia.

'There's this conversation that we gotta close these communities, that they're not viable,' says Dr Anne Poelina, Nyikina traditional custodian and Indigenous-rights activist, to-camera in the film. '[T]his is part of the ongoing colonial regime to clear Aboriginal people off country. So that we go back to the *terra nullius* [concept] – nobody, empty country, empty wilderness, nobody cares about it, bring in the mining company.' She is, of course, referring to the famous 1992 victory of Meriam man Eddie Mabo in the High Court, which threw out the legal doctrine of *terra nullius* in favour of Australian First Peoples' native title claims to their lands.[5] *Undermined* is keen to show us how this victory has been only partial, and is under attack in in everyday practice.

Moreover, as its press kit states, *Undermined* is 'a hybrid style documentary film, investigative by nature, but driven by character – the micro speaking to the macro'.[6] It's at the micro level that it's best understood. One of the film's subjects is Kevin Oscar, Bunuba traditional owner and long-time station manager of Leopold Downs, a struggling outback cattle farm. From him, we learn that one-third of Kimberley cattle stations are Aboriginal-owned, but that they have suffered from a lack of access to capital and an inability to sell or borrow against their properties. Wrangling jeeps, horses and helicopters, Oscar heads up a small family business that also employs his rangy, bright-eyed grandsons, who work as stockmen. Promising to bring a capital investment and a joint venture to the station is Richard Paterson, a charismatic white man from the Eastern Guruma Pastoral Company, with *Undermined* following the two men's story from hopeful beginnings and mutual respect through to disillusionment. Exactly how and why the relationship breaks down remains a little murky. What lingers are the heartbreak that ensues and the resultant lack of work for the young station hands, who must now move into town or interstate. The spectres of alcohol, drugs and suicide are mentioned in this and so many of the film's other stories.

> Perhaps the most disturbing impetus for the film is that, in practice, native title means little more than the right for Indigenous groups to sit at the table and negotiate with these giant corporations' interests, with what various subjects liken to having a metaphorical gun to their heads.

Perhaps the most disturbing impetus for the film is that, in practice, native title means little more than the right for Indigenous groups to sit at the table and negotiate with these giant corporations' interests, with what various subjects liken to having a metaphorical gun to their heads.[7] As former Kimberley Land Council CEO Wayne Bergmann explains on camera, if consensus cannot be reached within six months, then development goes ahead. As for the rights that the *Native Title Act 1993* enshrines – those that legally enable traditional owners to camp, fish and hunt on their native lands – the film shows many cases in which these privileges bang up against locked gates, unanswered mobile phones and unpleasant skirmishes with white land users. Poelina, one of the documentary's clearest voices, again sums it up succinctly: 'Native title is the weakest, [most] racist and most oppressive law that we have in this country for

Aboriginal people. And how the Native Title Tribunal has been set up [… is] to fast-track development.'

But, if there is one shining star in *Undermined*, it's Wiggan. He's young, handsome and eloquent – a natural leader and entertainer. He accompanied Wrathall and King to the premiere of the film at MIFF, bringing his guitar and performing a song he had composed himself. Having trained at the Western Australian Academy of Performing Arts, he has toured internationally with John Butler and featured in the 2009 SBS documentary *Old Country New Country*, which chronicles how he was taught raft-making by his uncle. Not only is Wiggan a skilled media performer, but he also brings passion and intelligence to his activism. He has a gift for bridging the gaps – for being a connector between 'the best of both worlds', as he put it at the post-screening Q&A.[8] There, Wiggan charmed the audience with the inclusive idea that we are all ultimately connected, our differences less important than our similarities: 'You go back two-and-a-half thousand years and all of us here in this room were connected to the ancestors. We all come from an indigenous bloodline somewhere. We are all indigenous.'[9]

On screen, Wiggan's journey encompasses so many of the issues wrestled with in the documentary's other stories, while proposing some practical solutions. As a boy, he grew up with a father who loved hunting and fishing on the remote islands off the Dampier Peninsula. Wiggan Sr's best friend was the white wildlife filmmaker and crocodile hunter Malcolm Douglas, and the two men had worked together in showcasing and protecting the beauty of the region. In contrast, Wiggan's mother was a Catholic mission–schooled woman ('assimilated', in his words). She valued Western education highly and insisted on sending her son away to a private boy's school in Perth, where he was the sole Indigenous student among 2500 kids. We're shown photos of him from that time period: the one dark face on the football team, or dressed up in tuxedos at school balls accompanied by white female classmates.

As a young man, Wiggan had come home, fallen in love with a local girl and, with her, had a baby too young. The dreamy look of disbelief he gets on his face when he reflects on love is one of the film's sweetest and funniest moments: 'Talk about mysteries. Love – I can never understand that thing!' he says, shaking his head as if that's a topic for another film. Rocked by his father's death around the same time that his child was born, Wiggan rediscovered country through a trip he was taken on by Douglas (whom he has described as his 'white second father'[10]). He then became a vocal activist in the much-publicised 2013 victory against the Woodside gas development at James Price Point.[11]

At the time, he was opposed to the Kimberley Land Council's methods; now, as a director of the council, he is trying to work within it rather than against it, and even talks about the need to bring young blood into an organisation that has been dominated by elders. Wiggan also works as a land ranger, collecting data about endangered species, particularly the region's native bilby, about which he's a recognised expert. Within the film, he preaches compellingly about the ways in which Indigenous science uses the same practices of observation and trial-and-error as Western science, and about how the council's land-ranger program is an example of sustainable Indigenous industry.

Asked by a MIFF audience member what he wanted *Undermined* to achieve, Wiggan gave the kind of response that deserves reproducing in full:

*Help us. All we need is that little bit of capital. Unfortunately, the only people prepared to extend us capital at the moment are mining and agriculture. That's not something we are totally opposed to as Indigenous people. We understand the importance of developing healthy economies and supporting our state and national economies. We get those concepts. But we want people to help us, as Indigenous people, to develop our own Indigenous industries.*[12]

*Undermined* may be an overflowing bag of heavy and unfinished stories, but it wisely chooses to conclude with Wiggan's wise words and impassioned delivery. 'Aboriginal Australia doesn't want to go into your backyard, doesn't want to disturb you. It doesn't want to exploit your resources or your privacy [or] your inheritance,' he says as the music swells. 'Whereas, every single day, Aboriginal people are facing that dilemma. We will have a really meaningful conversation about this. That's the opportunity that's here in the Kimberleys.'

Whatever questions might remain, the film's portrait of this emerging Indigenous leader is crystal-clear and unforgettable – and a very good start to that conversation he's asking for.

http://underminedfilm.com

*Rochelle Siemienowicz is a writer and critic with a PhD in Australian cinema. She is a journalist for* screenhub *and is co-host of the long-running film podcast* Hell Is for Hyphenates. **m**

Endnotes

1. The Australian Bureau of Statistics (ABS) estimates that the proportion of residents of Indigenous descent is around 42 per cent, while the filmmakers, referring exclusively to long-term residents, put the figure closer to 75 per cent. See ABS, 'Kimberley', 2016 Census QuickStats, <http://quickstats.censusdata.abs.gov.au/census_services/getproduct/census/2016/quickstat/51001>, accessed 11 February 2019; and Amnesia Productions, *Undermined: Tales from the Kimberley* press kit, 2018, pp. 5, 8.
2. See, for example, Sherryn Groch, 'In Black and White: Racism and the Mainstream Media', *Overland*, 17 October 2016, <https://overland.org.au/2016/10/in-black-and-white-racism-and-the-mainstream-media/>, accessed 14 February 2019.
3. See 'Q&A with *Undermined: Tales from the Kimberley* Director Nicholas Wrathall', Melbourne International Film Festival website, 27 July 2018, <http://miff.com.au/blog/story/qa-with-undermined-tales-from-the-kimberley-director-nicholas-wrathall>, accessed 11 February 2019.
4. ibid.
5. See Australian Institute of Aboriginal and Torres Strait Islander Studies, 'Mabo Case', 11 September 2015, <https://aiatsis.gov.au/explore/articles/mabo-case>, accessed 19 February 2019.
6. Amnesia Productions, op. cit., p. 10.
7. ibid., p. 9.
8. Albert Wiggan, in *Undermined: Tales from the Kimberley* post-screening Q&A, Melbourne International Film Festival, 8 August 2018.
9. ibid.
10. ibid.
11. Amanda Cavill, 'Woodside Abandons James Price Point Gas Hub', *SBS News*, 26 August 2013, <https://www.sbs.com.au/news/woodside-abandons-james-price-point-gas-hub>, accessed 11 February 2019.
12. Wiggan, op. cit.

# HOME ON THE ROCKS

## Blue Lucine on Displacement and *The Eviction*

Gentrification and commercial interest, along with insufficient government intervention, are key threats faced by publicly funded welfare accommodation in inner-city areas – as recent examples in Sydney attest. **Jasmine Crittenden** speaks to filmmaker Blue Lucine about her eye-opening documentary that not only confronts these very issues but also captures the laments of brave, now-evicted residents.

'It was a film that everybody was telling me to stop making, the whole time I was making it,' says director Blue Lucine, referring to her documentary *The Eviction*, which premiered at the 2018 Antenna Documentary Film Festival. 'People would say, "No-one's going to watch it," or, "The story's already over."'

The seed for *The Eviction* was sown on the evening of 19 March 2014. Lucine was having dinner with friends shortly after the New South Wales (NSW) Government had announced it would sell 293 public-housing properties in Sydney. These included the famed Sirius building, made in the brutalist style, as well as other dwellings in Millers Point, Dawes Point and The Rocks. The sale would affect 579 tenants, who received two years' notice to relocate.[1] Lucine recalls:

*My friends knew elderly people who lived in Millers Point. They were distraught, wondering […] how it would impact everybody. Meanwhile, most of the media was presenting a different story: That the tenants were bludgers who lived in a rich area. That they should be kicked out, and it would be a really good thing for the rest of NSW. The simplicity of that made me question what was really happening and why.*

By 22 March, Lucine had borrowed a camera from a friend and begun filming. Her first stop was a public meeting at Abraham Mott Hall, Millers Point. Convened by Alex Greenwich, the independent Member for Sydney in the NSW Legislative Assembly, the event attracted more than 300 local residents. 'It was like a mass wake,' Lucine recalls.

*The hall was filled with people sobbing and holding each other. I was introduced to ninety-year-old women who were saying to me, 'I've lived here all my life. What's going to happen to me?' The contrast between that and the headlines was so stark […] For a government to make a decision on a grand scale, that has a huge impact on the individual, but [which] isn't represented as such, I find that really dishonest – not as a public-housing tenant or even as a resident of Sydney, but just as a human being.*

**Opposite, clockwise from bottom right:** Barney Gardner; Myra Demetriou; Cherie Johnson; a local resident protests the evictions  **Above:** The Sirius building

*The Eviction* traces the four years from this meeting up to 1 February 2018, when the Sirius building's last remaining tenant, the legally blind 91-year-old Myra Demetriou, moved out. Lucine narrates the events of this period from Demetriou's standpoint and those of four other local residents: Barney Gardner, Bob Flood, Molly Clark and Cherie Johnson. Their personal histories and emotional journeys interweave with their fight against their eviction, a fight galvanised by sympathetic politicians and public figures and pursued at all levels – from grassroots protests to legal action against the NSW Government.

'I chose the subjects I did foremost because of the relationships,' says Lucine.

*When I started filming, everybody else was filming at the same time.* A Current Affair *was trying to get stories. Reality-television shows were looking for content [...] As someone three months out of film school, it was really daunting. I couldn't compete. I couldn't promise anything. So my strategy was to be as honest and open as possible. The relationships I formed ended up being really, really strong. They've stood the test of time.*

The resulting intimacy enabled Lucine to travel deep into her subjects' worlds. The first individual we meet in the film is Flood; his face fills the screen in an eye-level close-up. 'My name is Robert William Flood,' he says to-camera, his gaze unflinching. 'I've lived in Millers Point all my life. I'm sixty-four years of age.' As the camera cuts to a black-and-white photo of two toddlers holding hands, Flood reveals that his connection to the area spans generations. 'My mother and father lived here. Grandmother, grandfather, lived up The Rocks.'

The same is true of Gardner, a childhood friend of Flood's, born in 1949. 'I came home from hospital to number 12 High Street, which is next door,' says Gardner. 'So I've been in this area for near on sixty-five years.' The two recall swimming and fishing in Sydney Harbour together. Both are also friends with then-ninety-year-old Clark, who's lived in Millers Point for six decades.

Then there's Johnson, one of the first residents of Sirius, an apartment complex built and owned by Housing NSW (formerly the Housing Commission of NSW). Completed in 1980, its purpose was to rehouse tenants displaced in the 1970s following a redevelopment of The Rocks.[2] In the film, Johnson recalls the signing of the lease: 'Mama said, "Before I put my signature to this, if I pass away, what's going to happen to my daughter?" And they said, "Don't worry. It's your home for life."'

Framing the subjects' stories is a voiceover by Australian actor Michael Caton, perhaps best known for his role as Darryl Kerrigan in *The Castle* (Rob Sitch, 1997), a fictional film about a working-class family who, threatened with eviction by the government, pursue their case all the way to the High Court. His opening line in *The Eviction* evokes this cinematic lineage: 'A bloke far smarter than I once said, "A man's home is his castle." But he didn't live on the Point.' Beyond its intertextual allusions, Caton's narration provides context about the area, recounting events that not only tie Lucine's subjects together, but also played a key part in Australia's industrial development. 'Millers Point has a rich maritime history,' says Caton. 'From the 1820s, the Maritime Services Board built houses for workers and their families – a short commute to compensate for gruelling twenty-four-hour shifts.' Black-and-white archival footage cuts between mammoth-size cargo ships arriving at the wharves and men hard at work lifting wool bales and shovelling.

This historical evidence gains colour and emotional resonance from Flood's and Gardner's recollections of their fathers, both of whom worked on the wharves. Interspersed with close-ups of the men reminiscing are family photographs. 'My old man started as a blacksmith, then he went to war,' recounts Flood.

*He went to the Middle East and New Guinea. He was a nervous wreck when he came home [...] They used to call him 'The Nerve' – that was his nickname. He went on the wharves. Pretty tough times, working [...] in his days. Very tough times.*

Not all of the subjects' memories are about hardship, however; also forefront of their minds are images of a close-knit community. 'If a family didn't have enough food or they didn't have enough money to pay a bill,' Gardner says, 'or they needed something done to a house, the whole community would pitch in.' In a similar vein, Flood recalls, 'Everybody was so close. It was like a village, which it was. Everybody trusted one another, helped one another. They all stuck together around here.' Through these testimonies, Lucine carefully crystallises the idea that the eviction represents not just the removal of 579 individuals from public housing, but also the destruction of a longstanding community bound by deep genetic, cultural and social ties.

For the filmmaker, this sense of community is epitomised – both historically and at the time of filming – by Clark. 'I met Molly through Bob, [who took] me around to her house. The first day, I felt like I was visiting my nan,' muses Lucine.

*She gave me Monte Carlo [biscuits] and a cup of tea, and started giving me life advice. She represented something that felt so special to me and that doesn't get seen a lot [...] Molly was like all of Australia's grandma – like everybody's nan.*

Another aspect of this generation is represented in Demetriou.

*The irony of Myra's story was quite strong. She had this beautiful view that she couldn't even see. She'd worked all her life for the city and, now, at ninety years old, she was getting turfed out. Her struggle was something that anybody could go through. She also represented [...] that stoic generation of really loving women who were so capable and took care of everybody and had this steely resolve. She's a really funny, feisty lady, and someone I really look up to as well.*

*The Eviction* paints the tenants' relationships founded on intimacy and trust in stark contrast to the government's focus on the properties' monetary value. Just after Flood states, 'It was like a big bloody family,' the camera cuts from his lounge room to long shots of the Sydney Harbour Bridge, foregrounded by leafy trees. Percussive music hastens the pace as Caton's narrative enters: 'Being smack-bang in the middle of Sydney, The Rocks is prime real estate – and, despite its social and cultural significance, from the 1960s, it's had the eye of developers.' Indeed, rather than an isolated or new event, the subjects' fight is the continuation of a struggle between the NSW Government and public-housing residents that has gone on for decades.

The viewer meets Jack Mundey, a renowned anti-development campaigner. Archival footage shows him being carried off by police in the middle of a frenetic protest. Sitting in his lounge room in the present day, but speaking of the 1970s, he asserts in the documentary:

*The Rocks was a turning point, where they put the brakes on the wholesale development of Sydney. I think all the approaches to the bridge – all that area of eastern Sydney – would have been destroyed. The workers who were going to build these giant buildings were the ones who were staying, 'Stop. All development is not necessarily good.'*

Like these workers and the past tenants they fought for and beside, Lucine's subjects are not mere victims. They might be at the mercy of a government decision that endangers their homes, but they are far from accepting of it. In this way, *The Eviction* is as much a study of fierce, determined and multifaceted activism as it is of the values and personalities of its subjects.

In fact, when the filmmaking process became challenging, Lucine found strength in their courage:

*When you see people like Bob and Myra and how hard they fought, bearing witness to that, I could never justify giving up, just because it was a little bit difficult. I think that's something that's unique about documentary. Your participants are the thing that inspires you to finish. You've taken on their story, and they've shared so much of their time and energy with you. So it's your duty to get it out there.*

This courage is established in the opening scenes, with footage of various tenants expressing their opposition to the eviction, loudly and clearly. Early in the film, an unidentified man sings 'Waltzing Matilda' a cappella before turning around and yelling, 'Bugger the housing commission!' Another fronts a crowd, declaring, 'This is not about one home. This is not about one street. This is the social cleansing of an entire suburb.'

Their initial protests, as the film reveals, turn into a four-year-long campaign, executed across an array of fronts. Sheets scrawled with handwritten messages such as 'No surrender. Millers Pt. Not 4 Sale' hang from verandahs. Small groups of tenants stand outside real-estate agents' offices shouting appeals to conscience. A line of protesters covers the footpath outside the NSW Parliament on Macquarie Street, Sydney, their bright, multicoloured umbrellas suggesting hope against a grey sky and pouring rain. Hundreds of people march through Sydney's CBD, joined by Lord Mayor Clover Moore and NSW opposition members, such as then–shadow planning minister Michael Daley. The decision of the state government not to list the Sirius building on the State Heritage Register – despite the recommendation of the Heritage Council of NSW – leads to a case in the Land and Environment Court.[3]

By complementing her documentation of the subjects' activism with statements of fact, Lucine demonstrates the contradictions in the NSW Government's policies. For instance, the viewer witnesses Minister for Social Housing Pru Goward's public announcement that the sale of Sirius is for the overall benefit of the state because the money will go towards the construction of new properties. Soon after, however, Caton reveals some disconcerting data: as of 2014, 57,000 people in NSW were waiting for social housing, yet 1500 houses and apartments remained vacant. Adding a human perspective to these startling figures are Flood's observations. After leading Lucine to a concealed area behind Clark's house – which is in a woefully dilapidated condition, filled with rubbish, broken wood and overgrown plants – he explains:

*The Maritime Service had their own workers. They had their own plumbers, electricians […] and they used to keep it right*

*up to scratch. As soon as the Housing Commission took [Millers Point] over, it started falling down, down, down, down, down, until it's got to now – they're doing nothing, really.*

The implications that this might suggest a more insidious plot on the government's part find backing in the comments of then–deputy lord mayor Robyn Kemmis, who also appears in the documentary: 'Well, it suggests that the thought of selling the whole estate in Millers Point has been on somebody's table for some time.'

*The Eviction* is a brave and conscientious documentary that burrows deep into one of the most controversial NSW Government decisions of the twenty-first century. The four-year journey Lucine takes viewers on – from eviction notice to the final resident's departure – offers both poignant, perceptive character studies and an astute chronicle of a powerful political campaign that began with the anger and resistance of a few. 'None of the people I filmed were "Woe is me". They'd all had really difficult lives, even before this happened. They'd struggled,' Lucine says.

*Yet, despite that, they didn't play the victim card […] Every single one of them, in any way they could, fought. I wasn't telling the story of a whole community of victims. I was making a film about a community fighting against everything to try and stay – and, to be honest, I didn't think they'd lose.*

*Jasmine Crittenden is a Sydney-based freelance writer whose interests include film, music, literature, sustainability and human rights. She's a senior writer at* Concrete Playground, *a regular contributor to* Metro *and* Screen Education, *and a member of the Australian Film Critics Association.* **m**

Endnotes

[1] See Alan Morris, *Gentrification and Displacement: The Forced Relocation of Public Housing Tenants in Inner-Sydney*, Springer, Singapore, 2019, p. 1.
[2] See 'Sirius Building | 1975/1980 | NSW', DOCOMOMO Australia website, <https://docomomoaustralia.com.au/dcmm/sirius-building-1975-1980-nsw/>, accessed 26 February 2019.
[3] Morris, op. cit., pp. 19–20.

# AGE OF ACCEPTANCE

## Community and Inclusion in Sue Thomson's *The Coming Back Out Ball Movie*

Australia's attitudes towards LGBTQIA+ people have shifted dramatically over the last half-century, yet – as Sue Thomson's eye-opening documentary highlights – many of the older members of these communities face a distressing return back *into* the closet before entering aged care. **Stephen A Russell** talks to one non-binary elder who refuses, and to the filmmaker who captured her and other elders' stories.

After a life lived fighting for queer and women's liberation as well as championing other marginalised voices, including those of Australia's Indigenous peoples, 78-year-old Pink Floyd fan and former police officer Nance Peck refuses to be disappeared.

Embracing a non-binary gender identity in recent years, after a life lived largely as a lesbian, she's just as happy being called 'mate' as she is going by female pronouns. What she won't accept, however, is being pushed out of the way by oblivious pedestrians. It's a red line she clearly demarcates with candour in Sue Thomson's gloriously life-affirming 2018 documentary *The Coming Back Out Ball Movie* (*TCBOBM*). Debuting on the closing night of last year's Melbourne International Film Festival (MIFF), it follows eleven elders spanning the gender and sexuality spectrums as they prepare to attend the eponymous gala held in their honour at the Melbourne Town Hall on 7 October 2017 – just over a month shy of the release of the results of Australia's postal vote on marriage equality on 15 November.

Sparrow-like in frame but larger than life, Peck notes, in *TCBOBM*, that she engages an Australian Football League player's darting elbow or swift hip thrust to clear her path. This exact premise plays out as I sit down with Peck and Thomson in a Richmond cafe on a stinking-hot Melbourne summer's day that would try anyone's patience. The big lug who blunders into her, unthinkingly, on his way to the counter is unlikely to do so again in a hurry.

Growing up in Queensland during the 1940s and 1950s, Peck describes the state as being a 'land of bloody ignorance', with stiflingly backwards politics and socially conservative views that were anathema to her increasingly progressive outlook on life. As an adult, she began to push back, embracing activism: 'overcoming ignorance is important to me,' Peck insists.

### No Cinderella

The inaugural Coming Back Out Ball, held as part of the Victorian Seniors Festival in association with the third National LGBTI Ageing and Aged Care Conference, directly addressed this sidelining of older people who are gender- and sexually diverse. Organised by social-equality and community-arts outfit All The Queens Men, led by Tristan Meecham and Bec Reid, the project

*is informed by growing research around isolation and loneliness plaguing elderly populations, which is deemed even more acute for LGBTI people. Research also reveals that some LGBTI elders conceal their sexual, gendered or cultural identity or variation(s) when they access aged care services – because they believe they are not safe.*[1]

This worrying phenomenon is underlined by findings released by the Australian Institute of Health and Welfare:

DOCUMENTARY

**Opposite, L–R:** Bec Reid with David Morrison; Tristan Meecham (right) dances with Derek Christian  **Above:** Heather Morgan and Lizzi Craig

**Above, L–R:** Nance Peck; Ardy Tibby and director Sue Thomson

*The history of discrimination experienced by older Australians who identify as LGBTI can be a source of anxiety in disclosing sexual orientation and gender identity. Approximately 34% of people who identify as LGBTI reported hiding their sexuality or gender identity when accessing services.*[2]

On the surface, the ball's mission statement fits perfectly with the impassioned Peck's determination to be seen and heard. But the prog-rock and world-music fan was less convinced by what she saw as a very narrow view of what appealed to an older audience: the event had a showtune focus, spearheaded by cabaret star and producer Robyn Archer, opera singer Deborah Cheetham and celebrity showgirl Carlotta. Initially wary of Meecham's intentions, Peck took some convincing to attend and to be filmed by Thomson, but her own politics – along with the widespread harms posed by the postal vote – eventually drew her in.

*I was suspicious, because I've done a bit of filming myself, but when the plebiscite came in, that convinced me to come out of my comfort zone and be involved [...] If there's a reason to speak, then, fuck, I'm old enough to stand up. I need to. So I did.*

## Loud and proud

After moving from Bundaberg to Sydney in the 1960s, Peck found herself politically fired up and, since then, has seen film as an invaluable tool for social change, pointing to Open Channel's foray into public-broadcast television, C31 and NITV as great community-led examples. She's optimistic about the democratisation enabled by new technological tools such as smartphones:

*I think film is more powerful now than it ever was – [especially] in terms of digital, which has been revolutionary. It doesn't mean it's all going to be quality, but it does mean listening to new voices and accessing the world [...] It's all about access, the degree to which film is reflecting you. Do you see anybody like yourself? That's the most important thing.*

Peck joined the police force after returning to Queensland, working in the Juvenile Aid Bureau, but ultimately left to study anthropology and sociology, then a postgraduate degree in psychology at the University of Queensland. Becoming an active protester there, she marched against the Vietnam War and the Springboks' planned South African tour during apartheid, among other causes. She also helped set up multiple women's support groups and refuges in Brisbane, despite the oppressive reign of then–Queensland premier Joh Bjelke-Petersen. With federal funds made available by then–prime minister Gough Whitlam – to support young people at risk of offending, people facing homelessness and women fleeing domestic violence – she wielded the black-and-white video camera she was given by fellow volunteers to great effect. 'The Whitlam government's "video access" policy opened up a way to show what we were dealing with while helping run a women's shelter,' she recalls. 'It was an exciting and exhilarating time where everyone "had a go" at everything, but many of us were blacklisted.'

Peck had always loved weekend trips to the movies as a kid despite her father's off-putting addiction to westerns, but it was a screening of *2001: A Space Odyssey* (Stanley Kubrick, 1968) that truly awoke her to the power of cinema – even as she pushed back against the 'dickhead pontificating' of overly academic film fans. Looking back, she remembers how she and her peers put that newfound power into action while revelling in some gallows humour: 'They had found this piece of video that was still extant, and there we are [...] saying, "Yes, these shelters are up and running, and we are going to end family violence in five years."'

Although that fight continues, Peck, who moved to Melbourne in 1977, remains determined – and her belief in activism-charged cinema is undimmed after many years of working with the likes of Open Channel's predecessor Melbourne Access Video and Media Cooperative, which have provided opportunities for continued community involvement.

*Digital is great for queer stuff. It brings us into a different, non-gendered diversity that actually can be extremely confusing or confronting. But it puts the question back on everybody who watches it: what is your attitude?*

## Attitudes evolve

When Thomson first met Peck, the pair soon realised they shared similar pathways and mutual friends. Neither went to film school, instead having learned on the job. 'I did everything from directing to audio, editing to catering,' Thomson says, of her time at C31. 'Women could do anything – there was no gender depreciation in that organisation.'

Despite this solid connection, it still took time to build a trusting relationship, with Thomson spending months with Peck before the cameras rolled on *TCBOBM*. 'I wouldn't have done it if Sue hadn't been making it,' says Peck, 'because you really expose yourself [...] Sue and her team came into my space and I felt comfortable.' According to Thomson, this was time well spent:

*Initially, Nance was reticent – as a lot of people were – but I wanted to represent as many of the community as I could and knew I had to include her [...] I admire her humanity, her*

acceptance of everyone, no matter their gender or sexual identity, or their colour, and her wonderful humour, feisty spirit and genuine self-deprecating humbleness. Nance is a humanist, and that's what I aspire to [be].

Thomson, whose roots lay in theatre, was drawn to film's ability to reach more people more easily. 'What I loved about public broadcast was the immediacy and the lasting impact, whereas, with theatre, you might be on for a week and then it's gone. There's no record.' Today, Thomson regularly funnels her interest in social work into her filmmaking; one of her earlier documentaries, *Tempest at the Drop-In* (2013), narrated by Eric Bana, features professional actors working with people with mental-heath issues to stage a production of William Shakespeare's *The Tempest*. 'I've always wanted to help people, and documentary is a way of combining my own passions with trying to effect change.'

### Changed perspectives

It was Thomson's friendship with Meecham's boyfriend, screenwriter and producer Roger Monk, that led to her being brought on board early to document the creation of The Coming Back Out Ball. But she soon realised the film needed to be more about the elders than the event itself. The resulting documentary has become a fascinating record of the particular travails – and triumphs – of the LGBTQIA+ community in all its wonderful diversity, with Peck joined by the likes of Ardy Tibby, a lesbian who has proudly grown out her beard and who thinks balls are a bad idea because they screw with her bedtime, and leather-loving David Morrison, who only felt able to come out in his mid seventies, after the death of his wife of several decades. Then there's Michelle McNamara, who fully embraced her transition over the course of filming; Indigenous artist Peter Waples-Crowe, the youngest of the bunch, who seeks to reconcile his racial and sexual identities; and intersex woman Trace Williams, who notes that the 'I' in the acronym is already pretty invisible within the broader gender-and-sexually-diverse community, never mind the general population, and that's before age is even taken into account.

Shining the spotlight on this charismatic bunch, *TCBOBM* employs an empowering and uplifting tone without shying away from the hardships faced by many of its contributors. As critic Glenn Dunks puts it, the film

*gains much of its power from the strength and resilience of its subjects […] Whether it's the erasure that many elderly people feel from a community despite their agility, their passion, and their desire to contribute, or something more specific to the queer experience like the elation that comes from a transgender individual no longer seeing their deadname on office nameplates. Their stories remain important and relevant in a society that many still feel unsafe in and disrespected by.*[3]

Peck wasn't sure what to expect when she attended the film's premiere at MIFF:

*It was an interesting exercise for me. I'm seventy-plus now, so I'm basically a new person, really. I've been on a mission to find my own truth, to not care what others think about me, to let go of that kind of responsibility.*

However uncomfortable she may have been at the thought of revealing such intimate details about her personal journey, she remains committed to sharing her story, standing up and not fading away. 'I am friends with people of all ages because I have never seen age as defining who you are,' she says, chuckling as she recalls how one friend asserted that she has a 35-year-old attitude in a 78-year-old body.

Expressing joy that her cheeky humour 'isn't too in-your-face' in the film, Peck says that humour is an important tool in tackling a big issue like the fate of Australia's ageing LGBTQIA+ population. But it's not all levity, with Peck harbouring serious concerns about the monetisation of the aged-care industry.[4] Thomson has reservations, too. 'I learned so much working on this project, and I'd like to say that things have changed for the better, but, in some ways, I think it's getting worse.' Pointing to the continued existence of discriminatory practices and policies, both at home and overseas, she suggests that constant vigilance – and Peck's particular brand of impassioned activism – is required. 'I hope *The Coming Back Out Ball Movie* has changed a few minds. I know it has within my circle, but there's a big fight and it's not over yet. Some of what's happening out there is terrifying.'

Reluctant to wrap up on a negative note, Thomson reiterates that working with the LGBTQIA+ elders has been life-changing for everybody.

*Every single person involved in this film – from Nance to Ardy to Michelle – has very different politics, and yet they all managed to get their voices across. And they have all seen each other in a different light that, perhaps, sitting at the ball, they wouldn't have. They have heard each other's stories and actually respect each other more as a result, and that's what I'm most proud of. It's incredible.*

> 'When the plebiscite came in, that convinced me to come out of my comfort zone and be involved … If there's a reason to speak, then, fuck, I'm old enough to stand up. I need to. So I did.'
> —NANCE PECK

https://www.thecomingbackoutballmovie.com

*Originally hailing from Glasgow, Stephen A Russell is a Melbourne-based freelance arts writer who has indulged a lifelong passion for film.*

### Endnotes

1. 'The Coming Back Out Ball', All The Queens Men website, <https://allthequeensmen.net/projects/coming-back-ball/>, accessed 7 February 2019.
2. Australian Institute of Health and Welfare, 'Older Australia at a Glance', 10 September 2018, <https://www.aihw.gov.au/reports/older-people/older-australia-at-a-glance/contents/diverse-groups-of-older-australians/older-australians-who-identify-as-lesbian-gay-bisexual-transgender-or-intersex>, accessed 7 February 2019.
3. Glenn Dunks, '*The Coming Back Out Ball Movie* Is a Valuable Resource for the Australian Queer Community', *Flicks.com.au*, 5 December 2018, <https://www.flicks.com.au/reviews/australian-documentary-the-coming-back-out-ball-movie-is-a-valuable-resource-for-the-queer-community/>, accessed 7 February 2019.
4. See Matt Wade, 'The "Marketisation" of Aged Care', *The Sydney Morning Herald*, 22 September 2018, <https://www.smh.com.au/politics/federal/the-marketisation-of-aged-care-20180921-p5057m.html>, accessed 7 February 2019.

# RHETORIC AND REMINISCENCE

## Graham Freudenberg, Political Memory and *The Scribe*

Perhaps no other profession evidences the societal influence of words more than that of the speechwriter, tasked with tapping into both emotion and political nous when devising rousing orations. And perhaps no other speechwriter is as renowned in Australia as Graham Freudenberg – a fact attested to by Ruth Cullen's documentary, which profiles its subject's illustrious career alongside illuminating, if lean, reflections on rhetoric, writes **Anders Furze**.

'Friends and flukes have been the making of me.' So says storied Australian Labor Party (ALP) speechwriter Graham Freudenberg in Ruth Cullen's *The Scribe* (2018). Cullen's documentary is a portrait of the man and his musings on the role that rhetoric has played in politics, with a brief incursion into how that might be changing. The result is a hybrid of sorts: a filmic profile of Freudenberg and an insider's account of a few tumultuous decades in Australian politics.

Proclaimed by journalist Laurie Oakes to be 'the greatest speechwriter this country has produced',[1] Freudenberg – known as 'Freudy' to his colleagues – crafted words that were spoken by an assortment of ALP heavyweights, beginning in 1961 with then–federal opposition leader Arthur Calwell and ending in 2005 with the resignation of New South Wales (NSW) premier Bob Carr. As a teenager, the documentary tells us, Freudenberg read voraciously and, precociously modelling himself after nineteenth-century British prime minister Benjamin Disraeli (whose biography he read at age ten), he embarked on a journalism career with a grand plan of eventually moving into politics.

As he 'never had the great hunger for a story that really makes a great reporter', he notes in *The Scribe*, he made the shift across after hearing about a press-secretary job in Calwell's office. He landed the gig, which initially involved just liaising with the Canberra Press Gallery, writing press releases and keeping up with information. But he quickly found himself writing the ALP leader's speeches, even though doing so was not in the original position description.

Freudenberg recounts that he learned about the job midway through a party and raced out to immediately apply. Crucially, he found out about the opportunity at the beginning of the night. 'If the conversation hadn't occurred early in the party,' he says, 'before I was blotto, the whole course of my life would have been completely different.' This frank admission is not the last time alcohol comes up in *The Scribe*; indeed, beer is something of a recurring theme. 'Drink, of course, did play a large part in the political affairs of this nation,' Freudenberg observes, describing how parliamentarians and their staff frequently find themselves stuck in the same building for hours on end until the house adjourns, often well after midnight.

The speechwriter identifies beer as his 'great love', and indeed it played a vital role in several key moments in his political career. As former prime minister Bob Hawke – interviewed in the film as one of a few recurring talking heads – muses, he and Freudenberg 'sculled a few together. It was during one of those sessions that he said I was going to be the next prime minister, and that he wanted to work with me.' Freudenberg even took to

DOCUMENTARY

**Above:** Renowned speechwriter Graham Freudenberg

measuring the difficulty of his speeches by how much beer he consumed while writing them. 'At a certain stage in most speeches, I needed some liquid refreshments,' he says. 'The average speech [is] a six-can job. A great speech might be a thirteen- or fifteen-can job.'

Yet, as shambolic as that sounds, Carr – another talking head – notes that Freudenberg never once missed a deadline. So trustful of his work was Carr that the two didn't even meet to discuss the contents of big speeches before Carr would deliver them. He says he trusted 'the depth of [Freudenberg's] history, and the diamond-hard quality of his memory'; he merely ensured his speechwriter had the necessary tools for the job, then would receive the speeches by fax.

As with elsewhere in the film, Cullen shows little interest in critically evaluating her talking heads' claims. With most of them being ALP insiders, we're left to take these claims at face value and without much in the way of context. As it is, the moments when *The Scribe* gets more critical of rhetoric in politics are when Freudenberg himself reflects.

From the evidence presented in *The Scribe*, we encounter a Freudenberg with an abiding respect for the canonical figureheads of his field – particularly former US president Abraham Lincoln, whose portrait hangs on his wall at home. Intriguingly, to illustrate excerpts from Lincoln's Gettysburg Address, *The Scribe* makes use of scenes from little-seen drama *Saving Lincoln* (Salvador Litvak, 2013), whose central gimmick involves actors being green-screened in front of vintage civil-war photographs. In the context of a documentary mostly consisting of talking heads and archival and stock footage, the strangeness of seeing these transplanted scenes from another film risks swamping the power of Lincoln's words. Yet it does inevitably remind the viewer of the extent to which Lincoln has been lionised by American popular culture, and how words can be reinterpreted in myriad ways and for different purposes. That's a truth Freudenberg knows only too well – he openly borrows phrases and rhetorical techniques from Lincoln, William Shakespeare et al. in his speeches. It's also reinforced by Tom Amandes' performance in *Saving Lincoln*'s title role, which refocuses attention to the language.

And what language. Lincoln's speech has, by Freudenberg's own admission, become the ultimate cliché, yet the latter's passion for the address cuts through all that. Reflecting on the speech, which comprises a grand total of 272 words, Freudenberg observes that it's 'really the distillation of all the great speeches of Lincoln, which were not high rhetoric but fierce, rigorous logic from his mighty mind'.

In a further example of Freudenberg's appreciation of both humour and history, he and former NSW premier Neville Wran, with whom he worked for a decade, used 'Gettysburg' as shorthand to describe any inspirational speech on grand themes. They also coined the term 'Chatham' to describe the kind of speech that's less concerned with grand ideas and more with pandering and vote solicitation. As the film reveals, the latter was named in honour of a town where then–British prime minister Harold Wilson was heckled. Wilson, politicking in the dockyard town of Chatham, was expounding on the benefits of the British navy when he asked the audience, rhetorically, 'And why am I saying all this?' Before he could continue, a member of the crowd yelled out, 'Because you're in Chatham!'[2] Ultimately, Freudenberg notes that most speeches are a mixture of the two categories, a reflection of the messy reality of politics – flitting between high and low, lofty and direct, aspirational and transactional.

It's in these moments that *The Scribe* transitions from straight biography to a more interesting rumination on language in politics. For one, its subject is not judgemental about the ostensibly less savoury aspects of the system (deal-making, for example), remaining a passionate advocate for democracy. 'I think the most majestic thing that ever happens in Australia happens every polling day,' Freudenberg remarks at one point, his observation accompanied by footage of politicians visiting schools and knocking on doors, and of ballot papers being collected. 'The getting of votes is the essence of democratic politics. This is nothing to be apologetic about. When it's all said and done, it does come down to persuading people to vote your way.'

\*

Writing is often seen as a solitary profession, but Freudenberg says that, throughout his career as a speechwriter, he was 'never alone'. For one thing, there were the great orators who inspired him, offering him a 'mind or cultural companionship'. Then there were the more concrete relationships he had with ALP politicians.

'I think we were a bloody good combination,' Hawke observes – and, indeed, *The Scribe* spends a good deal of its running time documenting Freudenberg's relationships with both Hawke and former prime minister Gough Whitlam. The speechwriter's tie with the latter was particularly close: 'It's a process of osmosis, not deliberate study or imitation,' Freudenberg reflects in the film. 'I did get into his head, as he got into mine.'

After citing Whitlam's 1972 'It's Time' oration as one of his key early-career highlights, Freudenberg says that there was something uniquely Australian about these so-called Policy Speeches ('capital "P", capital "S"', he notes). According to him, no other democracy in the world had 'this contract, a mixture of high endeavour and pork barrelling'. It's not hard to see why Whitlam had the impact he did. Archival footage shows him proclaiming to a rapt audience, including a young Hawke in the front row, that 'there are moments in history when the whole fate and future of nations can be decided by a single decision. For Australia, this is such a time.' As the audience applauds enthusiastically, Whitlam struggles to conceal a smile. The energy is palpable.

So, in Freudenberg/Wran parlance, that's a Gettysburg. But what about a Chatham? Freudenberg points out that, at the time of Whitlam's speech, many of the suburbs in Sydney, Melbourne and Brisbane were un-sewered. So his speech-making would veer from grand proclamations that 'it's time' right through to quotidian promises to fix suburban sewerage systems. He admits that 'Whitlam was pilloried for it.' Still, he had the last laugh. His shrewd interweaving of the mundane and very real with the lofty and abstract clearly resonated with voters: as Freudenberg

> For the most part, *The Scribe* is a laudatory profile of its subject. That comes at the expense of a fuller – and, given our current political state, badly needed – consideration of rhetoric's role in politics, and how that might be changing.

asks the viewer with a sparkle in his eye, 'Which was more interesting to people?'

Yet, of all the Freudenberg speeches featured in it, *The Scribe* spends most of its time on Hawke's oration on the seventy-fifth anniversary of the landing at Gallipoli. Watching the speech now, you get a sense of the seriousness with which Hawke treated the occasion. Writing from a twenty-first-century perspective, academic Marilyn Lake has argued that there has been a marked shift in Australia's relationship with Anzac Day:

*New narratives about our troops fighting for 'freedom and democracy' and 'a nation forged in battle' began to be promoted by federal government departments.*

*Anzac Day thus appropriated an imperial war and re-cast it as a story of national independence to be taught to new generations of school children.*[3]

By choosing to focus on this speech, Cullen presents a powerful example of speechwriting's ability to influence our national sense of ourselves. That this is also noticeably different from the contemporary idea of Anzac Day suggests that this power is impermanent.

'None of us come here to glorify war,' a visibly emotional Hawke begins, in the archival footage presented.

*For us, no place on Earth more grimly symbolises the waste and the futility of war, this scene of carnage in a campaign which failed. It is not in the waste of war that Australians find the meaning of Gallipoli, then or now.*

'That was a remarkable speech,' Hawke reminisces, citing the occasion as the most moving experience he had as prime minister – a statement that's clearly reinforced by his emotional delivery in the archival footage shown. In a telling moment of bathos, Cullen cuts from this footage to Freudenberg reading the script for the speech. His reaction? 'Yeah, it's not bad.' He then attributes its power to the fact that he borrowed heavily from Shakespeare, before eventually conceding that it was the 'nearest [he] could come – like, a thousand miles away – from Gettysburg'.

\*

If there's a spectre haunting *The Scribe*'s celebration of political rhetoric, it's the election of Donald Trump. The incumbent US president intermittently makes his way into the film via campaign-rally footage, which is intercut with other examples of politicking. But it's not until the end of the film that Freudenberg directly addresses the growing popular disenchantment with establishment politics. He often worries that speechwriting has helped '[diminish] the spontaneity of things' in politics; then, enter Trump, who 'cuts through all that'. While competing presidential candidate Hillary Clinton could give a 'very good speech', Freudenberg reflects that her flaw was not appearing as authentic as Trump's 'brawling, undisciplined, sometimes almost illiterate form of speeches'.

It's in these fleeting moments that *The Scribe* becomes a more interesting exploration of the role rhetoric plays in politics. At times, interviewees gesture towards more complicated reflections – Carr, for example, notes that Freudenberg's writing enhanced Calwell's leadership so dramatically that it turned him into a 'figure of more authority and of some style, more than he was really entitled to be'.

Towards the end of the film, Freudenberg argues that speechwriters for ex-president George W Bush may have done active harm to the global political order. Referring to Bush's State of the Union address that popularised the concept of an 'axis of evil', he asserts:

*That was put in by speechwriters simply because they thought it sounded good and had echoes of the war against [Adolf] Hitler and [Benito] Mussolini. And, of course, referring to Iran in particular as part of an 'axis of evil' has distorted US relations with Iran ever since, perhaps irreparably.*

*This is a case where the satisfaction that one gets from writing a stirring phrase can be damaging.*

It's a moment that highlights the lasting impact that rhetorical manipulation can have on the real world. But brief clips of Trump and Adolf Hitler aside, for the most part, *The Scribe* is a laudatory profile of its subject. That comes at the expense of a fuller – and, given our current political state, badly needed – consideration of rhetoric's role in politics, and how that might be changing. It does, however, lead to some interesting reflections from a man who's used to sticking his words in other people's mouths.

In *The Scribe*'s conclusion, the director herself – in the form of her off-screen voice – enters the film, asking Freudenberg whether he's looking forward to his upcoming Whitlam Oration. The renowned speechwriter will be reading his own work aloud for a change. 'No, I'm dreading it,' he abruptly responds, cigarette in hand. He pauses, then softens slightly. 'Because I don't know what the hell I'm going to say.' The feeling is not, Freudenberg clarifies, unique to this speech. Indeed, he approaches 'every speech with a feeling of dread', as if 'this speech will be the one that I can't do'.

Now in his eighties, Freudenberg reflects with wry amusement that age has turned him into the 'last surviving expert on the past', at least as far as the ALP is concerned. Certainly, his great collaborators have progressively passed into history. The 'chameleon', as Hawke called him, has run out of camouflage, and he can no longer wrap the rhetoric of history – from Shakespeare to Lincoln – around the political personalities of the present. 'This time,' he says of that pre-speech dread, 'it's even worse. I'm on my own.'

https://www.thescribefilm.com

*Anders Furze is a journalist and film critic based in Melbourne. His work has appeared in* The Guardian, Meanjin, The Age, The Sydney Morning Herald, Crikey *and elsewhere.*  **m**

Endnotes
1. Laurie Oakes, 'Politicians Have Lost the Art of Making Great Speeches Thanks to Sound Bites', *The Herald Sun*, 3 June 2017, <https://www.heraldsun.com.au/news/opinion/laurie-oakes/politicians-have-lost-the-art-of-making-great-speeches-thanks-to-sound-bites/news-story/ab733b3d583797b4e19124e227e6d8cb>, accessed 13 February 2019.
2. See Michael White, 'A Brief History of Heckling', *The Guardian*, 28 April 2006, <https://www.theguardian.com/politics/2006/apr/28/past.labour>, accessed 13 February 2019.
3. Marilyn Lake, 'Beyond Anzac: What Really Shaped Our Nation?', *Pursuit*, 23 April 2018, <https://pursuit.unimelb.edu.au/articles/beyond-anzac-what-really-shaped-our-nation>, accessed 21 February 2019.

**This spread, L–R:** Argokhi resident Jimmy; Jimmy with his parents Otar and Ano

DOCUMENTARY

# GREENER PASTURES

## Tradition and Modernity in Grace McKenzie's *In the Land of Wolves*

A remote, arcadian town seemingly lost to time, Argokhi forms the focal point of Grace McKenzie's meditative sophomore work. As her documentary reveals, this Georgian community is simultaneously out of step and in touch with the world: encumbered by its affinity for tradition, entrapped by its post-Soviet context, yet also emancipated from alienating consumerism by its direct engagement with the land, writes **Gabrielle O'Brien**.

Life isn't easy for the residents of Argokhi, Georgia. Their small rural village huddles in the foothills of the imposing Caucasus mountain range, where the natural beauty of the terrain is mostly untouched by modern intervention. This is a place that seems to resist the pull of technology and the other trappings of contemporary life. Most villagers live hand-to-mouth, working the land to produce food for themselves and their neighbours. Animals are either slaughtered for meals or sold on for profit. The land itself is diligently tended using agricultural practices that date back to the Middle Ages; as one resident explains, 'We all grow our own wheat and mill it into flour. You can't make a living out of working in the village. We work just to live.'

*In the Land of Wolves* (2018), writer/director Grace McKenzie's sophomore documentary feature, presents a fascinating snapshot of a community that appears to stand outside of time. Yet, as the film shows us, there is a universality to the human condition that time

> *In the Land of Wolves* uses the rhythms of the seasons as a framing device … McKenzie refers to the film as 'a pastoral symphony', a lovely description of her freewheeling approach that responds to the vagaries of nature and to the relationship between it and the film's subjects.

and place cannot alter. Building on the intimate filmmaking of McKenzie's award-winning debut, *Audrey of the Alps* (2012), *In the Land of Wolves* also exudes a gentle poignancy that takes its cues from the unhurried rhythms of slow cinema. A broad definition of that mode of filmmaking will usually note features like 'the employment of (often extremely) long takes, de-centred and understated modes of storytelling, and a pronounced emphasis on quietude and the everyday'.[1] Certainly, the film's effect on the viewer is gently hypnotic as it homes in on details: a donkey's hoofs punching out little grooves in the snow, a hand caressing a newborn calf, fingers kneading dough. Produced by McKenzie's father, Brian, with assistance from Screen Australia, this is a lucid, assured cinematic work from a talented young Australian director.

## In and out of time

*In the Land of Wolves* uses the rhythms of the seasons as a framing device, eschewing a formal narrative structure. It tracks the lives of a handful of residents over the course of a year, dropping in and out of their lives like an old friend. McKenzie refers to the film as 'a pastoral symphony',[2] a lovely description of her freewheeling approach that responds to the vagaries of nature and to the relationship between it and the film's subjects. After all, the seasons shape the Argokhi villagers' daily toil, determining the cycles of growth and harvest that provide them with food and income.

Frenchman Jean-Jacques is an expatriate living in the village; he sells his artisanal bread at a weekly market stall in the capital city of Tbilisi. He brings contemporary methodology to the way that he farms and produces – biodynamic techniques that would make any urban hipster proud. European students come to volunteer at his farm. While the presence of these young travellers might seem strange in such an isolated rural location, Argokhi, in fact, welcomes outsiders. The village's population is primarily composed of Georgians and Ossetians; McKenzie's film shows us how the two ethnicities are harmoniously blended, often via marriages. But, while the lands of North Ossetia remain under modern-day Russian control, Georgia gained its independence from the former Soviet Union in 1991, with South Ossetia contentiously subsumed into it. Tensions and violence over territory there, as well as in other parts of Georgia, still take place. It's unsurprising, then, that the Ossetian population is not-so-happily integrated elsewhere in the country.[3]

Sveta, Jean-Jacques' Ossetian neighbour, acts as a friendly go-between connecting farming families. At times, her function in McKenzie's film recalls that of a solitary Greek chorus, as she elucidates the actions of other villagers or provides context for their struggles. But Sveta's commentary becomes particularly enlightening when she speaks about the predicament of Jimmy, a deaf turkey farmer who can't speak but who has a preternatural kinship with animals. Gradually, Jimmy's story becomes

**This spread, L–R:** Villagers at work in the field; Argokhi townsfolk Sveta and Emzari

**Above:** Sveta and Ano

**The importance of communication for human survival and for the preservation of hope is a subtle but pervasive trope in *In the Land of Wolves*. The farming families are a self-supporting network, a real flesh-and-bones community that functions on physical interaction and shared labour.**

the compelling centrepiece of *In the Land of Wolves*. Despite his disability and the isolation that this creates for him within his community, his experiences offer a bridge between the world depicted in the film and that of foreign audiences.

Jimmy is arguably the most sympathetic figure in the documentary, and there is a comforting familiarity to his circumstances that transcends the very specific (and, in many ways, otherworldly) setting and subjects that the film tracks. Having recently returned to Argokhi after a failed marriage, Jimmy is caught between the pull of family, the village and an independent life. He misses his daughter, who remains with her mother in the city. Devoted to supporting his family, he proudly grows the largest turkeys in the region so that he can make a good profit from their sale. Yet his own identity seems to oscillate between pragmatic, hardworking villager and lonely young man yearning to find his tribe.

Ano, Jimmy's kind, down-to-earth mother, worries about her son and wants him to settle down with a new wife. But Otar, his father, is existential in outlook – the result of a life in which uncertainty is a dominant keynote. He personifies the stoic temperament of the villagers with reflections such as this:

*We are tormented. Sometimes, we have joy in our life; sometimes, we have tragedy. One cannot have a life without such things. No smooth road exists. One just has to stumble somewhere.*

## Disconnection and connection

When McKenzie arrived in the village, her initial impression of it was that it was an idyllic refuge where old ways of living were preserved rather than destroyed. However, on closer examination, a different picture gradually emerged:

*In reality life is harsh in the village and there is a battle to make ends meet. It would be naïve to think that the residents do not know what is going on elsewhere. Everyone dreams of living in the city with all the modern appliances. The young are bringing in cars and have a reckless obsession with the [W]est. After the war with Russia, America is favoured and graffiti at the bus stop reads 'Buy U.S.' The elderly are disappointed with the shift but tired of working hard. The young want to leave and the old cannot look after themselves. Pressure mounts for consumer items and the haphazard network of subsistence growers is not able to deliver what the young people want.*[4]

This idea of an intergenerational disconnect is significant. The older villagers aren't plugged in to the technological networks that are so ubiquitous in the West. Some of the younger residents have a small taste of these forms of communication, and they want more. While the film largely follows the older villagers, there is a brief glimpse of this disjuncture when we see Ano puzzling over Jimmy's night-time online chats, wondering how on Earth he could stay up so late on his computer. Perhaps, for Jimmy, online communities might be especially important, but for all of the other subjects in the film, EM Forster's epigraph 'Only connect!'[5] resonates sharply. The importance of communication for human survival and for the preservation of hope is a subtle but pervasive trope in *In the Land of Wolves*. The farming families are a self-supporting network, a real flesh-and-bones community that functions on physical interaction and shared labour. In contrast to the digital relationships of online worlds, here is a place where communication is a pressing material commodity.

Interestingly, communication posed extradiegetic hurdles for the filmmakers. Brian McKenzie recounts, for instance, that distance was an issue:

*For two years, our collaboration took place from opposite sides of the globe – Grace was in Bristol and I in Melbourne. We were in the village together four times during production (and again during post production), often meeting on the way in Istanbul.*[6]

More pressingly, communication posed challenges due to the complex language barriers. When shooting footage of the villagers, Grace McKenzie could only speculate as to what they were saying to one another. Adding another layer of difficulty was the fact that some spoke Georgian while others conversed in Ossetian. And then there was Jimmy, who expressed himself using sign language. As a result, the filmmakers required an elaborate chain of interpreters to pin down what the subjects were saying. In a way, this process replicates Jimmy's experience, as a deaf man, of being an outsider in a predominantly hearing world. At the same time, it reaffirms the capacity for reciprocal understanding despite differences – a very moving and humbling comment on the expansiveness of human connection.

Some of the loveliest moments in *In the Land of Wolves* celebrate the residents' intimate connections. McKenzie makes wonderful use of a series of tableaux featuring family members; these images are highly constructed and static, recalling photographs, yet she also includes some footage of her subjects preparing to get into frame, jostling each other for prime position or smiling nervously at one another. Yet, despite their artificiality, these staged images, much like the rest of the film's scenes, are nevertheless anchored in the moment. Complementing these visuals, sound is used to convey a sense of place and of Georgian culture – particularly in the form of diegetic music and singing by locals. Together, image and sound reinforce the film's organic sensibility in a way that is both moving and insightful.

## From farm gate to plate

Death is never too far away in Argokhi. The precarious balance between life and death is a part of the villagers' largely unmediated interaction with the natural world. In contrast with the West (and with cities more broadly), where death is a latent presence, here, the practical reality of death is unmuted.

The film opens with a confronting sequence that demystifies the process of birth; depicting a calf being unceremoniously dumped into a cruel and indifferent world, it discards any romantic connotations we commonly associate with new life. The calf struggles to feed from its mother, and needs Jimmy's help to stay alive. The proximity to death is immediately emphasised – and this theme becomes a recurring trope in the film. Some baby chickens thrive while others don't last long enough for a first breath. The villagers chase a pig around before ritually slaughtering it for a traditional feast. Otar tells us his donkey has had a sad life as a mother: two of her offspring were stillborn. And, when Ano's cousin passes away, we are invited to the funeral.

Arguably, this acceptance of the arbitrariness of life and death partly comes from the subsistence farmers' pragmatic relationship to animals. Otar recalls his mother scolding him as a boy for protesting against the slaughter of a pet lamb. The dissociation between food source and food consumption that we in the West take as a given is, clearly, not part of the Argokhi consciousness. In fact, one of the film's most interesting messages concerns this same unmediated relationship between agriculture and food consumption: it reminds us that our experiences with over-packaged supermarket products are a sadly sanitised reality. It offers us an opportunity to reflect on the enormous distance we tend to have between what we eat and its origins. Perhaps an appreciation of the provenance of our food might help us to consume more carefully, and to reconsider our relationship to animal products.

*In the Land of Wolves* brings us up close to the day-to-day minutiae of village life, with each season bringing its own hardships and pleasures. Beyond its old-world beauty, however, Arghoki is a place at a sociocultural crossroads. Much like the world it shines a light on, this film, too, is at a crossroads. Its Sydney and Melbourne film-festival sessions were warmly received, and, while it is showing for the first time in Georgia at this year's CinéDOC-Tbilisi documentary festival, McKenzie is still on the hunt for a distributor. Mirroring her team's difficult journey while making the film, this process hasn't been easy. '[*In the Land of Wolves*] doesn't have a driving story or clear theme, so it's hard to describe, let alone sell,' she explains. 'It is a thoughtful film with a lot of heart and care, and audiences seem to appreciate it, but it's a process to get it viewed.'[7]

'Thoughtful' indeed, but not just that – this is a thought-provoking glimpse into unseen lives that deserves to find an audience.

*Gabrielle O'Brien is a Melbourne-based freelance film writer. The Australian Film Critics Association recently conferred her the Ivan Hutchinson Award for best long-form film criticism.* **m**

Endnotes

1. Matthew Flanagan, 'Towards an Aesthetic of Slow in Contemporary Cinema', *16:9*, vol. 6, no. 29, November 2008, <http://www.16-9.dk/2008-11/side11_inenglish.htm>, accessed 19 February 2019.
2. Grace McKenzie, in 'About the Making of *In the Land of Wolves*', Brian McKenzie Film Productions & Screen Australia, *In the Land of Wolves* press kit, 2018, p. 5.
3. See Giorgi Sordia, *Ossetians in Georgia: In the Wake of the 2008 War*, European Centre for Minority Issues, working paper no. 45, September 2009, pp. 4–15, available at <https://www.files.ethz.ch/isn/106675/working_paper_45_en.pdf>, accessed 18 February 2019.
4. Grace McKenzie, in 'About the Making of *In the Land of Wolves*', op. cit., pp. 4–5.
5. EM Forster, *Howards End*, The Floating Press, Auckland, 2009 [1910], p. 335.
6. Brian McKenzie, in 'About the Making of *In the Land of Wolves*', op. cit., p. 6.
7. Grace McKenzie, email to the author, 8 February 2019.

CRITICAL VIEWS

# Cinema for Claustrophiles

## Virtual Reality at the Adelaide Film Festival and Beyond

VIRTUAL REALITY PROMISES ESCALATED LEVELS OF IMMERSION AND INTERACTIVITY – YET, IN ITS CURRENT TEETHING STAGES, EXEMPLARS OF THE FORM REMAIN TETHERED TO THE CONVENTIONS AND CONSTRAINTS OF TRADITIONAL FILMIC STORYTELLING. **KIT MACFARLANE** EXAMINES FOUR AUSTRALIAN VR TITLES TO ILLUMINATE DEVELOPMENTS IN THIS STILL-NASCENT BUT INCREASINGLY POPULAR MEDIUM.

Previous spread, L–R: *Carriberrie*; *The Unknown Patient* **This spread, clockwise from top left:** *The Unknown Patient*; *Carriberrie* (three images)

Unobtrusively situated next to the entrance of the main 2018 Adelaide Film Festival (AFF) venue on Hindley Street, the Jumpgate VR Lounge boasted a selection of packages that offered audiences an opportunity to engage with a range of virtual reality (VR) titles from Australia and around the world. Despite the name, there wasn't much lounging to be done. There, VR didn't involve lounging; VR required *swivelling*. Functional swivel stools were scattered around some unassuming tables while a row of computers for the more interactive VR texts lined the back wall. It was also not particularly 'virtual' – several staff members were present to divvy out headsets encasing mobile phones as well as handheld controllers (which I carefully looped around my arm, certain of my non-virtual clumsiness). For my first session, I was the only participant, with five staff waiting to help or casually chatting; the unwieldy physicality of the preparation process made me feel like I was the one on display.

Fritz Lang jokes in Jean-Luc Godard's *Contempt* (1963) that CinemaScope is 'only good for snakes and funerals'. Using similar(ly incorrect but still somewhat revealing) logic, it might be worth suggesting that VR is particularly good for audiences who enjoy the sensation of being surrounded; 'claustrophile' is the closest term I could find. While VR can create, or at least suggest, open and expansive surroundings – I remember my unease upon returning to the 'smallness' of an ordinary computer room after my first stint playing some VR games a few years ago – the Australian VR pieces on offer at AFF tended instead to evoke enclosure. As viewers/participants themselves were often the focal point of the ensuing narrative, even the seemingly 'open' simulated surroundings produced a sense of confinement. We may don a headset to 'see' the VR text and 'move' through its world, but we also can't help imagining a phantasmic crowd with their gaze turned steadfastly back on us.

Despite this sense of enclosure – whether in physical or narrative terms, or through an awareness of being a captive audience of one – the Australian VR pieces at AFF nevertheless covered a broad range of styles and genres. One of them, *The Unknown Patient* (Michael Beets, 2018), won AFF's award for best VR title as well as screening in competition in the VR sidebar of the 2018 Venice International Film Festival, suggesting the possibility of a strong and diverse Australian presence in what is still a nascent artform. Of the four titles examined here, three present direct narratives about Australian history and/or culture through fairly familiar communication methods, notwithstanding the lure of VR's encapsulating technological frame. Film criticism can be a game of historical surveying, finding antecedents for new products and examining their place in some speculative sense of ongoing development; VR is not videogames or video art, but elements of these must inevitably influence – through prior exposure – a participant's subjective experience of this realm. Yet what I witnessed largely mirrored established film techniques, with creators using the still-developing medium as a marketable, novel platform for direct cultural, political and social exposure and awareness-raising.

## Carriberrie

*Carriberrie* (Dominic Allen, 2018), described on its promotional website as 'a multi-platform immersive journey across Australia celebrating the depth and diversity of Indigenous dance and song from the traditional to the contemporary',[1] propels the viewer to a variety of stunning locations, utilising music and movement to weave together the piece's sprawling story. There's no question that *Carriberrie* is a vital cultural document as well as a vivid and energising experience, but there's also an interesting tension at the heart of its 'immersive' form: despite its focus on the performances in the surrounding circular space, the viewer's position at the centre of this space always feels foregrounded. Indeed, the viewer's entry into

*Carriberrie* is a vital cultural document as well as a vivid and energising experience, but there's also an interesting tension at the heart of its 'immersive' form ... the viewer's position at the centre of this space always feels foregrounded.

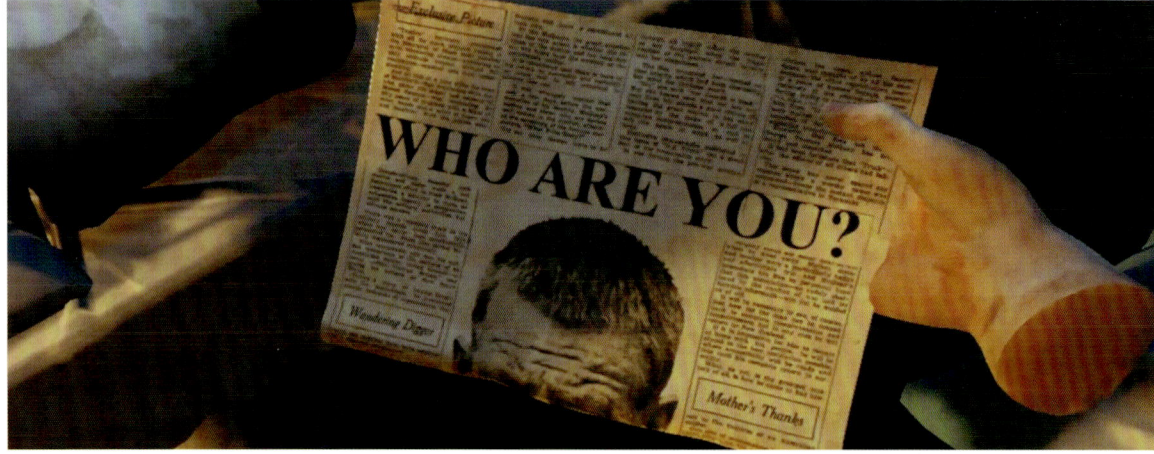

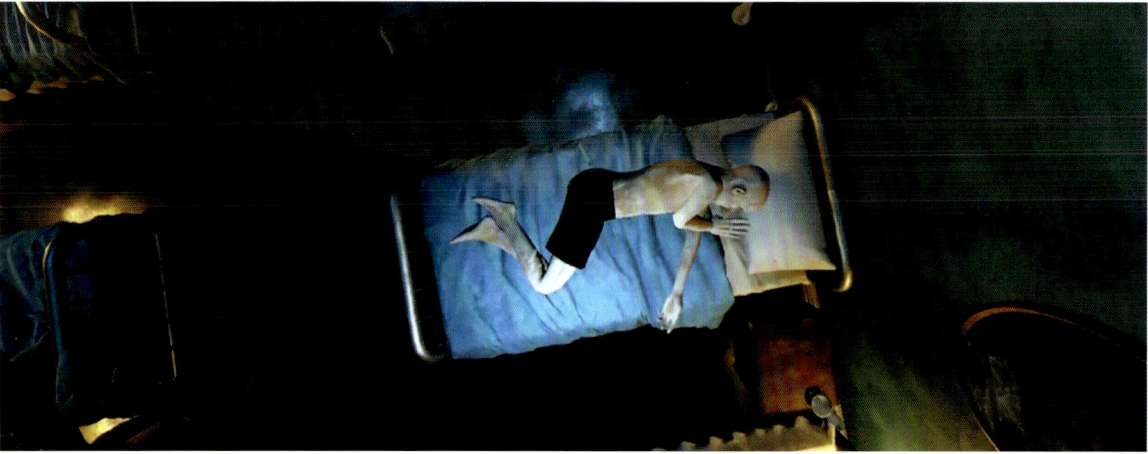

**Above:** *The Unknown Patient* (two images) **Opposite:** *Parragirls Past, Present: Unlocking Memories of Institutional 'Care'*

the diegetic world is via a theatre stage, after which we're shifted through the various performances. The vividness of all of these fiercely talented dancers and singers[2] sits awkwardly with our awareness of them performing into this 'empty' core: the space now occupied by the viewer. The feeling of being looked at – or performed to – so intimately while simultaneously being both 'there' and not there reinforces too strongly that we are never really seen.

On another level, being propelled through a variety of different cultures experienced through landscape, dance and song may seem to re-create the tourist's passing, flimsy gaze. Again, the performances are enrapturing, but the generated feeling of merely 'browsing' remains: passing moments rather than extended connections and understandings. Similarly, and perhaps counterintuitively, the sense of personal address that comes with VR can't help but imbue gravitas to the watching of this artwork: *Who wants to let down these wonderful dancers who are performing for us? And how can/should non-Aboriginal viewers feel about being a privileged audience of one for a practice so culturally significant to First Nations Australians?*

None of these are criticisms of the text per se; instead, they suggest some of the baggage that comes, if not from VR technology itself, then from making the viewer's gaze so central to VR storytelling and the difficulty of communicating culture using mere snippets and spectacle. *Carriberrie* employs wonderful footage that undoubtedly provides the viewer with a vibrant and visually engrossing experience – but it's too soon to say exactly how well performances of this sort work in the VR space.

### The Unknown Patient

Presented as the first episode of a possible five-part series, *The Unknown Patient* uses VR as a slightly unwieldy amalgam of prestige-style historical drama and interactive game, not quite inhabiting either form nor effectively distancing VR from them. Its interactive aspects are fairly perfunctory: in particular, the viewer is commanded to repeatedly 'find that coin' before the narrative can continue.

While *The Unknown Patient* does allow for some interaction with elements of the environment, its main task remains that of, essentially, looking, listening and swivelling. The piece's central point of interest is its underlying narrative: the true story of an ANZAC soldier who was found wandering the streets of London in 1916 and ended up in a Sydney hospital for twelve years. Placing the viewer in the shoes of someone without a known name or backstory gives the mystery a personal impetus (a technique that obviously predates VR storytelling, but is given additional weight by the medium's heightened faculty for point of view), as does the effectively perturbing ambience of the hospital setting.

As the storyline unfolds in a largely traditional manner, *The Unknown Patient* never quite allows the viewer to feel truly lost in the character's identitylessness. A conveniently earnest and talkative nurse, Diana (Lily Sullivan), and some fragmentary flashbacks (which are fairly generic in terms of narrative, but also surprisingly effective in the way they appear within, and overwhelm, the surrounding virtual environment) ensure that the narrative's momentum never threatens to disappear. But direct involvement here still feels like a token element in a passive narrative realm: interaction, but not yet 'real' contribution. Nevertheless, *The Unknown Patient*'s strong use of historical detail and visual design makes the prospect of further instalments an intriguing one for Australian VR.

### *Parragirls Past, Present: Unlocking Memories of Institutional 'Care'*

*Parragirls Past, Present: Unlocking Memories of Institutional 'Care'* (2017) – written, designed and produced by a team including Lily Hibberd, Bonney Djuric, Jenny McNally, Volker Kuchelmeister and Alex Davies – summons confronting memories of life in the Parramatta Girls Home, which operated under different guises from 1887 until 1983. It positions the viewer within the establishment's high-walled grounds as former residents, returning some forty years later, recount the abuses and torments they experienced there. While 'residents' is the term used in promotional material, the stories relived in *Parragirls Past, Present* may lead viewers to feel that 'prisoners' might be a more apposite word.

The VR experience is largely fixed in its format: we drift through the dark premises, shifting through standard film-style transitions into new locations and buildings as the narration details life in that particular section or in the general confines of the institution. The generated sensation of drifting can initially be frustrating, but the feeling of powerlessness that this elicits ultimately contributes to the work's overall depiction of physical and emotional confinement. The slow, powerless drift – almost like being wheeled around unwillingly – suggests the impetus of an ominous dream, an aesthetic that effectively paints the home as a nightmarish site of trauma from the not-so-distant past. Indeed, the filmmakers talk of their desire not to follow the standard CGI pursuit of 'ever more realistic depictions', instead opting for an 'abstract reconstructed reality' that 'can be interpreted as being compatible with how human memory operates. It is mutable, constructed and fragmented.'[3]

Yet, at times, this dreamlike presentation can be evocative of a horror movie's constructed CGI setting – we witness stock-standard motifs like shadowy spaces and techniques like the (highly overused) low drone on the soundtrack. This is far from tonally inappropriate, of course, but it does mean that the depicted location can occasionally feel generic rather than specific. At the

> By allowing viewers to hear the voices of the victims directly, in an approximation of the real location within which they suffered, *Parragirls Past, Present* offers a vital contribution to Australia's historical record and future understanding of institutional abuses.

> *Summation of Force* is the only title of the four that doesn't make the viewer's presence central to the sense of the surrounding action ... its packaging of simulated space far exceeds the surround-and-stare or drag-through approaches that have often been default choices for VR works to date.

end of the piece, the viewer floats back to see the home isolated in space, not only reinforcing its status as an imprisoning context for suffering but also reminding us of the lack of historical and cultural specificity within the text itself.

One particularly upsetting detail (although there's no shortage of upsetting stories) involves a subject describing having to respond to doubts about the abuse claims. The Royal Commission into Institutional Responses to Child Sexual Abuse may have released its findings into the Parramatta Girls Home,[4] but, ultimately, a traumatic history can never be declared closed. By allowing viewers to hear the voices of the victims directly, in an approximation of the real location within which they suffered, *Parragirls Past, Present* offers a vital contribution to Australia's historical record and future understanding of institutional abuses.

### Summation of Force

Perhaps the most formally ambitious of the titles being looked at here, *Summation of Force* (Trent Parke, Narelle Autio & Matthew Bate, 2017) engages most overtly with the possibilities that come with VR's encapsulating space. Rather than relying on the viewer to swivel in order to 'survey' the text's portrayed surroundings, *Summation of Force* is carefully designed to encourage smaller, less certain evaluations of the enveloping space, with certain visual elements appearing in particular parts of the frame rather than forming constitutive parts of a generalised environment.

*Summation of Force*'s move away from the focal points of the aforementioned three works – narration in *Parragirls Past, Present*; flashback and dialogue in *The Unknown Patient*; linked vignettes in *Carriberrie* – sees it drawing instead on the tradition of experimental filmmaking, and this arguably leads to it feeling more fully developed as a VR-specific work.[5] The film's description in its promotional material of the way it examines, and (to some extent) elevates, sport and childhood growth may be avowedly blunt – its official synopsis describes it as a 'a paean to collective dreams, youthful determination, and the bonds that sporting ambition can create'.[6] In reality, however, its abstract images, occasional use of extreme slow motion and lack of exposition will, for many viewers, present a somewhat less comfortable and comforting view of the childhood sporting realm.

Interestingly, *Summation of Force* is the only title of the four that doesn't make the viewer's presence central to the sense of the surrounding action, offering instead a somewhat more detached and, as a result, more dramatically intriguing experience. In fact, its packaging of simulated space far exceeds the surround-and-stare or drag-through approaches that have often been default choices for VR works to date. In the opening scene, for example, the viewer is in the middle of a suburban backyard, a batter on one side and some hanging laundry on the other, against the backdrop of a black night-time void. As the slow-motion approach of the bowler becomes apparent, the viewer is faced with two planes of action: it's impossible not to regard the batter even if the approach of the ball seems to be the movement that dominates the frame. It's this type of tension between spaces – rather than a uniformity – that sparks *Summation of Force*'s VR environment into life. As David Bordwell notes in relation to VR's role of guiding viewers, 'Narrative, we've known since forever, depends on controlling attention'[7] – and *Summation of Force* offers us an intriguing mix of controlled *and* uncontrolled experiences.

*

It's difficult to look into any VR work's promotional material (including those of the above titles) without running into some variation of the word 'immersive'. This is entirely reasonable, but the near-ubiquity of the term carries certain problems, since it can feel like a general functional description of the *overall* nature of the technology has just been extrapolated (each time) into a defining feature of the individual VR work – a bit like (meaninglessly) referring to a film's 'visuality'. This ambiguity as to how we're supposed to understand the word suggests that, just as VR has a long way to go in terms of determining exactly what its defining properties and possibilities are, the way we talk about and analyse it is also still evolving. The pursuit of some phantasmic idea of 'immersion' is likewise a fairly dominant trend in traditional film, which therefore couches VR as a logical extension of its forebear rather than a real game changer in an artistic sense. Like Bordwell, most viewers may still (for now) be finding 'close affinities between VR and cinema'.[8]

It may be boorish to point out that, currently, public VR spaces such as the one I visited at AFF are far from able to compete with some of the higher-end professional

**Above:** *Summation of Force*

products and home set-ups that accommodate powerful user-directed motion within virtual spaces, online communication, and a more immediate sense of action and interaction. But the uneasy dynamic between VR as film, VR as game, VR as interactive tool, VR as public installation and VR as immersive experience isn't one that's likely to be 'settled' in any specific way; rather, these shifting characteristics are likely to define the medium's development into the future. Moreover, the range and variety of VR titles presented at AFF demonstrate Australia's engagement with the VR realm's multiple formats and approaches – as well as its ongoing pursuits in this media space to increase and promote cultural, historical and political knowledge through art and new technologies.

https://www.carriberrie.com

http://www.michaelbeets.com/the-unknown-patient-2/

https://parragirlsmovie.com

http://closerproductions.com.au/films/summation-force

*Kit MacFarlane has a PhD in film and literature studies, and is a lecturer in the School of Creative Industries at the University of South Australia.*     **m**

Endnotes

1. *Carriberrie* official website, <https://www.carriberrie.com>, accessed 11 February 2019.
2. A list of the featured performances can be found on *Carriberrie*'s official website, ibid.
3. *Parragirls Past, Present: Unlocking Memories of Institutional 'Care'* official website, <https://parragirlsmovie.com>, accessed 11 February 2019.
4. Royal Commission into Institutional Responses to Child Sexual Abuse, *Report of Case Study No. 7: Child Sexual Abuse at the Parramatta Training School for Girls and the Institution for Girls in Hay*, October 2014, available at <https://www.childabuseroyalcommission.gov.au/sites/default/files/file-list/case_study_7_-_findings_report_-_parramatta_training_school_for_girls.pdf>, accessed 11 February 2019.
5. Even though it was produced in conjunction with an installation piece; see David Knight, 'Trent Parke and Narelle Autio's *The* [sic] *Summation of Force*', *The Adelaide Review*, 21 June 2017, <https://www.adelaidereview.com.au/arts/visual-arts/trent-parke-narelle-autios-summation-force/>, accessed 11 February 2019.
6. '*Summation of Force*', Closer Productions website, <http://closerproductions.com.au/films/summation-force>, accessed 11 February 2019.
7. David Bordwell, 'Venice 2018 College Cinema: Landscapes, Portraits', *Observations on Film Art*, 7 September 2018, <http://www.davidbordwell.net/blog/2018/09/07/venice-2018-college-cinema-landscapes-portraits/>, accessed 11 February 2019.
8. ibid.

# Other Voices

## Grace, Who Waits Alone and New Australian Underground Cinema

AUSTRALIA'S UNDERGROUND FILM MOVEMENT IS UNDERGOING A RENAISSANCE, BUT THE FILMS THEMSELVES REMAIN OUT OF REACH FOR MANY CINEMA-GOERS – THE RECENT *GRACE, WHO WAITS ALONE* BEING AN EXCELLENT CASE IN POINT. SPEAKING TO THE FILM'S DIRECTOR, GEORGIA TEMPLE, ALONG WITH LOCAL SCREEN FIGURES BILL MOUSOULIS AND CHRIS LUSCRI, **DAVID HESLIN** EXAMINES THE CHALLENGES AND CHARMS OF THIS CINEMA ON THE PERIPHERIES.

**This spread:** *Grace, Who Waits Alone* (three images)

A young woman, clad in loose white fabric, stands with her back to a wall, her attention devoted to the iPhone in her hand. Everything around her is sparse: a window faces onto the peeling weatherboard of the neighbouring property, its horizontal wooden slats contrasting with the vertically panelled interior. Nothing within the frame suggests the possibility of colour; only the woman's achromatic skin definitively reveals the shot to be black-and-white.

This first, stationary, shot of *Grace, Who Waits Alone* (Georgia Temple, 2016), which lingers for over a minute, is both representative of one of the film's recurring visual motifs – detached depictions of a human body and technological device encased together in mausoleum-like interiors – and indicative of its status as an underground film. Such rigorous minimalism has its antecedents in the international film canon (the cinema of Chantal Akerman, Jean-Marie Straub and Danièle Huillet, Mark Rappaport), but it is unlikely to be found nowadays among the slate of even the most adventurous independent picture houses, let alone the multiplexes. Certainly, it's difficult to imagine a recent Australian production with any kind of theatrical release that looks like this.

But then, this is a work that exists entirely beyond the realm of the local film industry. Shot over the course of two weeks for an estimated budget of A$1500[1] and featuring only one character (the titular protagonist, played by the director herself), *Grace, Who Waits Alone* has only had sporadic showings in Australia, most notably at the 2017 Queensland Film Festival. Other viewers, including this author, were first introduced to Temple's feature in late 2018, at a single screening in a theatrette at the back of a cocktail bar in Melbourne's inner north, a venue with a maximum capacity of thirty. It is no slight on the film to acknowledge that its potential audience reach is narrow. Indeed, if ever we were to apply the adjective 'underground' to an artwork, it's hard to think of a case that could be more apt than a film like this.

What do we mean when we talk about underground film, though? For independent director and *Senses of Cinema* founder Bill Mousoulis, who organised the Melbourne screening of *Grace, Who Waits Alone* as part of a program entitled The Australian New Wave,[2] the term may be loosely applied to filmmakers 'who are actually making bold and formally inventive films' but are 'struggling to get noticed'.[3] He divides the broader Australian indie cinema scene into two streams: more 'genre-oriented' work – that is, those films that are able to achieve some exposure by slotting into the various B movie categories catered for by events such as the Melbourne Underground Film Festival (MUFF) and Monster Fest – and 'no-budget' art films, which are caught between a rock and a hard place: not trashy enough for the grindhouse circuit, but also frozen out of more highbrow platforms. These are titles that, for the most part, 'the major film festivals won't touch […] presumably because there's no funding or distribution attached to them'.[4]

Underground film, in one form or another, has a rich history in Australia. Since the earliest days of modern Australian cinema, aesthetically daring works put together on a shoestring budget have existed alongside more popular, industry-backed fare. In the 1960s, even before

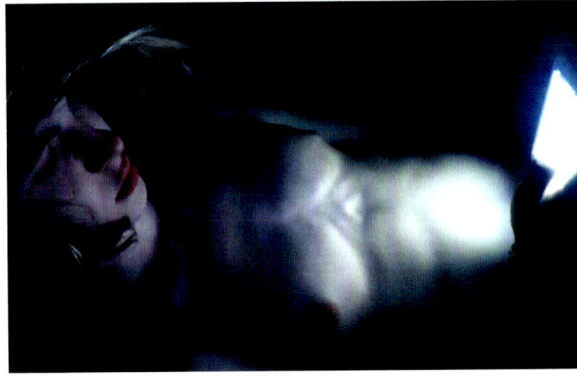

**Above, from top:** *Strange Colours*; *Je, tu, il, elle*; *Youth on the March*; *The Plastic House*

the country had a film industry to speak of, filmmakers such as Giorgio Mangiamele in Melbourne and the Ubu collective in Sydney were making work that had more in common with European new wave and avant-garde movements than anything from the much-vaunted New Australian Cinema of the following decade,[5] and Mousoulis traces this alternative canon of local cinema through the 1970s and 1980s to what he sees as a new resurgence today.[6] But it's clear that, even in comparison with the relatively niche work of overseas underground filmmakers like Akerman, Rappaport, Marcel Hanoun and Ulrike Ottinger, Australian underground films are little celebrated or even known in cinephile circles – in Australia or anywhere else. There's a grim irony that this should be the case in a country whose broader cinematic output is so often treated with derision at home;[7] it seems as if, rather than encouraging audiences to seek out alternative local creative voices, the cultural reluctance to attend industry-backed Australian films is only serving to bury their underground counterparts even more deeply.

This is not to say that radical filmmaking is completely absent from Australian screens. A few relatively experimental works have, in recent times, made their way onto more established film platforms: Amiel Courtin-Wilson's *Hail* (2011), *Ruin* (co-directed with Michael Cody, 2013) and *The Silent Eye* (2016) all received major festival exposure, while Alena Lodkina's *Strange Colours* (2017) travelled around the country

> Even in comparison with the relatively niche work of overseas underground filmmakers ... Australian underground films are little celebrated or even known in cinephile circles – in Australia or anywhere else.

to acclaim following a well-received debut in Venice. These are films that, despite their visibility and relative success, possess – in their unconventional narrative constructions and visual language – artistic sensibilities that do not appear to have been compromised by commercial imperatives, something Mousoulis describes as a fundamental quality of 'great' underground filmmaking.[8]

While it lacks the profile or budget of those films, *Grace, Who Waits Alone* is an equally sophisticated work. Over the course of a series of vignettes, nearly all shot with a stationary camera, we mostly see Grace either working in a supermarket, traipsing through an underground carpark or, most frequently, engaging in quotidian rituals at home – eating, showering, vacuuming, putting on make-up, hanging out the washing in the backyard. In a recurring juxtaposition, she is seen bandaging a gaping abdominal wound, only to, a few scenes later, wake in the morning to find her nightdress and bedsheets drenched in blood. We gather, from her frequent texting and voicemails, that her partner has recently left her, and is not responding to her many messages.

The most obvious parallels to this work can be found in Akerman's early feature *Je, tu, il, elle* (1974), a similarly austere monochrome study of a female character played by the film's director, who, for the first third of the narrative, like Grace, inhabits a sparse, solitary domestic space in the aftermath of an apparent break-up with a lover. While

Temple was already well into the production of *Grace, Who Waits Alone* when she saw that film for the first time, she does speak of the more general influence of Akerman on her filmmaking, citing *Jeanne Dielman, 23, quai du commerce, 1080 Bruxelles* (1975) and *The Meetings of Anna* (1978) as key texts in her artistic development.[9] This admiration for Akerman is clearly shared by Lodkina, who has described her as the director who 'discovered the vertical and horizontal mysteries of cinema's space-time', and – addressing theorist Roland Barthes' remarks about the exclusive *actuality* of photographs – has written that Akerman's oeuvre 'is proof that cinema can be a lived experience'.[10]

That these two new Australian underground (or, at least, in Lodkina's case, underground-adjacent) directors should share a passion for the Belgian experimental filmmaker is not particularly surprising: Akerman has been a staple of film and gender studies courses for decades.[11] But what, then, can we make of the near-complete absence of anything comparable to her work in the visible Australian film industry, either in terms of the radicalism of her specific aesthetics or, more generally, her bold experiments with form? It is important not to overstate the case here: European underground filmmakers, by and large, have faced plenty of struggles on their own for funding and recognition. But there is a distinction between *niche* and *invisible*, and the fact that *Grace, Who Waits Alone* remains undistributed and mostly unknown to Australian cinephiles over two years since its completion indicates that the contemporary industry has little space for anything so aesthetically radical.

For Temple, this is not a wholly unwelcome state of affairs. While she observes that 'it's pretty clear we have a pretty massive problem as an industry' and doesn't believe that industry bodies' genre focus 'results in better films', she expresses a willingness to continue to remain outside the realm of the mainstream Australian film industry for the time being: 'I would much rather try to make, basically, no-budget films and really hone my skills before I even start to think about funding.'[12] Not all filmmakers working outside the establishment are quite as willing to make peace with this dynamic, however. Mike Retter, director of *Youth on the March* (2017),[13] has claimed in an interview that the script for his film (which he developed with fellow independent filmmaker Allison Chhorn) was rejected for funding on the grounds of 'sexism'.[14] Retter's diagnosis of the malaise surrounding mainstream Australian film is blunt: a 'university elite point of view that does not reflect the rest of society', which, he argues, forms part of a broader arts culture that is 'monolithic, stagnant, safe and politically correct'.[15]

For nearly two decades, the most visible claim to the mantle of underground cinema in Australia has been the aforementioned MUFF, founded in 2000 by filmmaker Richard Wolstencroft after his feature *Pearls Before Swine* (1999) was rejected by the Melbourne International Film Festival.[16] While the event has often attracted approbation for its controversial programming choices and Wolstencroft's own far-right political sympathies,[17] it provides an instance of a very different conceptualisation of the term 'underground', identifying itself far less with experimental or aesthetically radical filmmaking than with grindhouse cinema and outré political opinion. In his excoriating contemporaneous review of *Pearls Before Swine*, critic Adrian Martin described the festival as representing something that 'has very little to do with radically queer cinema, experimental art or authentically anarchist politics', describing the films in the program as, instead, 'ultra-low budget genre exercises' and 'exploitation rather than underground fare'.[18]

While it seemed at one time to have derived at least some cache from its branding – along with a deeper cultural desire to foster a cinema outside established channels – MUFF has always been dominated by, if not quite its founder's self-proclaimed 'transcendental fascism',[19] then certainly a form of aggressive libertarianism. In some ways, MUFF might be seen as a precursor to the emergence of the (particularly US) alt-right's transgressive 'underground' online subculture that has flourished over the last decade[20] and that has, while remaining broadly despised, derived self-declared mainstream legitimacy from the election of its political poster boy Donald Trump as US President in 2016.[21] For MUFF, this inversion of the concept of 'underground' was perhaps finally solidified last year; its program featured a pro-Trump propaganda documentary directed by none other than former White House chief strategist Steve Bannon.[22]

None of this is to suggest, of course, that politics ought to have no place in underground filmmaking. Chris Luscri – who executive-produced *Youth on the March*, is serving as co-producer on Courtin-Wilson's upcoming film *The Empyrean* and has curated or co-curated a range of independent film programs – argues for the importance of underground works that contain an intersection of minority voices: both 'minority as it pertains to class and also to film form, not merely the "top layer" (identity politics) that dominates a lot of leftist-liberalist discourse'. In his view, 'the best films being made […] in this country at the moment are by filmmakers whose "minority status" sits across all three of those spheres'.[23]

Political motivations were also not far away from the filming of *Grace, Who Waits Alone*, particularly regarding Temple's decision to play the lead role: '[Acting] felt like me pushing myself to expose but also just to get rid of [concerns] that feel damaging to myself, as someone who wants to do art,' she explains, describing the film as an attempt 'to not allow those preoccupations to remain – because I feel like there are a lot of behaviours or concerns I hold because of conditioning'. She continues:

*That act of putting oneself on screen in that kind of more open and unguarded way and then showing it to people is really terrifying. It does really just rid you of a lot of that. It's really cathartic to do […] And maybe that's why it's common for a lot of female artists to want to do that, especially early on in their careers.*[24]

One recent film that effectively synthesises Luscri's 'spheres' is Chhorn's mid-length work *The Plastic House* (2018), a project that mirrors *Grace, Who Waits Alone*'s minimalism, intimacy and claustrophobia but adds a layer of documentary realism by depicting the director's family members at work in an Adelaide greenhouse. Whereas, in Temple's film, dialogue is nearly entirely confined to the director's intermittent poetic voiceover, in Chhorn's, the only voices we hear are her parents and uncle occasionally speaking in English-subtitled Khmer. In both films, repetitive manual labour is juxtaposed with physical and psychological isolation; in *The Plastic House*, that loneliness is derived from the director's imaginative representation of what her life might be like after her parents' death, a loneliness that she explicitly compares to the times she has been left in Australia to fend for herself without them.[25]

**Above:** *Grace, Who Waits Alone*

The fact that *Grace, Who Waits Alone* remains undistributed and mostly unknown to Australian cinephiles over two years since its completion indicates that the contemporary industry has little space for anything so aesthetically radical.

Perhaps, then, the loneliness that Chhorn and Temple allow themselves to navigate in their respective films serves as an apt metaphor for underground filmmaking in Australia. These are films that might not quite fill a thirty-seat makeshift cinema in Melbourne's inner north, and it's highly likely that they will remain undistributed, unavailable to all but a lucky few. But in their intimacy and careful composition, even with all of the technical and budgetary limitations their creators have had to contend with, they are as cinematically pure as any Palme d'Or winner or massive international co-production, and they speak a language as radical as the best of their underground antecedents. Don't let anyone tell you that artistically ambitious Australian cinema is dead – you just have to know where to find it.

*David Heslin is editor of* Screen Education *and subeditor of* Metro, *and also edits and writes for online film journal* Senses of Cinema. *He has written articles on politics and ethics for* Overland, The National Times *and* New Matilda. **m**

Endnotes

1. Georgia Temple, video interview with author, 3 February 2019.
2. See Bill Mousoulis, 'The Australian New Wave at Long Play, Melbourne, Nov 2018', *Pure Shit: Australian Cinema*, 31 October 2018, <http://www.pureshitauscinema.com/new_wave_lp_18.html>, accessed 5 March 2019.
3. Bill Mousoulis, email interview with author, 3 March 2019.
4. ibid.
5. See Alex Gerbaz, 'The Legacy of the Experimental Film and Television Fund, 1970–78', paper presented at the National Archives of Australia, Canberra, 13 October 2009, available at <http://www.naa.gov.au/collection/publications/papers-and-podcasts/social-history/gerbax-transcript.aspx>, accessed 5 March 2019.
6. For a curated catalogue of some of these films, see Bill Mousoulis, 'Online Indie Australian Cinema', *Pure Shit: Australian Cinema*, <http://www.pureshitauscinema.com/online_cinema.html>, accessed 5 March 2019.
7. See Steve Dow, 'What's Wrong with Australian Cinema?', *The Guardian*, 26 October 2014, <https://www.theguardian.com/film/2014/oct/26/australian-film-australian-audiences>, accessed 5 March 2019.
8. Mousoulis, email interview with author, op. cit.
9. Temple, op. cit.
10. Alena Lodkina, 'Chantal Akerman and the Possibility of Intimacy in Film', *4:3*, 3 October 2016, <https://fourthreefilm.com/2016/10/chantal-akerman-and-the-possibility-of-intimacy-in-film/>, accessed 5 March 2019.
11. See Cristina Álvarez López & Adrian Martin, 'Chantal Akerman: A Primer', *Sight & Sound*, vol. 25, no. 2, February 2015, available at <https://www.bfi.org.uk/news-opinion/sight-sound-magazine/features/chantal-akerman-primer>, accessed 5 March 2019.
12. Temple, op. cit.
13. This film is covered in an earlier issue of *Metro*; see Anthony Nocera, 'Rebel on the Screen: Mike Retter on *Youth on the March*', *Metro*, no. 197, 2018, pp. 28–33.
14. Mike Retter, quoted in Malcolm Sutton, 'Political Correctness "Stifling Australian Cinema" as Indie Filmmakers Rebound in Adelaide', *ABC News*, 24 March 2018, <https://www.abc.net.au/news/2018-03-24/political-correctness-stifling-australian-cinema-filmmaker-says/9571006>, accessed 5 March 2019.
15. ibid.
16. Michelle Griffin, 'Bad Reputation', *The Age*, 26 June 2004, <https://www.theage.com.au/entertainment/movies/bad-reputation-20040626-gdy3sw.html>, accessed 5 March 2019.
17. See Tom Clift, 'Melbourne's [sic] Underground Film Festival Director Under Fire over a Homophobic Facebook Rant', *Junkee*, 18 November 2017, <https://junkee.com/richard-wolstencroft-homophobic-post/135573>, accessed 5 March 2019.
18. Adrian Martin, 'Pearls Before Swine', *Film Critic: Adrian Martin*, July 2000, <http://filmcritic.com.au/reviews/p/pearls_before_swine.html>, accessed 2 March 2019.
19. See Gerard Henderson, 'Intellectual Garbage, by David Irving', *The Age*, 8 July 2003, <https://www.theage.com.au/opinion/intellectual-garbage-by-david-irving-20030708-gdw0bg.html>, accessed 5 March 2019.
20. A subculture whose epicentre, online bulletin board 4chan, has been aptly described by Irish non-fiction writer Angela Nagle as 'the lowest form of a vacuous, faux ironic, sniggering moral imbecilism'; see Nagle, 'Paleocons for Porn', *Jacobin*, 22 February 2017, <https://www.jacobinmag.com/2017/02/paleocons-for-porn>, accessed 5 March 2019.
21. See Nicky Woolf, 'The "Alt-right" Thrives in Opposition. What Happens Now It's the Establishment?', *The Guardian*, 15 November 2016, <https://www.theguardian.com/us-news/2016/nov/15/alt-right-victory-donald-trump-mainstream-what-next>, accessed 5 March 2019.
22. See 'The Melbourne Underground Film Festival Returns for Its 19th Year', *Forté*, 18 October 2018, <http://fortemag.com.au/?p=42434>, accessed 5 March 2019.
23. Chris Luscri, Facebook Messenger exchange with author, 21 February 2019.
24. Temple, op. cit.
25. Allison Chhorn, '*The Plastic House*: Director's Statement', *Pure Shit: Australian Cinema*, 16 November 2018, <http://www.pureshitauscinema.com/features/plastic_house.html>, accessed 5 March 2019.

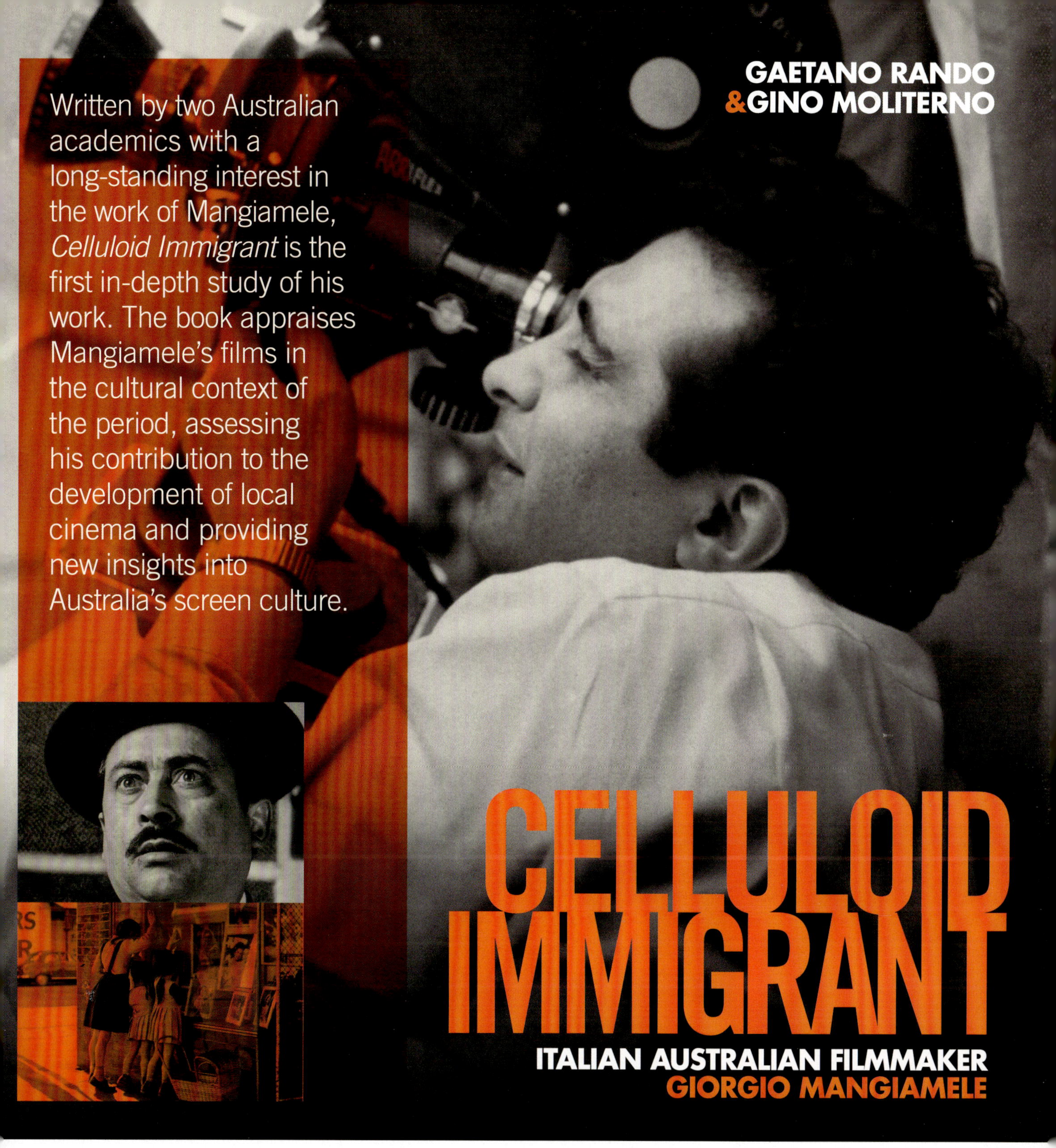

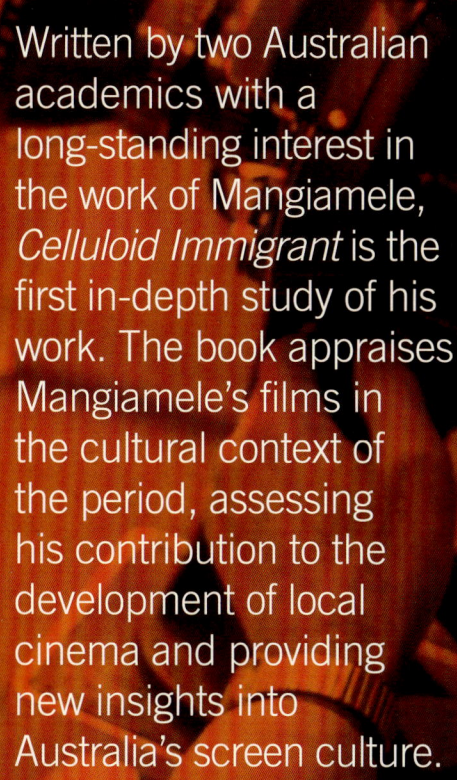

**GAETANO RANDO & GINO MOLITERNO**

Written by two Australian academics with a long-standing interest in the work of Mangiamele, *Celluloid Immigrant* is the first in-depth study of his work. The book appraises Mangiamele's films in the cultural context of the period, assessing his contribution to the development of local cinema and providing new insights into Australia's screen culture.

# CELLULOID IMMIGRANT

**ITALIAN AUSTRALIAN FILMMAKER**
**GIORGIO MANGIAMELE**

---

## CELLULOID IMMIGRANT ORDER FORM

☐ Please send me 1 copy of *Celluloid Immigrant: Italian Australian Filmmaker Giorgio Mangiamele* for $39.95. **Price includes Australia-wide shipping for a single copy.**
To combine shipping on multiple copies, or for international orders, please order online at The Education Shop – http://www.theeducationshop.com.au

Given name Surname Organisation

Mailing address State Postcode

Telephone (day) Fax Email

☐ I enclose purchase order number _____ ☐ I enclose a cheque / money order (cheques / money orders are to be made payable to ATOM).

Charge my: ☐ Bankcard ☐ Mastercard ☐ Visa ☐ Amex ☐ Diners Club Card number: ☐☐☐☐ ☐☐☐☐ ☐☐☐☐ ☐☐☐☐ Expiry date: ☐☐/☐☐

Cardholder name Signature

**A tax invoice will be issued upon receipt of your order. Prices include GST.** ATOM's ABN: 84 393 760 027

**FAX** (+61 3) 9537 2325 **TEL** (+61 3) 9525 5302
**EMAIL** editor@atom.org.au **POST** ATOM, PO Box 2040 St Kilda West, VIC 3182 Australia
http://www.theeducationshop.com.au
http://www.metromagazine.com.au

SUPPORTED BY

It is hard to believe that *Proof* was director Jocelyn Moorhouse's first feature, given its subtle, sophisticated texture as it deals with such tantalising issues. Those who admired her dexterous 2015 film, *The Dressmaker*, may well be interested in rediscovering the earlier work: in both, she demands serious attention from viewers, but, as Rose Lucas' very perceptive and admirably detailed study makes clear, such attention is amply rewarded. Moorhouse went on to film in the US, but arguably her first and latest films show her at her provocative best, and Lucas makes a brilliant case for re-evaluating *Proof*.

Brian McFarlane, Series Editor

**This spread, L–R:** Martin (Hugo Weaving); Andy (Russell Crowe), whom Martin befriends, among photos of him taken by his housekeeper

THE NFSA RESTORES COLLECTION

PART 44

# Proof

**ROSE LUCAS**

*The screen was lit with Weaving, Geneviève Picot, and an unknown*
    *Russell Crowe.*
*We agreed on how good* Proof *was and that now*
*Australia had at least three outstanding women directors, that*
    *Jocelyn Moorhouse*
*was on a par with Gillian Armstrong and Jane Campion.*

– Mark Rudman[1]

When Jocelyn Moorhouse released *Proof* as her debut film in 1991, its success marked an exciting new direction for Australian cinema. This was an intriguing narrative, clearly situated in a very recognisable urban Melbourne milieu of 1990, which was playing with the definitions and structure of genre.

It was also clearly driven by some serious philosophical questions regarding the relationship between the visual image and epistemology – how we might 'see' and know the world and our position within it. In addition, it provided an engaging study of human behaviour through a focus on an intense triangle of characters. As Mark Rudman's poem 'I Think About Australia Endlessly' suggests, *Proof* was instantly part of a familiar Australian cultural fabric, giving us all – at home and abroad – a new feeling of pride and understanding about how we fit into the world.

**MAIN CAST**
**Martin** Hugo Weaving
**Celia** Geneviève Picot
**Andy** Russell Crowe
**Mother** Heather Mitchell
**Young Martin** Jeffrey Walker

**PRINCIPAL CREDITS**
**Year of release** 1991
**Length** 90 mins
**Writer/Director**
Jocelyn Moorhouse
**Producer** Lynda House
**1st Assistant Director**
Tony Mahood

**Director of Photography**
Martin McGrath
**Sound Recordist** Lloyd Carrick
**Production Designer**
Patrick Reardon
**Editor** Ken Sallows
**Music** Not Drowning, Waving

## The narrative

*In 1986 someone told me that they had met a blind photographer. At the time I didn't think to ask why a blind person would take photographs, but I soon found the unknown answer haunted me. I'm fascinated by blindness and how blind people cope with not having visual knowledge – the everyday confirmations of 'what is' – that I take for granted. Blind people have to place their faith in others. I wanted to tell the story of a man who couldn't.*[2]

As Moorhouse has indicated in her director's note, the story of *Proof* is motivated by a curiosity both about how a blind man might use photography to engage with the world and about the nature of interpersonal relationships in general. While blindness might constitute an extreme case, Moorhouse's film explores how we might exercise control over ourselves and both trust in and influence other people – and the varieties of factors that determine that influence.

*Proof* focuses on the character of Martin (Hugo Weaving). Blind from birth, Martin now lives in his grandmother's house in urban Melbourne, alone except for his housekeeper, Celia (Geneviève Picot), who is in an obsessive and tortured state of unrequited love for him. Martin, however, is misanthropically withdrawn from the world, paranoiacally convinced that others

**Above, left:** Martin's housekeeper, Celia (Geneviève Picot), with his dog Bill  **This spread, all other images:** Andy and Martin

cannot be trusted; Celia becomes an object of this bitterness and mistrust, while also feeding it through her own perverse efforts to make Martin reliant on her.

The narrative in the present is intercut at a number of points by images or memories from Martin's childhood, powerfully suggesting the influence of the past on where Martin now finds himself. As a child (played by Jeffrey Walker), alone with his mother (Heather Mitchell), he listens to her describe the world outside his window – the seasons, the light, the gardener raking leaves. In these episodes, we see the origins of Martin's distrust: Was his mother telling him the truth about what was visible out in the world? Was there really a gardener? Could Martin trust his own senses? Could his mother be trusted, or was she lying to him – either 'because she could', as he accuses her, or because she was ashamed at having a blind child? As she pushes away his exploring fingers as they attempt to 'read' her hair, face and chest, telling him that it's 'rude', Martin is crushed, seeing it as another sign of his unworthiness and unloveability. Even when his mother grows ill and tells him she will die soon, he interprets it as further evidence that she wants to get away from him.

The film begins with a random narrative 'collision', as Martin walks with his cane and a bag of shopping down recognisably Melbourne streets and alleys, entirely careless of whom he bumps into. This combination of disregard and the vulnerability of his sightless condition brings him literally into the path of a young dishwasher at an Italian restaurant, Andy (Russell Crowe), when Martin knocks over some fruit crates and inadvertently crushes the stray cat Andy has been feeding. When Martin returns to the restaurant for an unsuccessful meal that evening, Andy confronts him about the cat, which he thinks is dead; examining the cat in the rubbish bin, Martin demonstrates a degree of knowing that exceeds simple seeing when he realises it is still alive. He and Andy then take it to the vet. While waiting there, Martin takes photos of Andy and the cat, as well as of the other pet owners in the waiting room – photos that we see as often off-centre, with key elements cut off. The next day, at the restaurant, Martin asks Andy to describe the photos – no more than ten words – which he then labels in braille. Quizzed by Andy, Martin explains that this is a way of providing himself with proof that a situation he has experienced was the same as the situation that others saw – proof of what really happened. Martin is drawn to Andy's straightforward and friendly style, and a tentative friendship with someone he feels he can trust begins.

The connection between Andy and Martin is consolidated during a visit to a drive-in, where Andy has the challenging task of describing the moving image of a film – a slasher/thriller. This is the film's most bizarre and comic scene, providing some light-hearted ballast against the intensity of much of the drama. When Martin – after 'feeling' his way across the contents of Andy's car, including his packet of condoms – is set upon by the thugs in a nearby vehicle, Andy swings into action to defend him. As the two speed away, they are pursued by police; the episode ends in humour, however, as Martin claims to have been 'blinded', and both end up in fits of laughter.

We know that their friendship is continuing to develop because at this stage we are given access to Celia's point of view; as she sneaks a look at Martin's developed photos – and as we look over her shoulder while she does so – she is enraged and worried to see a man's image emerging from the chopped fragments of Martin's photography. As she lays out the photos in a kind of cubist puzzle, we see what she sees: Andy at the centre of Martin's attention and 'gaze'. Celia intensifies her efforts to become the object of Martin's interest; having taken a photo of him on the toilet, she uses it to blackmail him into going out with her. She takes him to a classical-music concert, where Martin becomes profoundly moved by the experience of listening, as Celia is by Martin's openness to the experience. The evening ends with them back at Celia's house, where, surrounded by walls filled with photos of Martin that he is not aware of, Celia initiates a sexual encounter. Drawn in at first, Martin then fights to extricate himself from Celia, literally running away from her and out of the house, zip still undone.

Unable to secure Martin's love, Celia determines to poison his growing attachment to Andy by drawing the younger man into a web of sexual complication with her, which would force him to 'choose' between her and Martin and to compromise his description of a photo in order to protect her. When Martin discovers the couple's duplicity as they make love in his bed and on his couch, he throws them both out. While Andy initially naively confesses to Martin that he and Celia are 'in love', by the time she takes him back to her home and he sees the number of photos of Martin, he realises that he has been used by Celia to hurt Martin.

The film concludes somewhat open-endedly with Andy telling Martin that 'everyone lies, just not all the time'. Martin decides to show Andy his first, and 'most important', photograph, which Andy describes as being of a gardener raking leaves, looking 'old and kind'. This description confirms Martin's dawning understanding that perhaps his mother didn't lie to him, and that perhaps it's impossible to know absolutely – that trust is a more complex, less black-and-white form of relationship than simply looking for proof that the other person has, or hasn't, lied. The

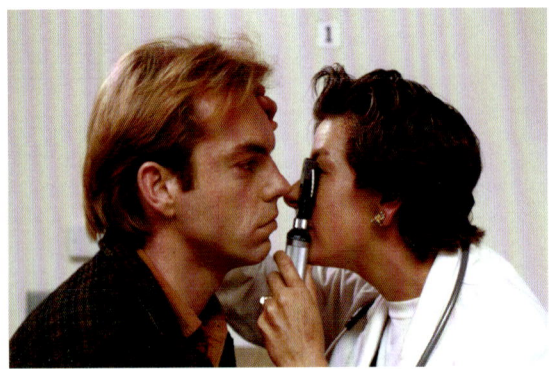

**Above, from top:** Martin has his eyes checked by a doctor (Belinda Davey); Martin and the cemetery caretaker (Cliff Ellen)

final scene returns us to the image of Martin as a boy, still inside in front of the window, but now with a sunny day instead of rain; in this tentatively positive scene, the child Martin is now putting his hand up to the light he cannot see, reaching out rather than closing down. It's an ambiguous image, but would seem to imply a new kind of hopefulness for Martin, a reanimated desire to touch the world outside himself – to reach out even though vulnerability and the lack of certainty remain.

## Production history

*Proof* was Jocelyn Moorhouse's debut feature film. A graduate of the Australian Film Television and Radio School (AFTRS) in 1984 ('Same year as Jane Campion. In case you were going to ask'[3]), Moorhouse had already worked in network television as both script writer and editor, with her 1986 short film *The Siege of Barton's Bathroom* made into a twelve-part 1988 TV series.[4] After the success of *Proof*, she collaborated with her filmmaker husband, PJ Hogan, on what was to become his hugely successful *Muriel's Wedding* (1994) – which she co-produced – and took further opportunities to direct in the US, on mainstream projects such as *How to Make an American Quilt* (1995) and *A Thousand Acres* (1997). Somewhat surprisingly, her next film as director, *The Dressmaker*, had to wait until 2017 and her return to Australia.

As the director herself has explained, the idea for *Proof* had originated some years previously, after she learnt of a blind photographer and found herself 'interested in characters that were a little isolated from the rest of the world … who have a different perception of reality'.[5] Moorhouse's interest in the point of view of the outsider, or the periphery – ironically, here, in terms of what can be perceived and understood from a position of sightlessness in such a vision-centric world, especially that of the cinema – is what gives *Proof* both its eccentricity and its acuity. As Mary Anne Reid recounts, Moorhouse first developed the film as a fifty-minute script, but funders Film Victoria and the Australian Film Commission (AFC) rejected it, encouraging her to instead develop it into a full-length feature.[6] Finally, with Moorhouse as scriptwriter and director and Lynda House as producer, the AFC provided the project with A$800,000, and Film Victoria A$300,000; with a total budget of A$1.1 million, *Proof* was, as Picot put it, 'a very, very low budget film […] and it was an independent, alternative, fringe element film […] it didn't fit, it wasn't like any of the other films being made at the time because of its subject matter'.[7] In 2016, the film was restored, courtesy of both the National Film and Sound Archive of Australia and crowdfunding,[8] and was screened at the Melbourne International Film Festival, marking a long-overdue acknowledgement and reappraisal of this important Australian film.

## Reception

Although not initially selected to screen in competition or as part of the Un Certain Regard section at Cannes, *Proof* premiered at the 1991 festival in the coveted spot of opening the Directors' Fortnight, where it was very well received by audiences and critics, and was runner-up for the Caméra d'Or.[9] This initial enthusiastic reception by the European film scene launched *Proof* on a path to success; while, in many ways, it could be understood as an 'Australian' film, it also had things to say to international audiences. The imprimatur of success at Cannes was no doubt instrumental in setting the stage for audiences, both at home and abroad, to take the film seriously, contributing to its reception as an independent or arthouse film.

It was then received with thunderous applause at the Sydney and Melbourne film festivals, followed by a release by Village Roadshow in August in Melbourne arthouse cinemas, where it enjoyed the support of audiences and critics. As it continued on the festival circuit, *Proof* made an ongoing impact, winning prizes in São Paulo, Tokyo and Chicago. A film that was engaging and intriguing, it clearly spoke in particular to arthouse and film-festival audiences looking for that blend of intelligence and entertainment. The film grossed A$2.1 million domestically at the box office, together with A$850,000 in rental returns to the distributor. As Roadshow managing director Alan Finney noted, this was well above expectation; comparing it to *Fried Green Tomatoes* (Jon Avnet, 1991), *Truly Madly Deeply* (Anthony Minghella, 1990) and *My Left Foot* (Jim Sheridan, 1989), he commented, '*Proof*'s at the top of that range of specialist product [in terms of domestic income], which I think is terrific.'[10]

While some critics were uncertain about the film, describing it as '[i]ntelligent but cold'[11] or 'slight in its spitefulness, and shallow in its "artiness"',[12] the vast majority of critics were extremely positive about *Proof*. *The New York Times*' Janet Maslin described it as a 'darkly clever Australian drama focusing on brilliant, wickedly manipulative characters';[13] David Stratton, in *The Weekend Australian*, claimed that the film should receive domestic acclaim as a 'unique approach to familiar cinema themes of male bonding, friendship and betrayal;'[14] *The Sydney Morning Herald*'s Lynden Barber wrote that the film is 'so startlingly fresh and clever that

[it] is hard to believe it is the feature debut of [...] Jocelyn Moorhouse'.[15] This very positive reception of the film was reinforced by the Australian Film Institute's awards in October 1991 – only seven weeks into *Proof*'s Australian screening season – where, up against films such as *Spotswood* (Mark Joffe, 1992), *Dingo* (Rolf de Heer, 1991), *Death in Brunswick* (John Ruane, 1990), the film scooped the pool with seven awards: Best Film, Best Actor (Weaving), Best Supporting Actor (Crowe), Best Editing (Ken Sallows), General Members Prize for Excellence (House), Best Director and Best Screenplay. As Barber had commented, *Proof* seemed to offer evidence of a new Australian film renaissance.[16]

Unfortunately, the film was not as successful internationally, grossing only A$105,000 in the UK, A$203,000 in the US and A$85,000 in France. As Fran Lanigan, the film's international sales agent from Kim Lewis Marketing, suggested, this may have been because 'it's a peculiarly Australian film. Maybe distributors didn't know how to promote it.'[17] House herself concurred with Lanigan, pointing out that overseas distributors released the film in mainstream cinemas simultaneously, rather than letting it grow by reputation in smaller venues, as had occurred in Australia. In addition, unfortunately, the film's release in the UK coincided with an Irish Republican Army bombing, and in the US with the Los Angeles riots – during which one of the cinemas showing the film was burnt down.[18]

## Film structure and genre

Critics have variously described *Proof* as belonging in a number of genre categories: 'art house', a 'romantic melodrama with a subtext of fear, jealousy',[19] a 'dark love story [... or] thriller',[20] an 'exploration of male bonding' (with 'homoerotic' undertones)[21] or an 'odd couple bromance [... that becomes] a story about temptation, betrayal and ultimately forgiveness'.[22] It could be seen explicitly as an Australian film, a 'psychodrama',[23] a 'black comedy'[24] or a work that foregrounds issues of blindness and visuality in the cinema and/or in experiences of physical disability.[25]

Perhaps the point here is that one of the really interesting things about Moorhouse's film is that it both touches on a number of these genre structures and expectations and also avoids being constrained by them. As an explicitly 'Melbourne' film, it evokes ideas of Australianness, and exists in explicit dialogue with earlier films about Australian history and identity. As Tom O'Regan puts it, *Proof* can be seen in the category of 'urban edge', with a 'group of Melbourne films focussing on that city's underbelly'.[26] Not concerned with the comparative safety of period dramas or literary adaptations (as had characterised earlier phases of the Australian film revival), *Proof* instead embodies what Garry Gillard describes in *Screen Education* as the 'quirkiness' that characterises so many examples of 1990s Australian cinema – a privileging of the '*un*expected, *un*characteristic'[27] subverting our expectations about what it means to be Australian, to be male or female, to be human in a social context. To Gillard, this tendency to unseat expectations has manifested across a range of Australian films, culminating in the cinema of the 1990s – *The Adventures of Priscilla, Queen of the Desert* (Stephan Elliott, 1994), *Bad Boy Bubby* (de Heer, 1993), *Sweetie* (Jane Campion, 1989), *The Castle* (Rob Sitch, 1997) and, perhaps especially, *Muriel's Wedding* – which reflects a stylistic trend of obliqueness, combining humour, irreverence and the unexpected. Perhaps most of all, *Proof* should be understood as an exploration of the human condition. As House puts it, 'On the surface you might think it is an exclusive arty-type production, but when you see the film you realise that it is something that affects everybody. It explores the need to trust and love and have friendships in life.'[28]

In many ways, the film can be read as an intense three-handed drama; the narrative revolves around the central character of Martin, but it is Martin as he operates in close and complicated relationship with the other two people in his limited orbit: Celia and Andy. The psychological nature of the drama – Martin's legacy of ambivalence toward his dead mother, which is played out again in relation to Celia; his hyper-anxieties about trusting a world he is so dependent on; the subcurrents of cross-relationships and agendas between Celia and Andy and Martin – is played out within the relative claustrophobia of largely interior scenes. In the cluttered mise en scène of Martin's home, we become aware of the very narrow divide between what is familiar and safe and what is confining.

Only in the scenes in the park, where Martin, with his dog Bill – interestingly, a companion animal, but not a guide dog – goes to take photographs, do we glimpse the possibilities of new formulations, new ways of seeing. Feeling the light, sensorily aware of leaves and movement, Martin appears freer, even joyful. However, this experience is repeatedly sabotaged by Celia's interferences and, ultimately, by Andy's compromises. As many critics have noted, this scene in the park is reminiscent of Michelangelo Antonioni's famous

> *Proof* is, paradoxically, also a film about how we see and grasp the world ... As such, it becomes very much a film about film, an exploration – via the technology of visual images, moving and still – of what the visual can bring into the orbit of our understanding.

*Blow-Up* (1966), which also poses questions about the relationship between the photographic image and a desire to find the 'answer', or the truth – a kind of epistemological puzzle. As Geoff Mayer has outlined, the multiple shots in *Proof*'s park sequence reflect the flicking points of view;[29] we move from Martin's 'perspective' to Celia's, to Andy's, to even the dog's, as the control of the scene is fractured. As the camerawork embodies, this kind of literalised 'seeing' is not about 'proof' or veracity so much as it is about having control, or a way of telling the dominant story. According to *Film Comment*'s Kathleen Murphy, it is during this scene that previous assumptions are painfully exposed, yet also finally lead to what she has described as Martin's 'epiphany': 'seeing is not always believing, and, though truth and beauty may be accessible in the perfect stasis of Keats' Grecian urn, real life rarely delivers up such pristine proofs'.[30]

A film about a blind photographer, *Proof* is, paradoxically, also a film about how we see and grasp the world. Just as Shakespeare explored the relationship between physical blindness and the possibilities of emotional or intellectual insight in *King Lear*, so too does Moorhouse's film examine the simple equation that seeing provides some kind of unmediated access to truth. As such, it becomes very much a film about film, an exploration – via the technology of visual images, moving and still – of what the visual can bring into the orbit of our understanding as well as where its limitations might lie. In this sense, the style of the film reflects that element of self-reflexivity, of a film reflecting on the business of seeing and the power relations it inevitably ushers in. This is signalled in the opening credits, when we see a series of snapshots of what we later learn are Martin's photos – images whose focal points are off-centre, in which elements we might have thought were central are rendered partial or peripheral. As Karl Quinn has commented about the film, 'Framing is […] a central metaphor: how we frame the world determines what we can know of and about it.'[31] We see this again as Celia 'discovers' the character of Andy through the fragments of Martin's photography, creating a collage of Martin's 'point of view'. The person behind the camera, making decisions about composition and framing is, as Laura Mulvey has long put it, the one in charge of shaping the gaze of the viewer.[32] In effect, by 'stealing' Martin's point of view, Celia, who photographs Martin herself, perceives his attraction to Andy through his perspective; if she can't draw Martin's gaze to herself, Celia decides instead to become the looker and to hijack Andy's reciprocal gaze.

The fabric of the film's mise en scène is heightened by the soundtrack. Not only does it include aspects of urban life – the city trams rattling past, overlapping voices and conversations, the tapping of Martin's cane on footpaths – but the non-diegetic sounds, produced by Melbourne band Not Drowning, Waving, also add a very contemporary, sometimes jarring, sometimes rhythmic, element to the narrative. With Martin paralysed by his past – the psychodynamics of the child who felt betrayed and deserted by his mother; the fussy, aged decor of his grandmother's house – the music provides a subliminal recontextualisation into a present moment, semiotically embodying a challenge to him to experience the world in new ways. Martin, who, it is implied, makes a living by writing music reviews, is open to the emotional and aesthetic charge of the classical music he hears at the concert with Celia; undistracted by sight, it is as though he experiences the fullest impact of that music as artform. Elsewhere, the Not Drowning, Waving soundtrack enacts the exciting and disruptive newness of his relationship with Andy, which challenges him to think about what more there might be in his world to experience, beyond the safety of what is already known. As Diana Sandars has argued in *Senses of Cinema*, it 'provides a [visceral] counterpoint to the images of entrapment that codes Martin and Celia's worlds'.[33]

## Key themes

There are a number of key, interlocking themes threaded throughout *Proof*, many of which circle around the central questions of how we might perceive, interpret and function in the world. In this philosophical sense, with its central protagonist being a blind photographer, the film embodies what Murphy has described as a 'blackly humorous exercise in epistemology'.[34]

This philosophical enquiry is explored primarily through the focus on visuality. This includes a number of modes: physical sight, with all its advantages and limitations; insight into self and the complex machinations of other people; the static visual image of the photograph and what it suggests about the containing, preserving or reactivating aspects of memory and knowing; as well as a reflexive view of cinema itself, a visual medium, thereby appearing to offer a metanarrative, a privileged form of seeing that makes sense of the rest. On one level, it is merely a matter of narrative complexity that Martin is blind; however, on another, it can be read as metaphorical. Moorhouse seems to be interested not only in the discrete phenomenon of how a person without sight might engage with the world and the sighted people within it, but also in using this condition as a trope for thinking about how sight and its apparatuses – eyesight, film, photography, etc. – can be understood as offering a particular access to truth and knowledge. Martin fears that his lack of sight leaves him fatally flawed – pathetically reliant on others to tell him what there is to be seen – and, therefore, he is constantly looking for ways to verify, to prove, that his experience correlates accurately with something that is actually there. Or, conversely, to prove the point that others are untrustworthy.

Commenting on Martin's use of photography, Dana Anderson draws attention to the way in which the visual image can seem to provide an unmediated access to ideas of truth – which is why Martin is so desperately dependent on others to provide him with the 'correct' interpretation of the images he takes:

*Martin needs people to describe the photographs so he can reify his other sense impressions, and it's clear that his desire to photograph objects comes not so much out of a need to see, as to be able to use sight to define existence or to prove, through the social interaction of the process of description, that what seems to exist is really present in the world.*[35]

Not only is this a central narrative component of how we understand the character of Martin, but it also reveals something of the role that the visual image – photograph, film, memory – plays in a more universal search for truth and reliable interpretations of the world. Using what he describes as an 'ethics of experiencing otherness', Bhaskar Sarkar examines how, in *Proof*, 'blindness put[s] pressure on the very notion of visuality, revealing the limits of its normative conceptions and stretching it beyond these limits'.[36] Also writing explicitly about *Proof*, Peggy Kamuf argues that it

*uses visual technology and technique to show the jealous search for truth operating in the blind relay between sense perception and its necessary prostheses or supplements. [The film] shows […] the blindness with which one sees and which all the technological supplements imaginable cannot fully correct or overcome.*[37]

Sight will never give us all the information we need to have, because 'truth' will always be endlessly elusive and multifaceted.

In this sense, Moorhouse has devised a film about the possibilities and limitations of filmmaking itself – about how seeing can certainly provide us with a particular set of sensory information, but also how, as Kamuf describes, it can never entirely close the gap between self and world. The visual image is, thus, a kind of talisman we hold on to, something we imagine gives us a better or special chance of showing us the world and its truths. As such, the visual image can also become a 'fetish', a way of attempting to 'fossilise' the past, as Sandars puts it.[38] However, like the teller of any story, the image can never be an entirely reliable narrator, and will always be susceptible to multiple extraneous factors – not the least of which being the many motivations of human actors. As Andy tells Martin in the film's concluding scene, the fact that people sometimes lie is no reason not to trust them; in other words, there is no simple equation between seeing and truth, and truth itself is, in fact, far more shifting and open to interpretation than Martin had at first thought. Friendship and connection have to move beyond the 'jealous search for truth' and, instead, take their chances on trust. As Moorhouse herself comments, Martin has 'learnt from Andy that faith and trust aren't about finding a method of proof. You can never have proof of those things [...] You have to decide to view the world in a more positive way'.[39]

While *Proof* is clearly driven by some of these serious intellectual questions, it is by no means merely animated theory. The film is also a captivating narrative study in human behaviour and relationships; through the drama involving Martin, Celia and Andy, it poses questions about why all of us do and feel as we do. As a result of the interspersed juxtaposing of Martin's past and his present, we see the ways in which his current anxieties and mistrust of others have their origins in his fraught, then lost, relationship with his mother. Even his retreat from the offering of Celia's 'extraordinary breasts' echoes the reprimand of being 'rude' for wanting to touch – and therefore 'see' – his mother's breasts as a child. In this sense, *Proof* is a psychological puzzle, claiming our fascination as we try to assemble the pieces of motivation and response.

The film is concerned with human relationships in their various modes and roles. This can be seen in the business of being male and female and what the nature of relationships between the two might be. Martin's intense anxieties and mistrust mean that he keeps Celia at a distance, tormenting her in order to avoid becoming the object of her pity; according to Moorhouse, Martin 'keeps [his mother] alive by hating her'[40] – and the same could be said of his relationship with Celia, who, in many ways, doubles for his betraying mother. Martin won't allow himself to soften towards her. Celia is a complex character, although we are not given any information regarding her background or why she might be so unhealthily obsessed with Martin. As she becomes more and more jealous of Martin's friendship with Andy, and more determined to disrupt it, she resorts to very stereotypical 'feminine' wiles in her own seduction of Andy – a motivation that Andy is initially blind to.

*Filmnews*' Peter Galvin has described Celia as a 'superbitch',[41] reducing her to a two-dimensional character and focusing instead on the film's depiction of the relationship between Martin and Andy. Indeed, the attention to relationships between men could be seen as a recurring interest across Australian film and culture, and, as Mayer has argued, this pattern has been particularly prevalent since the revival of the early 1970s.[42] However, the intensity of Martin and Andy's connection offers new insights into traditional representations of male bonding or mateship within Australian cinema. Writing for *Metro*, Barbara Creed has argued:

Although Proof *is not about a homosexual relationship its exploration of male bonding, based as it is on the exclusion of woman, suggests that all relationships between men involve a degree of homoeroticism. Woman is represented as an abject figure who must be located outside the territory of the male couple.*[43]

The intensity of Martin and Andy's connection offers new insights into traditional representations of male bonding or mateship ... the homoerotic subtext is built on the repudiation of the female figure as embodied by both Martin's mother and Celia.

Indeed, the homoerotic subtext is built on the repudiation of the female figure as embodied by both Martin's mother and Celia, and is made fleetingly explicit during the drive-in scene, in which Martin explores Andy's condoms and the two are set upon as 'perverts'; perhaps, if the film were made more recently, this theme of the primacy of connection between men would have been more readily able to take centre stage. Quinn describes their relationship as taking on 'elements of the suppressed homosexuality that seem to determine so many friendships in Australian cinema'.[44] As I have argued elsewhere, *Proof* can be seen to offer a

*narrative about a desire which exceeds the call of the conventional – as glimpsed in the potential relationship which Martin has with Celia [...] – and which haltingly, amongst the shadows of self-knowledge and propriety, explores an intimate and erotically charged connection between Martin and Andy [...] The sexualised relationship between Martin and Andy thus disrupts the conventional triangular relationship [... and] suggests that the primary bond is indeed between the 'mates'. Despite Andy's 'seduction' by Celia, this primacy is not displaced onto competition for the woman. In this way,* Proof *may actually illustrate [...] the homoeroticism that inevitably and implicitly informs any homosocial economy, leaving the way open for men such as Martin and Andy to explore different ways of enacting the masculine.*[45]

As Creed has also discussed, the relationship between mothers and sons is likewise important to the film. Martin's

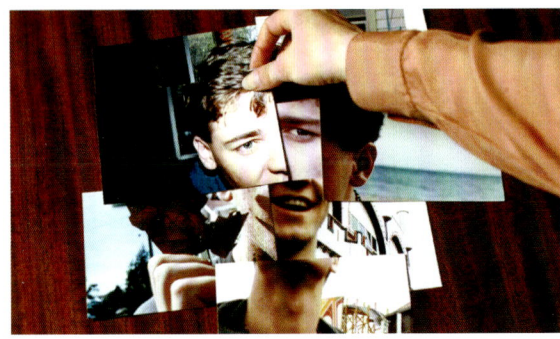

the 1990s, namely that it is not the success of such characters that the films focus upon, [but] rather "disablement and vulnerability"'.[48] While Moorhouse certainly portrays the ways in which Martin is both disabled and vulnerable, *Proof*'s narrative – and perhaps, in particular, the iconography of his photographs and his memories – also emphasises his capacity to learn and to change over the course of his experiences. When Martin finally gives Andy the earliest photo he took, and tells Celia he is finished with her services as housekeeper, it is as though an enchantment is broken. No longer paralysed by the dichotomous constraints of true/false and loyalty/betrayal, Martin takes tentative steps towards accepting himself – and others – in a new-found 'light' of self-understanding.

*This article has been refereed.*

*Rose Lucas is a regular contributor to* Metro *and* Screen Education. *She is a Melbourne poet and a senior lecturer at Victoria University.*  m

## Select bibliography

Lynden Barber, 'Rewind: The Making of the Aussie Classic, *Proof*', *FilmInk*, 27 July 2016, <https://www.filmink.com.au/rewind-the-making-of-the-aussie-classic-proof/>, accessed 13 March 2019.

Barbara Creed, 'Mothers and Lovers: Oedipal Transgressions in Recent Australian Cinema', *Metro*, no. 91, Spring 1992, pp. 14–22.

Kath Duncan, Gerard Goggin & Christopher Newell, '"Don't Talk About Me … like I'm Not Here": Disability in Australian National Cinema', *Metro*, nos. 146–147, 2005, pp. 152–9.

Katie Ellis, 'Disability as Visual Shorthand: Theme and Style in Australian Cinema in the 1990s', *Metro*, no. 152, April 2007, pp. 135–9.

Jan Epstein, 'Jocelyn Moorhouse: The Gift of *Proof*', *Cinema Papers*, no. 85, November 1991, pp. 4–12.

Garry Gillard, 'Quirkiness in Australian Cinema', *Australian Screen Education*, no. 29, Winter 2002, pp. 30–5.

Robert Horton, '*Proof* or Dare', *Film Comment*, vol. 28, no. 2, March–April 1992, pp. 29–30.

Peggy Kamuf, 'Jealousy Wants Proof', *REČ*, no. 59, 5 September 2000, pp. 429–45.

Rose Lucas, 'Dragging It Out: Tales of Masculinity in Australian Cinema, from *Crocodile Dundee* to *Priscilla, Queen of the Desert*', *Journal of Australian Studies*, vol. 22, no. 56, 1998, pp. 138–46.

Geoff Mayer, '*Proof*', *Metro Education*, no. 4, 1995, pp. 21–6.

Karl Quinn, '*Proof*', *Cinema Papers*, no. 85, November 1991, pp. 59–60.

Mary Anne Reid, '*Proof*', in *Long Shots to Favourites: Australian Cinema Successes in the 90s*, Australian Film Commission, North Sydney, 1993.

Diana Sandars, 'Affectively Trapped, Fossilised and Fetishised: Early 1990s Melbourne Through Stillness, Movement and Music in *Proof*', *Senses of Cinema*, issue 85, December 2017, <http://sensesofcinema.com/2017/screening-melbourne/proof-1991/>, accessed 13 March 2019.

Bhaskar Sarkar, 'Blindness, Visuality and the Ethical Turn', *New Review of Film and Television Studies*, vol. 3, no. 2, 2005, pp. 201–22.

relationship with his own mother was a tortured combination of love, dependency, eroticism, guilt and resentment. Even her death has been interpreted by him as proof of her rejection of him. It is not until his relationship with Andy, and the implication that they have survived the crisis of his infidelity with Celia, that Martin is able to share his 'originary' photo with Andy – who affirms both the veracity of his mother's description and the presence of the gardener, the missing father-figure in Martin's family romance.

Examining a group of 1990s films depicting a 'new' kind of Australianness – *Strictly Ballroom* (Baz Lurhmann, 1992), *Priscilla*, *Muriel's Wedding*, *Bad Boy Bubby*, *The Sum of Us* (Geoff Burton & Kevin Dowling, 1994) – Olga Seco Salvador writes: 'Not only did [these films] emphasise the individual and his/her individuality and personal concerns but, above all, they disclosed the existence and relevance of alternative Australian identities and the need to celebrate the diversity of the nation.'[46] In *Proof*, this diversity can be seen in relation to Martin's physical disability, the 'suppressed homosexuality' or homoerotic[47] that informs the relationship between the two men, and perhaps generally the intensity and eccentricity of the three central characters.

Writing in *Metro* about the important representation of disability within Australian cinema of the time, Kath Duncan, Gerard Goggin and Christopher Newell note that there is something about '"oddball" characters in Australian films of

Endnotes

1. Mark Rudman, 'I Think About Australia Endlessly', *The Kenyon Review*, vol. 27, no. 3, Summer 2005, pp. 122–3.
2. Jocelyn Moorhouse, 'Director's Note', in House & Moorhouse Films, *Proof* media kit, 1991, p. 7.
3. Jocelyn Moorhouse, quoted in Robert Horton, '*Proof* or Dare', *Film Comment*, vol. 28, no. 2, March–April 1992, p. 29.
4. Jocelyn Moorhouse, in interview with Peter Brunette, *Sight & Sound* supplement, November 1991, p. 10.
5. Jocelyn Moorhouse, quoted in Lynden Barber, 'Rewind: The Making of the Aussie Classic, *Proof*', *FilmInk*, 27 July 2016, <https://www.filmink.com.au/rewind-the-making-of-the-aussie-classic-proof/>, accessed 13 March 2019.
6. Mary Anne Reid, '*Proof*', in *Long Shots to Favourites: Australian Cinema Successes in the 90s*, Australian Film Commission, North Sydney, 1993, p. 13.
7. Geneviève Picot, quoted in Travis Johnson, 'Geneviève Picot: Looking Back on *Proof*', *FilmInk*, 1 September 2016, <https://www.filmink.com.au/genevieve-picot-looking-back-on-proof/>, accessed 13 March 2019.
8. Travis Johnson, '*Proof* Restored Thanks to Crowdfunding Drive', *FilmInk*, 29 June 2016, <https://www.filmink.com.au/proof-restored-thanks-to-crowdfunding-drive/>, accessed 13 March 2019.
9. Jan Epstein, 'Jocelyn Moorhouse: The Gift of *Proof*', *Cinema Papers*, no. 85, November 1991, p. 4.
10. Alan Finney, quoted in Reid, op. cit., p. 23.
11. Mick LaSalle, '*Proof* Explores Trust and an Odd Love Triangle', *San Francisco Chronicle*, 20 May 1992.
12. Peter Galvin, '*Proof*', *Filmnews*, vol. 21, no. 7, 1991, p. 12.
13. Janet Maslin, 'Acerbity and Escapism in *Proof*, from Australia', *The New York Times*, 20 March 1992, available at <https://www.nytimes.com/1992/03/20/movies/review-film-festival-acerbity-and-escapism-in-proof-from-australia.html>, accessed 13 March 2019.
14. David Stratton, 'Drama of Blind Trust Proves a Class Act', *The Weekend Australian*, 17–18 August 1991, p. 8.
15. Lynden Barber, 'Proven Renaissance', *The Sydney Morning Herald*, 15 August 1991.
16. ibid.
17. Fran Lanigan, quoted in Reid, op. cit., p. 27.
18. Lynda House, quoted in Reid, ibid., p. 27.
19. Elvis Mitchell, '*Proof* That Unbridled Talent Was Tamed', *The Age*, 5 January 2001.
20. Des Partridge, 'First-timer Offers Glossy Local Drama', *The Courier-Mail*, 28 September 1991, p. 8.
21. Barbara Creed, 'Mothers and Lovers: Oedipal Transgressions in Recent Australian Cinema', *Metro*, no. 91, Spring 1992, p. 16.
22. Luke Buckmaster, '*Proof* Rewatched – an Enormously Compelling Character Study', *The Guardian*, 28 November 2014, <https://www.theguardian.com/film/2014/nov/28/proof-rewatched-an-enormously-compelling-character-study>, accessed 13 March 2019.
23. Desson Howe, 'Australia's *Proof* Positive', *The Washington Post*, 5 June 1992, available at <https://www.washingtonpost.com/archive/lifestyle/1992/06/05/australias-proof-positive/1020cb02-8453-4352-ab5b-0bfc2c0c9552/>, accessed 15 March 2019.
24. Rita Kempley, '*Proof*: Every Picture Tells a Story', *The Washington Post*, 6 June 1992, <https://www.washingtonpost.com/archive/lifestyle/1992/06/06/proof-every-picture-tells-a-story/bcca153d-d91a-429e-9158-a709a4b8ab90/>, accessed 13 March 2019.
25. See, for example, Katie Ellis, 'Disability as Visual Shorthand: Theme and Style in Australian Cinema in the 1990s', *Metro*, no. 152, April 2007, pp. 135–9; and Kath Duncan, Gerard Goggin & Christopher Newell, '"Don't Talk About Me … like I'm Not Here": Disability in Australian National Cinema', *Metro*, nos. 146–147, 2005, pp. 152–9.
26. Tom O'Regan, 'Beyond "Australian Film"? Australian Cinema in the 1990s', *Culture & Communication Reading Room*, Murdoch University, 26 October 1995, <https://wwwmcc.murdoch.edu.au/ReadingRoom/film/1990s.html>, accessed 13 March 2019.
27. Garry Gillard, 'Quirkiness in Australian Cinema', *Australian Screen Education*, no. 29, Winter 2002, p. 30.
28. Lynda House, quoted in Shelli-Anne Couch, '*Proof* Takes the World by Storm', *The Border Mail*, 3 December 1991, p. 35.
29. Geoff Mayer, 'Effective Film Analysis aka Where the Hell Do We Start in Teaching *What's Eating Gilbert Grape?*, *Proof*, *Blade Runner*, et al?', *Metro Education*, no. 12, 1997, p. 4.
30. Kathleen Murphy, 'Illuminated Texts', *Film Comment*, vol. 27, no. 6, November–December 1991, p. 47.
31. Karl Quinn, '*Proof*', *Cinema Papers*, no. 85, November 1991, p. 60.
32. Laura Mulvey, 'Visual Pleasure and Narrative Cinema,' *Screen*, vol. 16, no. 3, Autumn 1975, pp. 6–18.
33. Diana Sandars, 'Affectively Trapped, Fossilised and Fetishised: Early 1990s Melbourne Through Stillness, Movement and Music in *Proof*', *Senses of Cinema*, issue 85, December 2017, <http://sensesofcinema.com/2017/screening-melbourne/proof-1991/>, accessed 13 March 2019.
34. Murphy, op. cit., p. 47.
35. Dana Anderson, 'Shooting Blind', *History of Photography*, vol. 27, no. 2, 2003, p. 200.
36. Bhaskar Sarkar, 'Blindness, Visuality and the Ethical Turn', *New Review of Film and Television Studies*, vol. 3, no. 2, 2005, p. 202.
37. Peggy Kamuf, 'Jealousy Wants Proof', *REČ*, no. 59, 5 September 2000, p. 439.
38. Sandars, op. cit.
39. Jocelyn Moorhouse, quoted in Epstein, op. cit., p. 12.
40. ibid., p. 10. There is also an interesting parallel here with the character of Norman Bates (Anthony Perkins) in Alfred Hitchcock's *Psycho* (1960), whose ambivalent feelings towards his mother mean that he literally 'animates' her, even as a corpse.
41. Galvin, op. cit., p. 12.
42. Geoff Mayer, '*Proof*', *Metro Education*, no. 4, 1995, p. 26.
43. Creed, op. cit., p. 16.
44. Karl Quinn, '*Proof*', in Scott Murray (ed.), *Australian Film: 1978–1992*, Oxford University Press, Melbourne, 1993, p. 322.
45. Rose Lucas, 'Dragging It Out: Tales of Masculinity in Australian Cinema, from *Crocodile Dundee* to *Priscilla, Queen of the Desert*', *Journal of Australian Studies*, vol. 22, no. 56, 1998, p. 145.
46. Olga Seco Salvador, '*Strictly Ballroom* (1992): Departure from Traditional Anglo-Australian Discourses or Veiled Confirmation of Old National-encouragement Mechanisms?', *Miscelánea: A Journal of English and American Studies*, issue 32, 2005, p. 106.
47. For a discussion of the prevalence of homoerotic or 'homosocial' subtexts within Western literature, see Eve Kosofsky Sedgwick, *Between Men: English Literature and Male Homosocial Desire*, Columbia University Press, New York, 1985.
48. Duncan, Goggin & Newell, op. cit., p. 154.

# Screen EDUCATION

## Looking for more teaching resources?

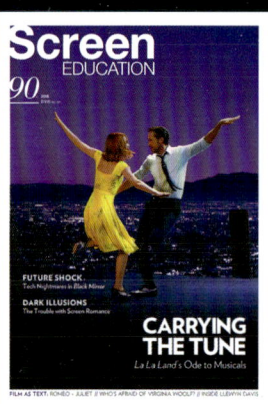

▲ **ISSUE 92**

*A Wrinkle in Time. Girls.* Cinema Science: *Ant-Man and the Wasp. Alice in Wonderland. The Blind Side.* Violence and gender roles. *The Truman Show.* Filmmaker profile: Stanley Kubrick. Stop-motion animation. **Film as Text:** *Moonrise Kingdom; The Last Picture Show; The Babadook.*

▲ **ISSUE 91**

*Call Me by Your Name. Mulan. Beauty and the Beast.* Cinema Science: *Annihilation.* Film and theatre. *The Square.* The ethics of viewing. *Perceval.* Filmmaker profile: Paul Thomas Anderson. Fake news. **Film as Text:** *Cool Hand Luke; All Quiet on the Western Front.*

▲ **ISSUE 90**

*La La Land. Black Mirror. Wonder.* Cinema Science: *Planet of the Apes.* Artificial intelligence. Romance genre tropes. *You Can't Ask That.* Filmmaker profile: Asghar Farhadi. **Film as Text:** *Romeo + Juliet; Who's Afraid of Virginia Woolf?; Inside Llewyn Davis.*

▲ **ISSUE 89**

*Sweet Country. 20th Century Women. The Handmaid's Tale.* Women in the games industry. Pornography. *Donkey Skin.* Filmmaker profile: Jane Campion. Same-sex marriage ads. *Wayne's World.* **Film as Text:** *The Sapphires; Remember the Titans; The Immigrant.*

### Pick up a copy of Australia's premier screen literacy magazine.

All of our back issues are packed with useful information and lesson ideas both for media teachers and for all primary and secondary teachers looking to use screen-based media in the classroom.

◄ **ISSUE 93**

*Moonlight. Custody* and *The Florida Project. Three Billboards Outside Ebbing, Missouri.* Cinema Science: *Pi.* Architecture in film. *Triumph of the Will. FernGully: The Last Rainforest. Simon of the Desert.* Women in horror. *Island of the Hungry Ghosts. Heathers* and identity politics. Filmmaker profile: Ingmar Bergman. Animation and reality. Adobe Premiere Rush tutorial. **Film as Text:** *Hail, Caesar!; Chariots of Fire; Birdman or (The Unexpected Virtue of Ignorance).*

**TO PURCHASE:** Visit The Education Shop at <https://theeducationshop.com.au>. Issues are $19.95 plus P&H (inc. GST).

Individual articles from back issues are also available as PDF downloads from The Education Shop.